CALIFORNIA

Prentice Hall
MEDIEVAL AND EARLY MODERN TIMES

Interactive Reading and Notetaking Study Guide

ADAPTED VERSION

PEARSON

Prentice
Hall

Upper Saddle River, New Jersey
Boston, Massachusetts

ISBN 0-13-119995-1

9 10 V069 10

Contents

How to Use This Book

The *Interactive Reading and Notetaking Study Guide* was designed to help you understand the content in your *Medieval and Early Modern Times* textbook. It will also help you build your notetaking and historical-thinking skills. Please take the time to look at the next few pages to see how it works.

The unit opener page prepares you to read and think about the chapters in each unit. Section Summary pages provide an easy-to-read summary of each section.

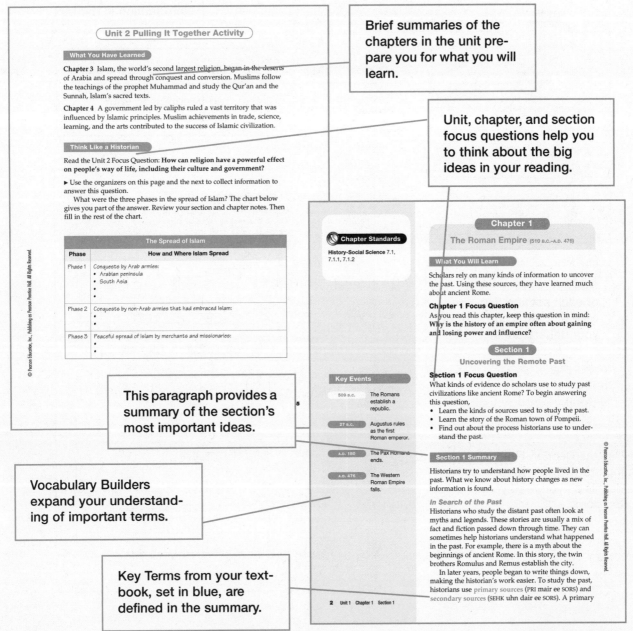

Brief summaries of the chapters in the unit prepare you for what you will learn.

Unit, chapter, and section focus questions help you to think about the big ideas in your reading.

This paragraph provides a summary of the section's most important ideas.

Vocabulary Builders expand your understanding of important terms.

Key Terms from your textbook, set in blue, are defined in the summary.

Unit 2 Pulling It Together Activity

What You Have Learned

Chapter 3 Islam, the world's second largest religion, began in the deserts of Arabia and spread through conquest and conversion. Muslims follow the teachings of the prophet Muhammad and study the Qur'an and the Sunnah, Islam's sacred texts.

Chapter 4 A government led by caliphs ruled a vast territory that was influenced by Islamic principles. Muslim achievements in trade, science, learning, and the arts contributed to the success of Islamic civilization.

Think Like a Historian

Read the Unit 2 Focus Question: **How can religion have a powerful effect on people's way of life, including their culture and government?**

▶ Use the organizers on this page and the next to collect information to answer this question.

What were the three phases in the spread of Islam? The chart below gives you part of the answer. Review your section and chapter notes. Then fill in the rest of the chart.

The Spread of Islam

Phase	How and Where Islam Spread
Phase 1	Conquests by Arab armies: • Arabian peninsula • South Asia
Phase 2	Conquests by non-Arab armies that had embraced Islam:
Phase 3	Peaceful spread of Islam by merchants and missionaries:

Chapter Standards

History-Social Science 7.1, 7.1.1, 7.1.2

Key Events

509 B.C.	The Romans establish a republic.
27 B.C.	Augustus rules as the first Roman emperor.
A.D. 180	The Pax Romana ends.
A.D. 476	The Western Roman Empire falls.

Chapter 1

The Roman Empire (510 B.C.–A.D. 476)

What You Will Learn

Scholars rely on many kinds of information to uncover the past. Using these sources, they have learned much about ancient Rome.

Chapter 1 Focus Question
As you read this chapter, keep this question in mind: **Why is the history of an empire often about gaining and losing power and influence?**

Section 1
Uncovering the Remote Past

Section 1 Focus Question
What kinds of evidence do scholars use to study past civilizations like ancient Rome? To begin answering this question,
• Learn the kinds of sources used to study the past.
• Learn the story of the Roman town of Pompeii.
• Find out about the process historians use to understand the past.

Section 1 Summary

Historians try to understand how people lived in the past. What we know about history changes as new information is found.

In Search of the Past
Historians who study the distant past often look at myths and legends. These stories are usually a mix of fact and fiction passed down through time. They can sometimes help historians understand what happened in the past. For example, there is a myth about the beginnings of ancient Rome. In this story, the twin brothers Romulus and Remus establish the city.

In later years, people began to write things down, making the historian's work easier. To study the past, historians use primary sources (PRI mair ee SORS) and secondary sources (SEHK uhn dair ee SORS). A primary

2 Unit 1 Chapter 1 Section 1

Questions and activities in the margin help you recall information from the summary. Section Notetaking Study Guides help you take notes as your read your textbook.

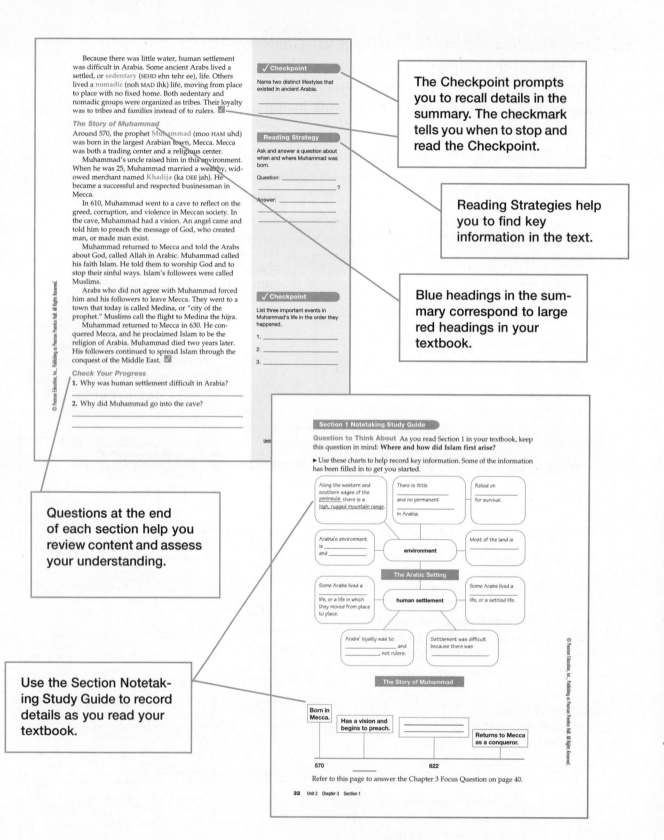

Because there was little water, human settlement was difficult in Arabia. Some ancient Arabs lived a settled, or sedentary (SEHD ehn tehr ee), life. Others lived a nomadic (noh MAD ihk) life, moving from place to place with no fixed home. Both sedentary and nomadic groups were organized as tribes. Their loyalty was to tribes and families instead of to rulers. ✓

The Story of Muhammad

Around 570, the prophet Muhammad (moo HAM uhd) was born in the largest Arabian town, Mecca. Mecca was both a trading center and a religious center.

Muhammad's uncle raised him in this environment. When he was 25, Muhammad married a wealthy, widowed merchant named Khadija (ka DEE jah). He became a successful and respected businessman in Mecca.

In 610, Muhammad went to a cave to reflect on the greed, corruption, and violence in Meccan society. In the cave, Muhammad had a vision. An angel came and told him to preach the message of God, who created man, or made man exist.

Muhammad returned to Mecca and told the Arabs about God, called Allah in Arabic. Muhammad called his faith Islam. He told them to worship God and to stop their sinful ways. Islam's followers were called Muslims.

Arabs who did not agree with Muhammad forced him and his followers to leave Mecca. They went to a town that today is called Medina, or "city of the prophet." Muslims call the flight to Medina the hijra.

Muhammad returned to Mecca in 630. He conquered Mecca, and he proclaimed Islam to be the religion of Arabia. Muhammad died two years later. His followers continued to spread Islam through the conquest of the Middle East. ✓

Check Your Progress

1. Why was human settlement difficult in Arabia?

2. Why did Muhammad go into the cave?

✓ Checkpoint

Name two distinct lifestyles that existed in ancient Arabia.

Reading Strategy

Ask and answer a question about when and where Muhammad was born.

Question: _____

_____ ?

Answer: _____

_____

✓ Checkpoint

List three important events in Muhammad's life in the order they happened.

1. _____
2. _____
3. _____

The Checkpoint prompts you to recall details in the summary. The checkmark tells you when to stop and read the Checkpoint.

Reading Strategies help you to find key information in the text.

Blue headings in the summary correspond to large red headings in your textbook.

Questions at the end of each section help you review content and assess your understanding.

Use the Section Notetaking Study Guide to record details as you read your textbook.

Section 1 Notetaking Study Guide

Question to Think About As you read Section 1 in your textbook, keep this question in mind: **Where and how did Islam first arise?**

▶ Use these charts to help record key information. Some of the information has been filled in to get you started.

Along the western and southern edges of the *peninsula* there is a *high, rugged mountain range.*

There is little _____ and no permanent _____ in Arabia.

Relied on _____ for survival.

Arabia's environment is _____ and _____

environment

Most of the land is _____

The Arabic Setting

Some Arabs lived a _____ life, or a life in which they moved from place to place.

human settlement

Some Arabs lived a _____ life, or a settled life.

Arabs' loyalty was to _____ and _____, not rulers.

Settlement was difficult because there was _____

The Story of Muhammad

Born in Mecca. → Has a vision and begins to preach. → _____ → Returns to Mecca as a conqueror.

570 — _____ — 622

Refer to this page to answer the Chapter 3 Focus Question on page 40.

Questions help you to assess your progress. Chapter Notetaking Study Guides help you to pull together the notes you took for each section and focus on important ideas.

Chapter 3 Assessment

Directions: Circle the letter of the correct answer.

1. Islam first emerged in
   A the Arabian Peninsula.
   B Mesopotamia.
   C Afghanistan.

2. The Qur'an and the Sunnah are
   A both the word of God.
   B key sources of Islamic thought.
   C Muslim holidays.

3. Muslim expansion
   A stopped when Muhammad died.
   B took place in three phases.
   C only happened by conquest.

Directions: Follow the steps to answer this question:

Why were different phases of Muslim expansion successful?

Step 1: Recall information: List the three phases of Muslim expansion.

Phase 1: _____
Phase 2: _____
Phase 3: _____

Step 2: Recall information: List five reasons the spread of Islam was successful.

1. _____
2. _____
3. _____
4. _____
5. _____

Step 3: Make a connection: Pick one phase of Muslim expansion. Write a topic sentence stating which reason was most important to the success of that phase. Write two or three sentences that support the topic sentence.

_____
_____
_____

Unit 2 Ch

> **Questions at the end of the chapter help you review content and assess your understanding of the summary.**

> **Critical-thinking questions are broken into manageable steps.**

> **Use the Chapter Notetaking Study Guide to organize your section notes to answer the chapter focus question.**

Chapter 3 Notetaking Study Guide

Now you are ready to answer the Chapter 3 Focus Question: **What are the origins and beliefs of Islam and how did it spread?**

► Complete the following charts to help you answer this question. Use the notes that you took for each section.

Origins

Arabian Setting
• _harsh_ environment
• people organized as _____
   with no loyalty to _____

Muhammad
• born around the year _____ in the city of _____
• fled to _____ on a journey called the _____
• conquered the city of _____ in the year _____

Beliefs

Qur'an
• tells about ____Allah____, the _____, and
• addresses _____, and _____ issues

Sunnah
• written version called the _____

Five Pillars of Faith
1. _____
2. _____
3. _____
4. _____
5. _____

Islam

Spread

First Phase
Arab soldiers were able to conquer because of their skill on _____ and the declines of the _____ and _____ empires.

Second Phase
Groups like _____ and _____ converted and took _____ back to their homelands.

Third Phase
Islam spread along trade routes by _____ and _____.

Refer to this page to answer the Unit 2 Focus Question on page 55.

The Pulling It Together Activity helps you to look back on your reading and focus on the unit's big ideas.

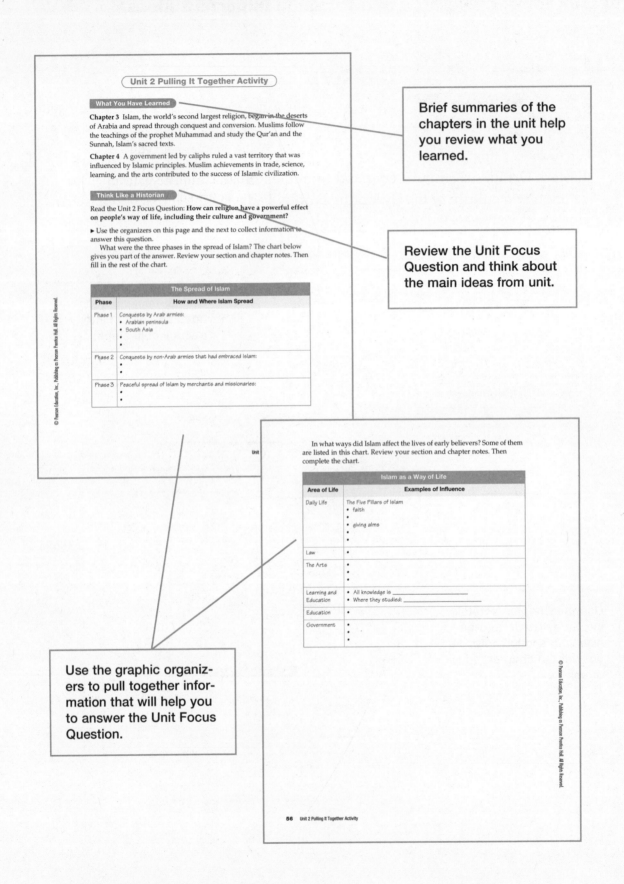

Unit 2 Pulling It Together Activity

What You Have Learned

Chapter 3 Islam, the world's second largest religion, began in the deserts of Arabia and spread through conquest and conversion. Muslims follow the teachings of the prophet Muhammad and study the Qur'an and the Sunnah, Islam's sacred texts.

Chapter 4 A government led by caliphs ruled a vast territory that was influenced by Islamic principles. Muslim achievements in trade, science, learning, and the arts contributed to the success of Islamic civilization.

Think Like a Historian

Read the Unit 2 Focus Question: **How can religion have a powerful effect on people's way of life, including their culture and government?**

▸ Use the organizers on this page and the next to collect information to answer this question.

What were the three phases in the spread of Islam? The chart below gives you part of the answer. Review your section and chapter notes. Then fill in the rest of the chart.

The Spread of Islam	
Phase	**How and Where Islam Spread**
Phase 1	Conquests by Arab armies: • Arabian peninsula • South Asia • •
Phase 2	Conquests by non-Arab armies that had embraced Islam: • •
Phase 3	Peaceful spread of Islam by merchants and missionaries: •

Brief summaries of the chapters in the unit help you review what you learned.

Review the Unit Focus Question and think about the main ideas from unit.

In what ways did Islam affect the lives of early believers? Some of them are listed in this chart. Review your section and chapter notes. Then complete the chart.

Islam as a Way of Life	
Area of Life	**Examples of Influence**
Daily Life	The Five Pillars of Islam • faith • • giving alms • •
Law	•
The Arts	• • •
Learning and Education	• All knowledge is _____ • Where they studied: _____
Education	•
Government	• • •

Use the graphic organizers to pull together information that will help you to answer the Unit Focus Question.

Rome and Byzantium

Chapter 1 Scholars rely on various sources of information to uncover the past. Using these sources, they have learned much about ancient Rome.

Chapter 2 Constantinople became the center of the Byzantine Empire. The Eastern Orthodox Church separated from the Roman Catholic Church. The religion and culture of the Byzantine Empire had a lasting impact on Eastern Europe.

Focus Your Learning As you study this unit and take notes, you will find the information to answer the questions below. Answering the chapter focus questions will help build your answer to the unit focus question.

Chapter 1 Focus Question
Why is the history of an empire often about gaining and losing power and influence?
(page 2)

Chapter 2 Focus Question
What were the origins and lasting effects of the rise of Constantinople and the Byzantine Empire?
(page 16)

Unit 1 Focus Question
How can the influence of an empire live on after the empire falls?
(page 27)

History-Social Science 7.1.1,
7.1.2

Key Events

509 B.C.	The Romans establish a republic.
27 B.C.	Augustus rules as the first Roman emperor.
A.D. 180	The Pax Romana ends.
A.D. 476	The Western Roman Empire falls.

Chapter 1

The Roman Empire (510 B.C.–A.D. 476)

What You Will Learn

Scholars rely on many kinds of information to uncover the past. Using these sources, they have learned much about ancient Rome.

Chapter 1 Focus Question

As you read this chapter, keep this question in mind: **Why is the history of an empire often about gaining and losing power and influence?**

Section 1

Uncovering the Remote Past

Section 1 Focus Question

What kinds of evidence do scholars use to study past civilizations like ancient Rome? To begin answering this question,

- Learn the kinds of sources used to study the past.
- Learn the story of the Roman town of Pompeii.
- Find out about the process historians use to understand the past.

Section 1 Summary

Historians try to understand how people lived in the past. What we know about history changes as new information is found.

In Search of the Past

Historians who study the distant past often look at myths and legends. These stories are usually a mix of fact and fiction passed down through time. They can sometimes help historians understand what happened in the past. For example, there is a myth about the beginnings of ancient Rome. In this story, the twin brothers Romulus and Remus establish the city.

In later years, people began to write things down, making the historian's work easier. To study the past, historians use primary sources (PRI mair ee SORS) and secondary sources (SEHK uhn dair ee SORS). A primary source is a record that was created at or near the time of an event. Its creator is usually an eyewitness. Primary sources include diaries, letters, poems, songs, and paintings. A secondary source is an account written after an event has occurred. An example is a history book.

Archaeologists also work with material culture (muh TIR ee uhl KUHL cher) to find out about the past. Material culture consists of the buildings, tools, and other objects that show how people live. Archaeologists also search places where people once lived to find artifacts. Artifacts (AHR tih fakts) are things made by humans. Tools, pots, weapons, and jewelry are examples of artifacts. ✓

When Time Stopped in Pompeii

One of the best places to study the material culture of Rome is Pompeii. Pompeii is a town that was buried by a volcanic eruption in A.D. 79. A young man named Pliny the Younger was near Pompeii during the eruption. He wrote: "Many… believed that there were no gods any longer and that this was one last unending night for the world…."

Pompeii was buried for about 1,700 years. When it was uncovered, it told us much about the ancient Romans. The city's buildings and artwork were preserved in the ash from the eruption. ✓

Interpreting the Past

Once they have studied the evidence, historians try to decide what it means. This can be hard. Sometimes sources disagree. Next, historians try to explain the meaning of what they've learned. Different historians may study the same facts and interpret them differently. Finally, historians combine facts and interpretations into a story. The best histories tell us what happened in the past, as well as why it happened. ✓

Check Your Progress

1. What kind of source is Pliny the Younger's letter?

_____

2. Why is analyzing evidence often hard?

_____

_____

Reading Strategy

Underline the sentence that defines a primary source. Next, circle the examples of primary sources, and draw an arrow from the examples back to the sentence you underlined. Do the same for secondary sources.

✓ Checkpoint

List two examples of primary sources.

_____

_____

✓ Checkpoint

List two things that were preserved in ash in Pompeii.

_____

_____

✓ Checkpoint

What do the best histories tell us?

_____

_____

_____

Question to Think About As you read Section 1 in your textbook and take notes, keep this section focus question in mind: **What kinds of evidence do scholars use to study past civilizations like ancient Rome?**

► Use these charts to record key information from the section. Some information has been filled in to get you started.

Sources of Information About the Past		
Source	**Definition**	**Examples**
Myths and Legends	An idea or story that many people believe but that is not true	Romulus and Remus
Primary Sources		
Secondary Sources		
Material Culture		Buildings and tools
Artifacts		

Interpreting the Past	
The Story of Pompeii	**Steps Historians Follow to Study the Past**
What happened:	1. Collect information
	2. Analyze information
Material culture found:	3.
	4.

Refer to this page to answer the Chapter 1 Focus Question on page 15.

Section 2

The Empire at Its Height

Section 2 Focus Question

What problems did Rome face as it expanded from a small republic into a vast empire? To begin answering this question,

- Learn how Rome grew from a small republic into a vast empire.
- Find out about the growth of the Roman Empire and the seeds of its decline.

Section 2 Summary

Rome began as a small republic and grew into a large empire. The empire was led by good and bad emperors. Over time, it became too large to manage, so it was divided.

From Republic to Empire

The Roman Republic conquered other lands in the Mediterranean, and it quickly grew into a large and growing empire. In a republic (ri PUHB lik), citizens have the right to vote and elect officials. This system worked well in a city, but it did not work well in an empire with people of different cultures.

The growth of the empire also created economic and social problems in Rome. In its military victories, Rome had taken thousands of prisoners. These prisoners were brought to Italy as slaves. Slaves took over many jobs once held by Romans. Both jobless Romans and slaves became unhappy, and riots and revolts resulted.

Romans wanted a strong leader to restore order, and they found one in Julius Caesar (JOO lee uhs SEE zer). Caesar was a famous war hero. When he led his troops into Rome, it sparked a civil war. But Caesar's forces won, and he took power in 44 B.C.

Many Romans worried that Caesar had too much power and would become a king. To prevent this, several senators assassinated him. To assassinate (uh SA sih nayt) means to murder an important person. After another civil war, Caesar's adopted son, Octavian, became the ruler of Rome in 31 B.C. ✓

Key Events

509 B.C.	The Romans establish a republic.
27 B.C.	Augustus rules as the first Roman emperor.
A.D. 180	The Pax Romana ends.
A.D. 476	The Western Roman Empire falls.

Reading Strategy

Based on the summary, number these events in the order they take place.

___ Julius Caesar becomes ruler of Rome

___ Roman republic conquers nearby lands

___ Rome stops being a republic

✓ Checkpoint

Name the leader who took power in 44 B.C.

_____

_____

The word *traditions* has several synonyms. Which of the following would best replace *traditions* in the underlined sentence?

A. customs

B. folklore

C. culture

The Empire Grows

<u>Octavian showed respect for the traditions of the Roman Republic.</u> He did, however, rule as an emperor with great powers. He took the title Augustus, which means "great and holy one."

Augustus (uh GUHS tuhs) founded more than 100 colonies. These colonies helped to spread Roman law and culture. The time of his reign began a period of peace and prosperity known as the Pax Romana (PAHKS roh MAH nuh), or "Roman Peace."

The first two rulers to follow Augustus took power smoothly. Later, however, there were plots and murders by families who wanted the throne. Some emperors were weak, some were good, and some were known for their insane behavior.

A group of rulers became known as the "good emperors." Trajan was a respected military leader who added Mesopotamia and lands in eastern Europe to the empire. He built roads, bridges, and harbors and tried to help the poor.

Hadrian was a fair and wise ruler and a military leader who worked to strengthen the empire's defenses. One of his projects was Hadrian's Wall, a defensive wall he built across northern Britain.

Marcus Aurelius was the last of the "good emperors." He was a peace-loving scholar, but he had to fight a number of wars along the empire's borders. When he died in A.D. 180, the Pax Romana ended.

Problems grew worse over the next century. Rome was plagued by civil wars at home and wars on the borders. The emperor Diocletian (di uh KLEE shun) saw that the empire was too large. He divided the empire into two parts. This division seemed to help at first, but it eventually weakened the empire. ✓

✓ Checkpoint

Name three of the "good emperors."

_____

_____

_____

Check Your Progress

1. What kinds of problems did the growth of the empire create?

_____

_____

2. What was the Pax Romana?

_____

_____

Question to Think About As you read Section 2 in your textbook and take notes, keep this section focus question in mind: **What problems did Rome face as it expanded from a small republic into a vast empire?**

▶ Use these charts to record key information from the section. Some information has been filled in to get you started.

Roman Leaders and Their Accomplishments		
Leader		**Accomplishments**
Caesar		• Conquered Gaul • Took power after civil war in Rome • Named "dictator for life"
Augustus		• Reformed government and army • •
"Good Emperors"	Trajan	• • •
	Hadrian	• • • Built Hadrian's wall
	Marcus Aurelius	•
Diocletian		•

Rome's Growing Empire		
Government of	**Territory Added**	**Significance of Expansion**
1. Roman Republic	Lands around the Mediterranean	Diverse cultures hard to govern
2. Augustus		Helped spread Roman law and culture
3. Trajan		

Refer to this page to answer the Chapter 1 Focus Question on page 15.

The Western Empire Collapses

Key Events

509 B.C.	The Romans establish a republic.
27 B.C.	Augustus rules as the first Roman emperor.
A.D. 180	The Pax Romana ends.
A.D. 476	The Western Roman Empire falls.

Vocabulary Builder

The words *economy* and *economic* have to do with the ways in which people make a living. List two words or phrases from the bracketed paragraphs that relate to the economy.

_____

_____

✓ Checkpoint

What effect did recruiting foreign soldiers have on the Roman army?

_____

_____

Section 3 Focus Question

How did internal weaknesses and external threats lead to the fall of the Western Roman Empire? To begin answering this question,

- Understand how internal weaknesses contributed to the collapse of the Roman Empire.
- Learn about the invasions that destroyed the empire.

Section 3 Summary

Several internal problems weakened the Roman Empire. Barbarian invasions destroyed the empire.

Rome's Internal Weaknesses

Even at its height, the Roman empire had problems. It was made up of diverse peoples, many of whom felt little loyalty to Rome. The emperor Caracalla tried to increase loyalty in the empire by giving all free people in the empire Roman **citizenship** (SIHT uh zuhn shihp). Citizenship is membership in a political community that brings rights and responsibilities. These people could take part in government and use the Roman courts. But this did not solve the economic problems.

As the empire expanded, the gap between rich and poor increased. Wars destroyed farms and hurt trade, and the poor grew poorer as a result. In addition, defending the empire's long borders was expensive, so taxes were raised.

Economic difficulties led to unrest in the cities. Wealthy people became afraid and fled to their country estates. There they raised their own food and hired guards to protect them. Poor people worked as farmers on the estates or joined the army. Some even became outlaws. Over time, the estates became self-sufficient "mini-towns," and cities became less important.

An army of well-trained citizens had built the empire. After the Pax Romana ended, the army began to recruit foreign soldiers. These new soldiers were not as loyal to Rome, and the army became weaker as a result. ✓

Threats From Outside the Empire

In addition to internal problems, Rome faced attacks on its borders. In Europe, the Rhine and Danube rivers marked the empire's eastern border. The areas across these rivers were settled by Germanic tribes, whom the Romans viewed as barbarian, or uncivilized.

Around A.D. 370, a new group of barbarians appeared. The Huns were fierce horsemen from Central Asia. They attacked peaceful Germanic tribes, who then fled into the empire. The Germanic Visigoths crossed into Greece. There they defeated a large Roman army, killing some 40,000 Romans.

A leader named Attila (uh TIHL uh) led the Huns into Gaul and Italy. When Roman troops were called away from the borders to defend Italy, more invaders poured in. Germanic tribes set up kingdoms in Gaul, Spain, and Italy. By the year A.D. 500, the empire had collapsed.

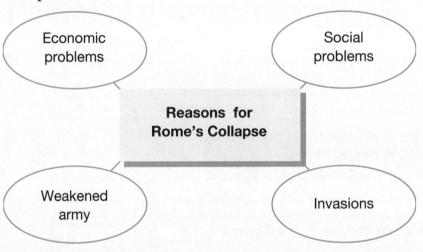

Historians disagree on which problem did the most to cause Rome to fall. Many modern historians believe that Rome could have survived if not for the barbarian invasions. ✓

Check Your Progress

1. When Roman people fled to country estates, how did the way of life in Europe change?

_____

_____

2. Why was Attila's invasion of Gaul and Italy so destructive to Rome?

_____

_____

How do the headings in the summary relate to the title of the section?

_____

_____

_____

✓ Checkpoint

List two groups of barbarians who contributed to the collapse of the Roman Empire.

_____

_____

Question to Think About As you read Section 3 in your textbook and take notes, keep this section focus question in mind: **How did internal weaknesses and external threats lead to the fall of the Western Roman Empire?**

▶ Use these charts to record key information from the section. Some information has been filled in to get you started.

Internal Issue	Effect on Empire
Diverse peoples, different cultures	Reduced loyalty to the empire
Wars	
Defending borders became _____ .	
Decline of cities	
	Emperor no longer had highest authority
Slavery	
	Army became less effective.

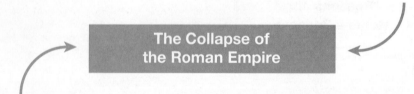

The Collapse of the Roman Empire

External Threats to the Empire

• Barbarian Invasions
  • The _____ from Central Asia attacked the borders.
  • _____ tribes fled into the empire.
  • The leader _____ led the Huns into Gaul and Italy.

• New Germanic Kingdoms
  • Germanic tribes settled and set up _____ kingdoms.
    • The Franks and the Burgundians settled in Gaul.
    •
    •

Refer to this page to answer the Chapter 1 Focus Question on page 15.

Section 4 Focus Question

What were the lasting contributions of Rome? To begin answering this question,

- Learn about the Romans' talent for art, architecture, and engineering.
- Understand the influence of Roman law and language today.

Section 4 Summary

The Romans created beautiful buildings, advanced roads, and public water systems. The law and languages of many countries today have their roots in Roman law and language.

Art, Architecture, and Engineering

The Romans created art and buildings that were both beautiful and practical. Most surviving Roman structures were public-works projects. **Public works** (PUHB lihk werks) are structures built by a government for public use. The Romans built public baths, temples, bridges, and marketplaces. Public places, as well as many homes, were decorated with statues, paintings, and mosaic floors.

The Romans invented concrete. Concrete was used in bridges, buildings, and roads. A network of more than 50,000 miles of Roman roads linked cities and military outposts. Roman roads helped the army move quickly. They also helped unify the empire and spread Roman culture.

Roman towns had very modern public water systems. Ordinary people got clean water from public fountains. Wealthier homes had private water supplies. The water flowed to the cities in aqueducts. These were covered channels supported by arches. ✓

Roman Law and Language

Rome's first law code was called the Twelve Tables. Roman laws were clearly stated so that every Roman could understand them. This was the beginning of a legal tradition that is still with us today.

© Pearson Education, Inc., publishing as Pearson Prentice Hall. All Rights Reserved.

Key Events

509 B.C. — The Romans establish a republic.

27 B.C. — Augustus rules as the first Roman emperor.

A.D. 180 — The Pax Romana ends.

A.D. 476 — The Western Roman Empire falls.

Reading Strategy

Identify the topic sentence in the bracketed paragraph and underline it.

✓ Checkpoint

List three types of construction and engineering projects in which the Romans used concrete.

_____

_____

_____

Think about what the word *international* means. Use context clues to help you if you need to. What do you think the prefix _____ means?

_____

_____

✓ Checkpoint

Name the two central ideas of Roman law.

_____

_____

_____

_____

✓

Name the emperor who allowed Christians to worship freely.

_____

The Romans believed that good government was based on the rule of law. They also believed that all Roman citizens had equal rights under the law. Early in the Roman Republic, only people who lived in Italy could be Roman citizens. As the empire grew, many more people were allowed to be citizens. This change brought a huge multicultural (muhl tee KUHL cher uhl) empire under Roman law. A multicultural empire consists of many different cultures dealing with foreigners as well. These rules are the foundation for modern <u>international</u> law.

Many countries in Europe and Latin America base their law on the Roman system. Roman law has also influenced U.S. law. The principle of equal justice, for example, is part of the U.S. system of government.

The Latin language also spread throughout the empire. Long after the empire collapsed, educated people continued to use Latin. Today, millions of people speak Romance languages ROH mans LAN gwihj ihz), or languages based on Latin. Romance languages include Spanish, Italian, French, Portuguese, and Romanian. Many English words come from Latin. English speakers use the Roman alphabet, too. ✓

The Christian Religion

For many people, Rome's most important legacy is Christianity. The Romans feared that the Jewish prophet Jesus might spark a rebellion. According to the Christian scriptures, the Romans executed him and persecuted his followers, the Christians. However, in the early 300s, the emperor Constantine (KAHN stehn teen) began allowing Christians to worship freely. With that protection, the Christian Church grew into a powerful religious institution. ✓

Check Your Progress

1. Why is Roman law so important to us?

_____

_____

2. What effects did the building of roads have on the empire?

_____

_____

Question to Think About: As you read Section 4 in your textbook and take notes, keep the section focus question in mind: **What were the lasting contributions of Rome?**

► Use these charts to record key information from the section. Some information has been filled in to get you started.

The Legacies of Rome	
Art and Architecture	
• statues • paintings •	• • •
Engineering	
• bridges • domes	• •
Law	
Characteristics of Roman Law	**Influence of Roman Law Today**

• First law code:
 	
• Important ideas about law and government:
 	
  •
 	
  •
	• Foundation of _____
	
	• Modern countries influenced:
	  • European countries
	
	  •
	
	  •

Language	

• Romance Languages: Spanish, _____, _____,
 	
  _____, _____
 	
• English:
  • Many English words come from Latin.
 	
  •	

Christianity	
Romans' part in the history of Christianity: • At the time of Jesus: • At the time of Constantine:	

Refer to this page to answer the Unit 1 Focus Question on page 15.

Chapter 1 Assessment

Directions: Circle the letter of the correct answer.

1. To determine what happened in the past, historians
    A   study only primary sources because they are the most reliable.
    B   study primary and secondary sources and interpret the information.
    C   learn myths and legends and decide what is fact and what is fiction.

2. The Romans invented
    A   roads.   B   concrete.   C   the concept of law.

3. The reign of Augustus began
    A   a movement of city dwellers to the country.
    B   a time of war and poverty.
    C   the Pax Romana.

Directions: Follow the steps to answer this question:

Did internal weaknesses or external threats contribute more to Rome's collapse?

Step 1: Recall the information: In the chart, list some of Rome's internal weaknesses and external threats.

Internal Weaknesses	External Threats

Step 2: Evaluate: In the chart, evaluate to what extent internal weaknesses and external threats affected the empire's strength. Circle the one you think contributed most to Rome's collapse.

Effects of Internal Weaknesses	Effects of External Threats

Step 3: Complete the topic sentence that follows. Then, write two or three more sentences that support your topic sentence.

Rome's collapse was mostly due to _____

_____

_____

_____

Now you are ready to answer the Chapter 1 Focus Question: **Why is the history of an empire often about gaining and losing power and influence?**

▶ Complete the following charts to help you answer this question. Use the notes that you took for each section.

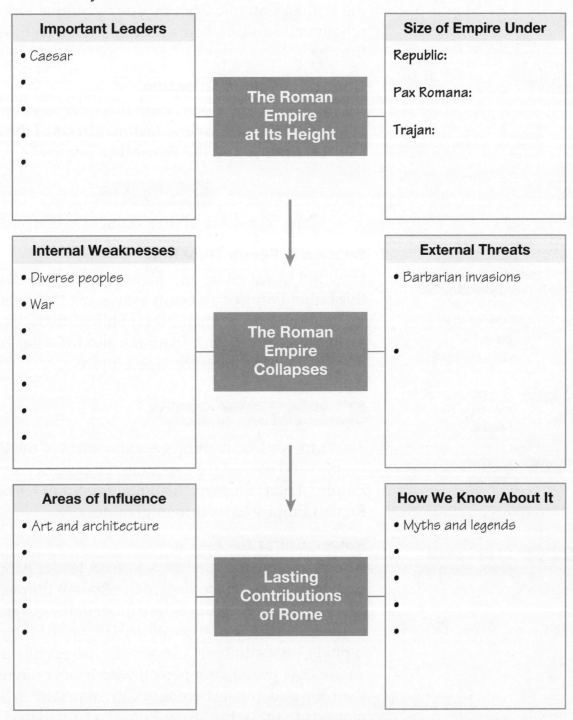

Important Leaders

- Caesar
-
-
-
-

The Roman Empire at Its Height

Size of Empire Under

Republic:

Pax Romana:

Trajan:

Internal Weaknesses

- Diverse peoples
- War
-
-
-
-
-

The Roman Empire Collapses

External Threats

- Barbarian invasions
-

Areas of Influence

- Art and architecture
-
-
-
-

Lasting Contributions of Rome

How We Know About It

- Myths and legends
-
-
-

Refer to this page to answer the Unit 1 Focus Question on page 27.

Chapter Standards

History-Social Science 7.1.3

Chapter 2

The Byzantine Empire (A.D. 324–A.D. 1453)

What You Will Learn

Constantinople became the center of the Byzantine Empire. The Eastern Orthodox Church separated from the Roman Catholic Church. The Byzantine Empire's religion and culture had a lasting impact on Eastern Europe.

Chapter 2 Focus Question

As you read this chapter, keep this question in mind: **What were the origins and lasting effects of the rise of Constantinople and the Byzantine Empire?**

Section 1

The Survival of the Eastern Empire

Section 1 Focus Question

How did Constantine and his successors establish the Byzantine Empire? To begin answering this question,
- Find out how Roman power shifted to the east.
- Learn how Emperor Justinian and his wife, Theodora, expanded the Byzantine Empire.

Section 1 Summary

The emperor Constantine gained control of the Roman Empire and moved the capital to the eastern part of the Empire. Later, Emperor Justinian fought to restore the Roman Empire to its former greatness.

Power Shifts to the East

After a great victory in 324, a Roman leader named Constantine gained control of the Roman Empire. Constantine decided to move the capital of his government to the eastern city of Byzantium. He named the new capital Constantinople. Constantine began life as a pagan (PAY guhn), or a person who believes in more than one god, but he became a Christian later in life. He planned to make his "New Rome" a Christian city.

Key Events

324	Constantine plans Constantinople.
532	Construction of the Hagia Sophia begins.
1054	Eastern and Western Christian churches split.
1453	Constantinople falls to the Turks.

Constantine chose an excellent location for his new capital. The city lay at the south end of the Bosporus, a strait that connects the Black Sea and the Mediterranean Sea. This location, plus its good harbors, made it a trading center. The trade made Constantinople rich.

Mostly surrounded by the sea, Constantinople was also easier to defend than Rome. Thick walls and a moat (moht), or trench filled with water, protected the city from attacks by land.

After Constantine's death, the Roman Empire split into an Eastern Empire and a Western Empire. The capital of the Eastern Empire was Constantinople. The Western Empire fell in 476, but the Eastern Empire survived. Historians later named the surviving empire the Byzantine Empire. ✓

Justinian and Theodora

The first great Byzantine Emperor was Justinian. Both Justinian and his wife, Theodora, were talented, intelligent, and confident.

The Byzantine Empire reached its largest size under Justinian. But his many wars left the empire with money problems, and the empire lost most of the territory Justinian had gained.

Justinian had other accomplishments. Many modern legal systems are based on a law code he created.

After Justinian halted an urban revolt in 532, he had absolute power (AB suh loot POW uhr), or complete authority, over the empire. The revolt had destroyed much of the city, so Justinian built many new buildings. One of the new buildings, a church called the Hagia Sophia, is often called one of the world's most beautiful buildings today. ✓

Check Your Progress

1. Why was Byzantium a good location for Constantine's new capital?

_____

_____

2. List two things that Justinian accomplished as emperor.

_____

_____

Vocabulary Builder

Read the following sentence to help you figure out what *strait* means: *The ship sailed through the Bosporus Strait to get from the Black Sea to the Sea of Marmara.* Define *strait* in your own words.

_____

_____

_____

Checkpoint

When did Constantine gain complete control of the Roman Empire?

_____

✓ Checkpoint

Name the church that Justinian built in his rebuilding program.

_____

Question to Think About As you read Section 1 in your textbook and take notes, keep this section focus question in mind: **How did Constantine and his successors establish the Byzantine Empire?**

▶ Use these graphic organizers to guide you as you take notes on your reading.

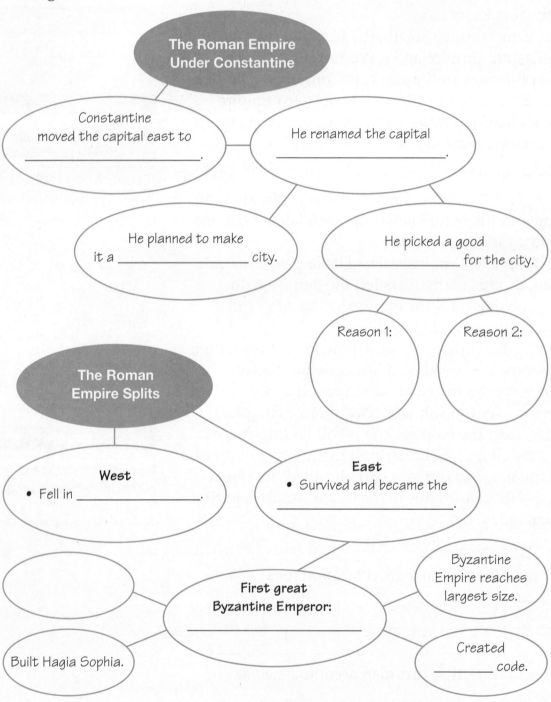

The Roman Empire
Under Constantine

Constantine moved the capital east to _____.

He renamed the capital _____.

He planned to make it a _____ city.

He picked a good _____ for the city.

Reason 1:

Reason 2:

The Roman Empire Splits

West
• Fell in _____.

East
• Survived and became the _____.

Byzantine Empire reaches largest size.

First great Byzantine Emperor:
_____

Created _____ code.

Built Hagia Sophia.

Refer to this page to answer the Chapter 2 Focus Question on page 26.

The Division of the Christian Church

Section 2 Focus Question

Why did the Christian Church split into the two distinct traditions—Eastern Orthodoxy and Roman Catholicism? To begin answering this question,

- Read about disagreements in the early Christian Church.
- Understand why the Christian Church split into two traditions in an event called the Great Schism.

Section 2 Summary

The early Christian Church had a strong organization. Disagreements among early Christians caused the Church to split into the Eastern Orthodox and Roman Catholic Churches.

The Early Christian Church

In the early years of Christianity, followers of Jesus founded churches in major cities of the Roman Empire. These early Christians were united in the belief that Jesus was a savior sent by God. Other issues divided Christians, such as issues about church organization or beliefs.

Even with competition from other religions, the early Church survived because of its strong organization. A bishop headed each local church, aided by deacons, deaconesses, and elders. Later, a bishop controlled all churches in a certain region.

The bishop's authority was based on an idea called "apostolic succession." This means that Jesus gave the original Apostles authority over his Church. The authority passes down to each following bishop.

The bishops of Rome, Jerusalem, Alexandria, Antioch, and Constantinople were called **patriarchs** (PAY tree ahrks). The five patriarchs had equal authority at first. But then the bishop of Rome claimed authority over all Christians. He called himself **pope** (pohp), which means father, or head, of the church. The pope said he had apostolic succession from the Apostle Peter. The eastern patriarchs disagreed.

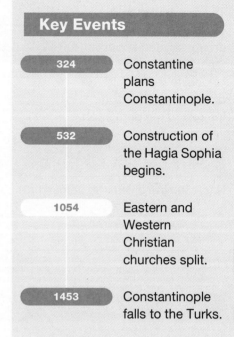

Key Events

324	Constantine plans Constantinople.
532	Construction of the Hagia Sophia begins.
1054	Eastern and Western Christian churches split.
1453	Constantinople falls to the Turks.

✓ Checkpoint

Name the five cities with patriarchs.

_____

_____

_____

Vocabulary Builder

The term *schism* comes from a Greek word meaning "split," or "division." To help you remember this, circle a context clue in the text.

✓ Checkpoint

Name the two churches that came out of the Great Schism.

_____

_____

As Christianity grew, groups also argued about the nature of Jesus. Constantine decided to settle the debate. He called a council of Church leaders. In A.D. 325, bishops met in Nicaea, in present-day Turkey. They approved a set of beliefs, or a creed (kreed), called the Nicene Creed.

Early Christians also argued about the use of icons. An icon (ī kahn) is a holy image, usually a picture of Jesus or a saint. In the 700s, many Byzantine emperors made their followers smash icons. To these emperors, using icons seemed like worshiping an object. The order to smash icons upset Christians in Western Europe. There, Church leaders saw icons as a way to teach people about God. ✓

The Great Schism

Over time, differences between the Eastern and Western Churches grew. In A.D. 1054, these two traditions split apart in an event called the Great Schism.

Traditions That Came Out of the Great Schism
The Eastern Tradition
• Led by the Byzantine emperor.
• Came to be known as the Eastern Orthodox Church. **Orthodox** (OR thuh dahks) means following traditional or established beliefs.
The Western Tradition
• Led by the pope.
• Came to be known as the Roman Catholic Church. **Catholic** (KATH uh lihk) means universal or concerned with all people.

The differences between the churches kept growing. Since A.D. 1054, the Eastern Church and Western Church have stayed apart. ✓

Check Your Progress

1. Which bishop claimed to be the pope?

_____

2. What is one difference between the Eastern Orthodox Church and the Roman Catholic Church?

_____

_____

Question to Think About As you read Section 2 in your textbook and take notes, keep this question in mind: **Why did the Christian Church split into the two distinct traditions—Eastern Orthodoxy and Roman Catholicism?**

▶ Use these charts to record key information from the section. Some information has been filled in to get you started.

The Early Christian Church

• The early Church survived because of its _____.
    • Each local church headed by:
      • Five _____ from: _____,
       _____,
       _____, _____, _____.
 	
 • Disagreements in the early Church
    • Pope claimed authority over Christians everywhere
    • The nature of _____
    • The use of _____

↓

The Great Schism

↓   ↓

Eastern Orthodox Church	**Roman Catholic Church**
_____ heads the Church.	_____ heads the Church.
Influenced _____ Europe.	Influenced _____ Europe.
_____ is the highest Church official.	_____ is the highest Church official.
Rituals and teaching are in _____.	Rituals and teaching are in _____.
Priests _____ marry.	Priests _____ marry.

Refer to this page to answer the Chapter 2 Focus Question on page 26.

Key Events

324	Constantine plans Constantinople.
532	Construction of the Hagia Sophia begins.
1054	Eastern and Western Christian churches split.
1453	Constantinople falls to the Turks.

Section 3 Focus Question

What lasting influence did Byzantine civilization have on Eastern Europe? To begin answering this question,

- Learn about the culture of the Byzantine Empire.
- Understand how Eastern Orthodox missionaries spread Byzantine culture to Eastern Europe.
- Examine why the Byzantine Empire ended.

Section 3 Summary

The Byzantine civilization preserved parts of classical Greek and Roman culture. Missionaries spread the Eastern Orthodox religion and Byzantine culture to Eastern Europe. Attacks reduced the size of the Byzantine Empire before it fell to the Turks.

A Unique Culture

Constantinople was at the crossroads between Europe and Asia. There, Eastern traditions mixed with classical Greek and Roman ideas. The result was a cultural blend that was unique, but also preserved tradition.

The Byzantine emperor Justinian worked to preserve the system of Roman law, but he organized it in a new way. He had a group of lawyers organize the laws he inherited from Rome into a unified code, or systematic body of law. Many law systems are based on this code today.

Byzantine artists also produced their own style of architecture and art. The most famous example of Byzantine architecture is the Hagia Sophia. The Hagia Sophia preserves tradition in the cross-shaped floor plan, which was typical of churches at the time. It breaks from tradition with its large dome.

Byzantine artists also found new ways to use old art forms. Mosaics (moh ZAY ihks), or designs made with colored stones and small pieces of glass, covered the walls and domes of their churches. Icons are another typical Byzantine art form. Byzantine art is usually flat, formal, and religious.

Reading Strategy

Read the bracketed paragraph. The first sentence is the main idea of the paragraph. Circle it. Then, underline each detail that supports the main idea.

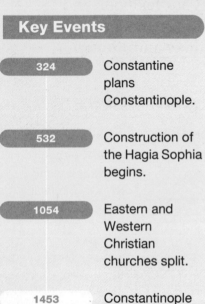

Learning was important in Byzantine culture. Children learned to read. Older students studied philosophy, math, and music. Libraries copied and preserved Greek and Roman manuscripts (MAN yoo skrihpts), or handwritten documents. ☑

The Spread of Byzantine Culture

Byzantine culture spread through the many visitors who came to Constantinople. <u>Merchants came to trade, and scholars came to study.</u> Byzantine rulers impressed their visitors with ceremonies, jewels, and rich clothes. The visitors took these ideas and products home.

Eastern Orthodox missionaries also spread Byzantine culture. A missionary (MIHSH uhn er ee) is someone sent to another country by a church to spread its faith. Eastern Orthodox missionaries went to Eastern Europe. They spread Byzantine culture to peoples who spoke Slavic languages, such as Russians, Serbs, and Bulgarians. They also traveled north to Rus—today called Ukraine, Belarus, and Russia.

Many in these areas converted (kuhn VERT uhd), or changed their religion, to Eastern Orthodox. Due to this missionary work, Eastern Orthodox Christianity is still practiced in these areas today. ☑

The End of the Byzantine Empire

The Byzantine Empire was almost always under attack. Germanic tribes invaded from the west. <u>Persians</u> were a threat to the east. Arabs invaded from the south. <u>Slavs</u> invaded from the north. Over time, attackers took over Byzantine lands. In 1453, Constantinople fell to the Turks. The Byzantine Empire was no more. ☑

Check Your Progress

1. How did the emperor Justinian preserve Roman law?

_____

_____

2. How did visitors spread Byzantine culture?

_____

_____

✓ Checkpoint

Name two forms of art that were typical of the Byzantine civilization.

_____

_____

Vocabulary Builder

Reread the underlined sentence. Write short definitions of *merchant* and *scholar*. Circle any context clues that helped you.

_____

_____

_____

✓ Checkpoint

List two ways Byzantine culture spread to other places.

_____

_____

✓ Checkpoint

When and to whom did Constantinople fall?

_____

_____

Question to Think About As you read Section 3 in your textbook and take notes, keep this section focus question in mind: **What lasting influence did Byzantine civilization have on Eastern Europe?**

▶ Use this chart to record key information from the section. Some information has been filled in to get you started.

Unique Culture			
Preserved Roman Law	**Produced Architecture**	**Created Art**	**Stressed Learning**
_____ had lawyers organize Roman laws. They created a _unified_ _____ _____ in 529.	The most famous example of Byzantine architecture is the_____ _____. This church had a huge _____.	Mosaics and _____ were common Byzantine art forms. Byzantine art is usually _____, _____, and _____.	Children learned to _____ in schools. Older students studied _____ _____, and _____. Libraries copied Greek and Roman _____.

The Byzantine Empire

Outside Threats	**Spread of Culture**
1. _____ tribes attacked in the west. 2. Persians threatened from the _____. 3. _____ invaded from the south. 4. _____ invaded from the north. 5. Constantinople fell to the _____ in 1453.	1. Visitors took _____ and _____ home. 2. Eastern Orthodox _____ spread their faith. 3. _____ came to trade. 4. _____ came to study. 5. The _____ alphabet helped Byzantine culture spread.

Refer to this page to answer the Chapter 2 Focus Question on page 26.

Directions: Circle the letter of the correct answer.

1. _____ moved the Roman Empire's capital from _____ to
   _____.

   A Constantine; Rome; Mecca
   B Justinian; Byzantium; Rome
   C Constantine; Rome; Byzantium

2. Where did the pope claim to get his authority?
   A It was passed to him from the Byzantine emperor.
   B It was passed to him from church members.
   C It was passed to him from the Apostle Peter.

3. The Hagia Sophia is an example of how Byzantine culture
   A worshiped a god named Sophia.
   B was unique, but also preserved tradition.
   C failed to produce lasting architecture.

4. The Byzantine Empire fell to the:
   A Turks.   **B** Arabs.   **C** Slavs.

Directions: Follow the steps to answer this question:

How did the location of Constantinople help Byzantine culture spread?

Step 1. List some reasons why Constantinople was an excellent location for
the capital.

_____

_____

_____

Step 2. Recall how Byzantine culture spread.

_____

_____

_____

Step 3. Make a connection. Finish the topic sentence below, and write three
or four more sentences telling how Constantinople's location helped
Byzantine culture spread.

The location of Constantinople helped _____

_____

_____

_____

Chapter 2 Notetaking Study Guide

Now you are ready to answer the Chapter 2 Focus Question: **What were the origins and lasting effects of the rise of Constantinople and the Byzantine Empire?**

► Complete the following charts to help you answer this question. Use the notes that you took for each section.

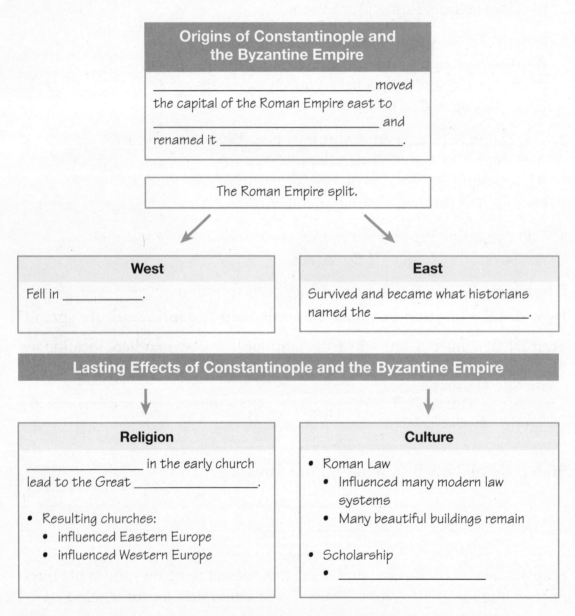

Origins of Constantinople and the Byzantine Empire

_____ moved the capital of the Roman Empire east to _____ and renamed it _____.

The Roman Empire split.

West

Fell in _____.

East

Survived and became what historians named the _____.

Lasting Effects of Constantinople and the Byzantine Empire

Religion

_____ in the early church lead to the Great _____.

- Resulting churches:
  - influenced Eastern Europe
  - influenced Western Europe

Culture

- Roman Law
  - Influenced many modern law systems
  - Many beautiful buildings remain

- Scholarship
  - _____

Refer to this page to answer the Unit 1 Focus Question on page 27.

Unit 1 Pulling It Together Activity

What You Have Learned

Chapter 1 Scholars rely on various sources of information to uncover the past. Using these sources, they have learned much about ancient Rome.

Chapter 2 Constantinople became the center of the Byzantine Empire. The Eastern Orthodox Church separated from the Roman Catholic Church. The religion and culture of the Byzantine Empire had a lasting impact on Eastern Europe.

Think Like a Historian

Read the Unit 1 Focus Question: **How can the influence of an empire live on after the empire falls?**

▶ Use the organizers on this page and the next to collect information to answer this question.

What legacies did the Romans and Byzantines leave behind? Review your section and chapter notes. Then complete these lists of key dates.

Key Events in the Roman Republic and Empire

509 B.C. Rome becomes a republic.

451 B.C. _____

_____

A.D. 180 _____

_____

A.D. 300s Christianity becomes official religion.

A.D. 476 _____

_____

Key Events in the Byzantine Empire

A.D. 324   Constantine plans new capital in the east.

A.D. 529   _____

_____

A.D. 532   Construction of Hagia Sophia begins.

A.D. 800s Eastern Orthodox missionaries travel to Eastern Europe.

A.D. 1054 _____

_____

A.D. 1453 _____

_____

What legacies did the Romans and Byzantines leave behind? The charts below give you a part of the answer. Use the information you have gathered to complete the charts.

Legacies of the Roman Republic and Empire	
Aspect	**Examples of Legacies**
Art, Architecture	• statues • public works
Engineering	• •
Law	• •
Language	•
Religion	•

Legacies of the Byzantine Empire	
Aspect	**Examples of Legacies**
Art, Architecture	• icons • mosaics • domes
Law	•
Language	•
Culture	•
Religion	•

Islamic Civilization

Chapter 3 Islam, the world's second largest religion, began in the deserts of Arabia and spread through conquest and conversion. Muslims follow the teachings of the prophet Muhammad and study the Qur'an and the Sunnah, Islam's sacred texts.

Chapter 4 A government led by caliphs ruled a vast territory that was influenced by Islamic principles. Muslim achievements in trade, science, learning, and the arts contributed to the success of Islamic civilization.

Focus Your Learning As you study this unit and take notes, you will find the information to answer the questions below. Answering the chapter focus questions will help build your answer to the unit focus question.

Chapter 3 Focus Question
What are the origins and beliefs of Islam and how did it spread?
(page 30)

Chapter 4 Focus Question
What were the political, social, economic, and cultural characteristics of Islamic civilization?
(page 41)

Unit 2 Focus Question
How can religion have a powerful effect on people's way of life, including their culture and government?
(page 55)

Chapter 3

Islam (570–1400s)

What You Will Learn

Islam, the world's second largest religion, began in the deserts of Arabia and spread through conquest and conversion. Muslims follow the teachings of the prophet Muhammad and study the Qur'an and the Sunnah, Islam's sacred texts.

Chapter 3 Focus Question

As you read Chapter 3, keep this question in mind: **What are the origins and beliefs of Islam and how did it spread?**

Section 1

The Origins of Islam

Section 1 Focus Question

Where and how did Islam first arise? To begin answering this question,
- Discover the geography and culture of Arabia.
- Learn the story of the prophet Muhammad.

Section 1 Summary

The religion Islam began in the Arabian Peninsula in the 600s. The prophet Muhammad founded Islam. Muhammad gained followers, and Islam became the religion of Arabia.

The Arabian Setting

Arabia is a large peninsula in southwest Asia. Arabia's environment—or the air, water, and land in which people and animals live—is dry and harsh. Most of the land is desert. There is a high and rugged mountain range along the western and southern edges of the peninsula.

In general, there is little water and no permanent rivers in Arabia. Arabians relied on oases for their survival. An oasis (oh AY sihs) is a fertile place in the desert where a spring or well provides a water supply.

Key Events

610	Muhammad begins to preach the message of Islam.
732	The Battle of Tours ends the Muslim advance into Europe.
1453	Constantinople falls to the Ottoman Turks.

Vocabulary Builder

Using context clues in the text, write a short definition of the others.

Ex. Arabia: *a peninsula in southwest Asia*

Arab: _____

Arabian: _____

Arabic: _____

Because there was little water, human settlement was difficult in Arabia. Some ancient Arabs lived a settled, or sedentary (SEHD ehn tehr ee), life. Others lived a nomadic (noh MAD ihk) life, moving from place to place with no fixed home. Both sedentary and nomadic groups were organized as tribes. Their loyalty was to tribes and families instead of to rulers. ☑

The Story of Muhammad

Around 570, the prophet Muhammad (moo HAM uhd) was born in the largest Arabian town, Mecca. Mecca was both a trading center and a religious center.

Muhammad's uncle raised him in this environment. When he was 25, Muhammad married a wealthy, widowed merchant named Khadija (ka DEE jah). He became a successful and respected businessman in Mecca.

In 610, Muhammad went to a cave to reflect on the greed, corruption, and violence in Meccan society. In the cave, Muhammad had a vision and began to receive revelations. An angel came and told him to preach the message of God, who created man, or made man exist.

Muhammad returned to Mecca and told the Arabs about God, called Allah in Arabic. He told them to worship God and to stop their sinful ways. The Qur'an names this religion Islam. Islam's followers were called Muslims.

Arabs who did not agree with Muhammad forced him and his followers to leave Mecca. They went to a town that today is called Medina, or "city of the prophet." Muslims call the flight to Medina the hijra.

Muhammad returned to Mecca in 630. He conquered Mecca, and he proclaimed Islam to be the religion of Arabia. Muhammad died two years later. His followers continued to spread Islam through the conquest of the Middle East. ☑

Check Your Progress

1. Why was human settlement difficult in Arabia?

_____

_____

2. Why did Muhammad go into the cave?

_____

_____

✓ Checkpoint

Name two distinct lifestyles that existed in ancient Arabia.

_____

_____

Reading Strategy

Ask and answer a question about when and where Muhammad was born.

Question: _____

_____ ?

Answer: _____

_____

_____ .

✓ Checkpoint

List three important events in Muhammad's life in the order they happened.

1. _____

2. _____

3. _____

Question to Think About As you read Section 1 in your textbook, keep this question in mind: **Where and how did Islam first arise?**

▶ Use these charts to help record key information. Some of the information has been filled in to get you started.

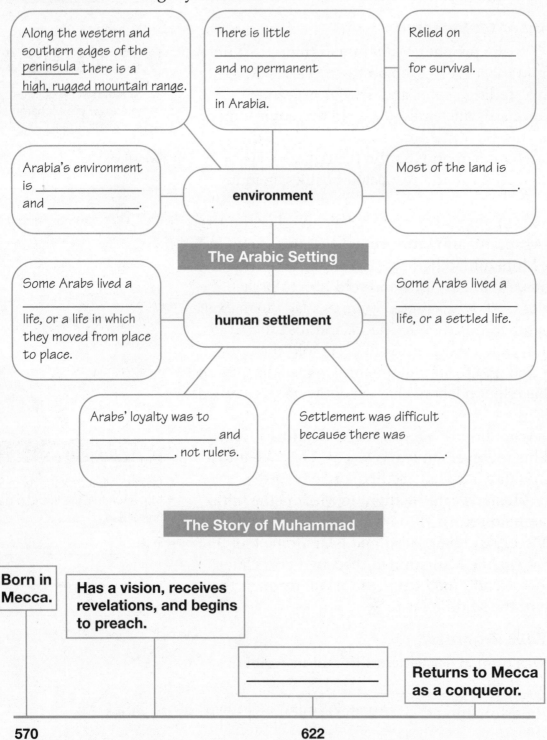

The Arabic Setting

Along the western and southern edges of the <u>peninsula</u> there is a <u>high, rugged mountain range</u>.

There is little _____ and no permanent _____ in Arabia.

Relied on _____ for survival.

Arabia's environment is _____ and _____.

environment

Most of the land is _____.

Some Arabs lived a _____ life, or a life in which they moved from place to place.

human settlement

Some Arabs lived a _____ life, or a settled life.

Arabs' loyalty was to _____ and _____, not rulers.

Settlement was difficult because there was _____.

The Story of Muhammad

Born in Mecca.

Has a vision, receives revelations, and begins to preach.

_____ _____

Returns to Mecca as a conqueror.

570

_____

622

Refer to this page to answer the Chapter 3 Focus Question on page 40.

The Beliefs of Islam

Section 2 Focus Question

What are the major beliefs of Islam, as revealed in the Qur'an and the Sunnah? To begin answering this question,

- Learn about the sacred writings of Islam.
- Discover the core beliefs of Islam.

Key Events

610	Muhammad begins to preach the message of Islam.
732	The Battle of Tours ends the Muslim advance into Europe.
1453	Constantinople falls to the Ottoman Turks.

Section 2 Summary

The Qur'an and the Sunnah are the two major sources of Islamic thought. The main belief that these sources teach is the existence of one God, called Allah in Arabic. Muslims have five religious duties that are central to their worship of Allah.

Sacred Writings

The Qur'an (koo RAHN) is the most sacred text in Islam. It is a record of Muhammad's visions over a period of 22 years. Muslims believe the Qur'an is the word of God, or Allah.

The Qur'an tells about the nature of Allah, creation, and the human soul. It also addresses moral, legal, and family questions.

The Sunnah, or the traditions of the prophet, is another major source of Islamic thought. It tells about Muhammad's words and actions and is based on stories from people who knew him during his lifetime. The written record of the Sunnah is called the Hadith. The Sunnah provides Muslims with a model for living a proper life. It also helps them interpret, or explain the meaning of, difficult parts of the Qur'an. ✓

Reading Strategy

Reread the bracketed paragraph. Underline the text that tells you how the Sunnah and the Hadith are related.

✓ Checkpoint

List the two main sources of Islamic thought.

_____

_____

Core Beliefs

The central belief in Islam is the existence of one God. Muslims honor Muhammad as a prophet, but they do not believe he was a god.

Muslims believe that each person has an individual and eternal soul. They also believe in heaven and hell, and that on a future judgment day, God will judge mankind and decide who will be saved.

Muslims have five key religious duties. These duties, listed below, are called the Five Pillars.

Vocabulary Builder

A creation is something that is created. A revelation is something that is revealed. What is a declaration?

_____

_____

✓ Checkpoint

Name the central belief in Islam.

_____

	The Five Pillars
1	**Declaration of Faith:** Muslims often recite the phrase, "There is no God but God; Muhammad is the messenger of God."
2	**Prayer:** Muslims are expected to pray five times a day, kneeling and facing the direction of Mecca.
3	**Almsgiving** (AHMZ giving): It is the duty of all Muslims to give goods or money to the needy or less fortunate.
4	**Fasting** (FAST ihng): Muslims are not to eat or drink from daybreak to sunset for a month every year.
5	**Pilgrimage** (PIHL gruh mihj), or *hajj*: If possible, Muslims must make a trip to Mecca, the holy city of Islam, at least once. A pilgrimage is a journey to a sacred place or shrine.

The Five Pillars guide Muslims in living a proper life. These duties form the foundations of Muslim life. ✓

Check Your Progress

1. What are three subjects that the Qur'an addresses?

_____

_____

2. List the Five Pillars. What purpose do they serve?

_____

_____

_____

_____

Question to Think About As you read Section 2 in your textbook, keep this question in mind: **What are the major beliefs of Islam, as revealed in the Qur'an and the Sunnah?**

▶ Use this chart to help record key information. Some of the information has been filled in to get you started.

Sacred Texts

_____

- Word of God

- _____
  revelations

- Used for_____
  and _____

- Discusses the nature of God,
  _____, and
  _____

The Sunnah

- Written down by _____
  _____

- Muhammad's _____
  and _____

- Guideline for living

- Written version called
  _____

Teachings

- One God, called _____

- Each person has an _____ and _____
  soul, and the belief in heaven and _____.

- Five Pillars, or the duties of a _____
  1. _____   4. _____
  2. _____   5. _____
  3. _____

Refer to this page to answer the Chapter 3 Focus Question on page 40.

The Spread of Islam

Key Events

610   Muhammad begins to preach the message of Islam.

732   The Battle of Tours ends the Muslim advance into Europe.

1453   Constantinople falls to the Ottoman Turks.

Reading Strategy

Reread the bracketed paragraph. What happened in between Abu Bakr being named caliph and the expansion of Muslim rule? Underline the sentence that tells you.

Vocabulary Builder

If "the rise of the Byzantine empire" is opposite in meaning from "the decline of the Byzantine empire," what does the word *decline* mean?

_____

_____

Section 3 Focus Question

How did Islam spread through three phases of expansion? To begin answering this question,

- Learn about the expansion of Muslim rule.
- Explore Islam's presence in the world today.

Section 3 Summary

After Muhammad's death, Muslim rule spread to new parts of the world. Today, more than one fifth of the world's population is united by the core beliefs of Islam.

Muslim Expansion

Except for rebel Arab tribes, most of the people on the Arabian Peninsula had converted to Islam by the time Muhammad died in 632. Leaders of the dominant Muslim group within the community chose **Abu Bakr** (uh BOO BAK uh) as Muhammad's successor, or **caliph** (KAY lihf). He led the conquest of the rebel tribes. He also united Arabs under the banner of Islam.

With Arabs united, Islam began to spread to new territories. The expansion had three phases. The first phase was conquest by Arab armies. Next came conquests by non-Arab armies. The third phase was peaceful conversion by merchants and missionaries.

The first phase began under **Umar ibn al-Khattab** (OO mahr IHB ihn ahl kah TAHB). It continued under other caliphs' rule. Only a hundred years after Muhammad's death, the Muslim empire included Mesopotamia, Palestine, Syria, Persia, Egypt, Afghanistan, India, North Africa, and Spain.

There were many reasons for the successful spread of Islam. One reason was the decline of the Byzantine and Persian empires. Years of warfare left these empires weak and vulnerable to the Arabs' attacks. The skill of Arab armies was a second factor in helping Islam spread. Arab soldiers were experts on horseback. They struck quickly and with deadly force. Arab warriors also fought with great religious zeal under the banner of **jihad** (jee HAHD), or holy struggle. *Jihad* refers to striving hard in God's cause. The struggle can be internal or waging war.

Another reason for the Arabs' success was their tolerance of other religions, customs, and beliefs. The Arab general **Khalid ibn al-Walid** (kah LEED IHB ihn ahl wah LEED) promised "security for [the] lives, property, and churches" of those he conquered. A final factor helping the Arabs was the appeal of Islam itself. Islam offered a direct path to God and salvation. It also emphasized the equality of all believers.

In the second phase, non-Arab peoples helped spread Islam through conquest. Groups such as the Turks and the Mongols converted to Islam while visiting Muslim lands. They took the new faith back to their homelands. Their efforts also spread Islam to Central Asia, southeastern Europe, western China, and India.

Conquests continued, but the third phase of Muslim expansion was entirely peaceful. Muslim merchants and missionaries who traveled with them spread Islam along trade routes. Southeast Asia and West Africa were exposed to Islam this way. ✓

Islam Today

Muslims are divided into two main groups today. The **Sunnis** (SOON eez) are the majority Islamic sect. The **Shiites** (SHEE īts) are the largest minority Islamic sect. The split was originally political. Some religious differences exist between the two groups, but their basic beliefs unite them.

Fewer than 20 percent of Muslims are Arabs. Nearly half live in South and Southeast Asia. Islam is the world's second-largest religion, and it continues to grow today. ✓

Check Your Progress

1. List the three stages of Muslim expansion.

_____

_____

2. What percentage of Muslims are Arabs? Where do nearly half of all Muslims live today?

_____

_____

✓ Checkpoint

Name the first caliph.

_____

✓ Checkpoint

List the two main groups in Islam. Circle the one that is the majority sect.

_____

_____

Question to Think About As you read Section 3 and take notes, keep this question in mind: **How did Islam spread through three phases of expansion?**

► Use the organizers below to record key information.

Muslim Expansion		
How Islam Spread		
Phase	**Spread by**	**How**
1	Arabs	conquests
2		
3		
Why the Spread of Islam was Successful		
Reason	**Why helpful**	
Decline of the Byzantine and Persian Empires	Years of warfare had left these empires weak and vulnerable to Muslim conquests.	
Skill of the Arab Armies		
Religious Zeal		
Appeal of Islam		

Islam Today

Islam's Two Main Groups

_____

• Belief about succesor:

_____
_____
_____

Common Beliefs
1. _____
2. _____
3. _____

_____

• Belief about succesor:

_____
_____
_____

Refer to this page to answer the Chapter 3 Focus Question on page 40.

Directions: Circle the letter of the correct answer.

1. Islam first emerged in
   A the Arabian Peninsula.
   B Mesopotamia.
   C Afghanistan.

2. The Qur'an and the Sunnah are
   A both the word of God.
   B key sources of Islamic thought.
   C Muslim holidays.

3. Muslim expansion
   A stopped when Muhammad died.
   B took place in three phases.
   C only happened by conquest.

Directions: Follow the steps to answer this question:

Why were different phases of Muslim expansion successful?

Step 1: Recall information: List the three phases of Muslim expansion.

Phase 1: _____

Phase 2: _____

Phase 3: _____

Step 2: Recall information: List five reasons the spread of Islam was successful.

1. _____

2. _____

3. _____

4. _____

5. _____

Step 3: Make a connection: Pick one phase of Muslim expansion. Write a topic sentence stating which reason was most important to the success of that phase. Write two or three sentences that support the topic sentence.

_____

_____

_____

_____

Now you are ready to answer the Chapter 3 Focus Question: **What are the origins and beliefs of Islam and how did it spread?**

▶ Complete the following charts to help you answer this question. Use the notes that you took for each section.

Origins
Arabian Setting
• _harsh_ environment
• people organized as _____ with no loyalty to _____
Muhammad
• born around the year _____ in the city of _____
• fled to _____ on a journey called the _____
• conquered the city of _____ in the year _____

Beliefs
Qur'an
• tells about _____Allah_____, _____, and the _____
• addresses _____, _____, and _____ issues
Sunnah
• written version called the _____
Five Pillars of Faith
1. _____
2. _____
3. _____
4. _____
5. _____

Islam

Spread
First Phase
Arab soldiers were able to conquer because of their skill on _____ and the declines of the _____ and _____ empires.
Second Phase
Groups like _____ and _____ converted and took _____ back to their homelands.
Third Phase
Islam spread along trade routes by _____ and _____.

Refer to this page to answer the Unit 2 Focus Question on page 55.

The Islamic World (632–1500)

Chapter Standards

History-Social Science 7.2.3, 7.2.4, 7.2.5, 7.2.6

What You Will Learn

A government led by caliphs ruled a vast area that was influenced by Islamic principles. Muslim achievements in trade, science, learning, and the arts contributed to the success of Islamic civilization.

Chapter 4 Focus Question

As you read this chapter, keep this question in mind: **What were the political, social, economic, and cultural characteristics of Islamic civilization?**

Section 1

The Expansion of Muslim Rule

Section 1 Focus Question

How did Muslim rule expand? To begin answering this question,
- Learn about the establishment of the caliphate.
- Find out about divisions in the caliphate.

Key Events

632	Muhammad dies.
800s	Golden age of Islamic civilization begins.
1258	Mongols conquer Baghdad and destroy the caliphate.
1453	Ottomans conquer the Byzantine Empire.

Section 1 Summary

After Muhammad's death, leaders called caliphs ruled Muslim lands. Under the caliphs, Muslim rule and influence expanded.

Establishing the Caliphate

To manage the new lands they conquered, the Muslims established a type of government called a caliphate (KAY luh fuht), which means rule by a caliph. *Caliph* was the title given to Muslim leaders after Muhammad's death.

The first four caliphs had close ties to Muhammad. They were selected by Muslim leaders, and they were guided by Muslim principles. After the death of the fourth caliph, the Umayyad family gained control of the caliphate. The Umayyads moved the capital from Medina to Damascus, and they founded Islam's first

Vocabulary Builder

The word *interact* can be broken into two parts, *inter–* and *act*. If *inter–* means "between," what do you think *interact* means? Use the context of the underlined sentences to help you.

_____

_____

✓ Checkpoint

List four cultures the Arabs came in contact with during the caliphate.

_____

_____

_____

_____

Reading Strategy

Underline the sentence that tells you when the Abbasid caliphate began. Draw an arrow to the sentence that tells you when it ended.

✓ Checkpoint

List two groups that contributed to the downfall of the caliphate.

_____

_____

dynasty (DY nuhs tee). A dynasty is a family that holds political power over many generations.

The caliphate expanded into North Africa, Spain, and Central and South Asia. Some expansion came about through treaties, rather than war. A **treaty** (TREET ee) is a written agreement between countries or peoples. The expansion led to cultural exchanges as Arabs interacted with Christians, Jews, Greeks, and Persians. Many non-Arabs adopted Islam and learned Arabic. Arabs were also influenced by other cultures. ✓

Divisions in the Caliphate

In the 700s, Muslim armies lost many battles and expansion ended. In 750, rebel forces overthrew the Umayyads. They installed a new caliph from the Abbasid family. The Abbasids built a new capital at Baghdad. Baghdad became the center of a golden age of art, science, and learning.

In the 900s, Turkish tribes began to invade Muslim lands. They eventually captured Baghdad. The Turks allowed the Abbasid caliphs to stay on the throne but stripped them of power. In the 1200s, Mongols attacked Baghdad, killing tens of thousands of people, including the last Abbasid caliph.

The caliphate ended, but individual Islamic states survived, each governed by its own **sultan** (SULT uhn), or Muslim ruler. The greatest of these Islamic states later became the Ottoman Empire.

The Ottomans were Turks. In the 1300s, they began attacking the Byzantine Empire, finally capturing Constantinople in 1453. In time, the Ottoman Empire stretched from Eastern Europe to Egypt. ✓

Check Your Progress

1. How were the "rightly guided caliphs" different from later caliphs?

_____

_____

2. What happened after the Mongol invasion destroyed the caliphate?

_____

_____

Question to Think About: As you read Section 1 in your textbook, keep this question in mind: **How did Muslim rule expand?**

▶ Use these charts to take notes on your reading. Some information has been filled in to get you started.

Leadership of the Caliphate		
	First Four Caliphs	**Dynastic Caliphs**
How they came to power		Power struggles, rebellions
Important names	•	• Umayyads •
Location(s) of capital	• Medina	• •

End of the Caliphate	
Internal problems	Parts of the empire were breaking away. • __Spain__ became independent. • Fatimids seized control of _____.
External attacks by	• __Turkish tribes_____ • _____
Results	• Individual Islamic states governed by a _____. • The greatest Islamic state became the _____.

Refer to this page to answer the Chapter 4 Focus Question on page 54.

Key Events

632	Muhammad dies.
800s	Golden age of Islamic civilization begins.
1258	Mongols conquer Baghdad and destroy the caliphate.
1453	Ottomans conquer the Byzantine Empire.

Section 2 Focus Question

What values, beliefs, and traditions influenced Muslims' daily life? To begin answering this question,
- Learn how Islamic law affected Muslims' daily life.
- Find out about Muslim society.

Section 2 Summary

Muslims believed that life should be conducted according to Islamic principles. Islamic laws helped guide people in their daily lives.

Islamic Law

Muslims believed that living a proper life meant following God's law as revealed in the Qur'an and the Sunnah. These laws were collected in a legal code known as the Sharia (SHAH ree uh), which means "the way that leads to God." The Sharia was based on the Qur'an and the Sunnah. It also included religious scholars' judgments on subjects not covered in those two books.

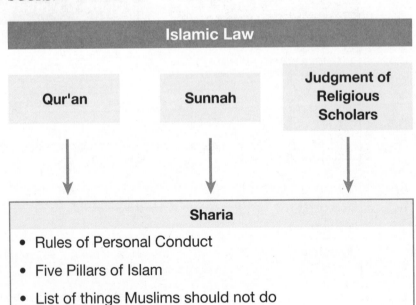

Islamic Law

| Qur'an | Sunnah | Judgment of Religious Scholars |

Sharia

- Rules of Personal Conduct
- Five Pillars of Islam
- List of things Muslims should not do
- Rules for resolving family issues and doing business

Prayer and worship were key elements of Muslim daily life. Muslims were required to pray five times a day in the direction of Mecca. A person called a muezzin called people to prayer from a tower called a minaret (mihn uh REHT). Communities gathered together in a mosque to pray and participate in other religious activities. An imam (ih MAHM), or religious leader, delivered sermons there, too. ☑

Muslim Society

Islam emphasized the value of a just and moral society. All human beings were considered equal, and Muslims were expected to give alms to the poor. However, social classes did exist in the Islamic world. In the early days of the caliphate, Muslim society was divided into four classes. Arabs were at the head of society. Next came non-Arabs who had converted to Islam. Third were Jews and Christians, who were respected as "People of the Book." At the bottom were slaves. Over time, however, class lines softened and people could rise in society based on their achievements.

Islam also laid out clear roles for men and women. Men were expected to support their families, and women usually stayed at home. Women generally had fewer rights than men, but before the spread of Islam, Arabic women had virtually no rights. Marriage was arranged by families, but the bride and groom had to approve the match. Men could practice polygamy (puh LIHG uh mee), or marriage to more than one spouse.

Education in Muslim society had a strong religious basis. Students began by studying the Qur'an. Later, they could study other subjects at a religious school, known as a madrasa (muh DRAHS uh). Because of this emphasis on education, the Islamic world produced many fine writers, scholars, and artists. ☑

Check Your Progress

1. What was Islamic law based upon?

_____

_____

2. How did Muslim society view education?

_____

_____

© Pearson Education, Inc., publishing as Pearson Prentice Hall. All Rights Reserved.

✓ **Checkpoint**

List three sources from which the Sharia is drawn.

_____

_____

_____

Vocabulary Builder

Read the underlined sentence. Use context clues to explain the meaning of the word *softened* in this sentence.

_____

_____

Reading Strategy

Read the bracketed paragraph. Underline the main idea of the paragraph and circle two details that support the main idea.

✓ **Checkpoint**

List the four social classes of Muslim society in the early days of the caliphate.

_____

_____

_____

_____

Question to Think About As you read Section 2 in your textbook, keep this question in mind: **What values, beliefs, and traditions influenced Muslims' daily life?**

▶ Use these charts to take notes on your reading. Some information has been filled in to get you started.

Islamic Law	
Sources of Islamic law (the Sharia)	• Qur'an • the Sunnah •
Laws of proper conduct	• Five Pillars of Islam • no gambling, stealing, eating pork, or drinking alcohol • •
Rules for prayer	• • Remove shoes, wash hands and feet, bow several times •

Muslim Society	
Feature	**Description**
Social classes	Emphasis on equality; four main classes: Arabs, Muslim non-Arabs, Jews and Christians, and slaves. Over time, class lines softened.
Role of women	
Marriage	
Education	

Refer to this page to answer the Chapter 4 Focus Question on page 54.

Section 3

The Growth of Cities and Trade

Section 3 Focus Question

How did Muslims develop and benefit from a thriving economy? To begin answering this question,

- Find out why Muslim cities prospered.
- Learn why the Islamic world was a center of trade.

Section 3 Summary

Under the caliphate, Islamic cities and trade thrived. Trade led to the exchange of goods, as well as ideas, throughout the Muslim Empire.

Muslim Cities

At its height during the Abbasid dynasty, the caliphate was united by a strong central government and a single language. These conditions fueled economic expansion and **urban** (ER buhn) growth. Urban means having to do with a city or cities.

By A.D. 1000, Islam had the largest and most developed cities outside of China: Mecca, Damascus, Baghdad, Córdoba in Spain, and Cairo in Egypt. A strong economy supported urban growth. Farms supplied food, wool, and other goods. <u>Traders brought silks and other exotic goods from distant lands.</u>

Among Islam's most famous and valuable products were **textiles** (TEHKS tĭlz), or woven goods, such as Egyptian cotton and Persian carpets. Other fine goods included steel swords from Damascus and leather goods from Córdoba. Traders carried goods all over the caliphate and beyond.

Traders and merchants were important to the urban economy. So, they were honored in the Islamic world. Successful merchants had great **social mobility** (SOH shul moh BIHL uh tee), or the ability to rise in society. Many merchants became important figures in the Islamic world.

The center of life for merchants was the **souk** (sook), or marketplace. Here, merchants bought and sold goods from around the empire. ✓

Key Events

632	Muhammad dies.
800s	Golden age of Islamic civilization begins.
1258	Mongols conquer Baghdad and destroy the caliphate.
1453	Ottomans conquer the Byzantine Empire.

Vocabulary Strategy

Exotic comes from a Greek root, *exo–*, meaning outside. Circle the phrase in the underlined sentence that might give you a clue about the meaning of *exotic* if you didn't know its root. Then write a short definition of the word *exotic*.

_____

_____

✓ Checkpoint

List three types of goods that Islamic merchants traded.

_____

_____

_____

Reading Strategy

Read the bracketed paragraph. Circle the main idea, and then underline a supporting detail in the paragraph.

✓ Checkpoint

List the three continents into which the Islamic empire expanded.

_____

_____

_____

Trade and Trade Routes

The location of the Islamic world was ideal for trade. It lay between the Mediterranean Sea and the Indian Ocean and covered parts of Europe, Africa, and Asia. Muslim traders sailed to Africa and India. On land they traveled by camel caravan. The most famous caravan route was from Baghdad to China. It was known as the Silk Road.

Merchants developed banking practices to improve trade. For example, banks issued letters of credit (LEHT erz uhv CREHD iht) that could be used anywhere in the empire. A letter of credit is a written record issued by one bank that allows a person to take money out of another bank. Carrying letters of credit was easier and safer than carrying coins.

With these methods, trade flourished in the Islamic world. Goods came to Islamic cities from three continents. Asia provided silk, paper, and dishes from China as well as spices, gems, coconuts, and tropical woods from India. Gold and salt came from Africa, while amber and furs arrived from northern Europe.

Ideas and inventions also spread along the trade routes. Muslim traders brought back the Chinese compass and the idea of Hindu numerals. In turn, traders spread Islamic customs and religious beliefs to other parts of the world. ✓

Check Your Progress

1. What conditions led to economic expansion and urban growth in the caliphate?

_____

_____

_____

2. How was the location of the Islamic empire good for trade?

_____

_____

_____

Question to Think About As you read Section 3 in your textbook, keep this question in mind: **How did Muslims develop and benefit from a thriving economy?**

▶ Use this chart to take notes on your reading. Some information has been filled in to get you started.

Islam's Cities and International Trade		
Major Cities of Islam	• Mecca • • • • Cairo	
Famous products of the Islamic world	**Goods**	**Region from**
	Carpets	Persia
	Leather goods	
Methods of transportation used by Muslim traders	• Ships •	
Goods traders brought to the Islamic world	**Goods**	**Region from**
	• • •	China
	• • • •	
	• •	
	• Amber • Furs	

Refer to this page to answer the Chapter 4 Focus Question on page 54.

Key Events

632	Muhammad dies.
800s	Golden age of Islamic civilization begins.
1258	Mongols conquer Baghdad and destroy the caliphate.
1453	Ottomans conquer the Byzantine Empire.

Reading Strategy

Read the bracketed paragraphs. Underline the main idea in each paragraph.

Section 4 Focus Question

How did cultural exchanges and the work of Islamic scholars produce lasting achievements? To begin answering this question,

- Find out about the great achievements of Muslim scholars.
- Learn how the arts flourished in the Islamic world.

Section 4 Summary

Learning and the arts were prized in Islamic culture. Muslim scholars, artists, and authors made many important contributions to the world.

Muslim Learning

According to the teachings of Islam, knowledge is sacred, so learning was highly prized in the Islamic world. The most famous center of learning was the House of Wisdom in Baghdad. Here, scholars translated works from Greece, Persia, and India. They also combined Islamic principles with foreign ideas, and created their own works.

The Muslim world produced many brilliant philosophers. One well-known philosopher, **Ibn Rushd** (IHB uhn rusht), tried to integrate, or combine, faith and reason. His work later influenced scholars in Europe.

Muslim physicians made great contributions to medical science. There were hospitals throughout the Islamic empire. There were also pharmacies where medicine was prepared. Muslim doctors were skilled surgeons. One doctor, **Ibn Sina** (IHB uhn SEE nuh), wrote a medical encyclopedia that covered every disease and treatment known at that time. It became the standard medical text in Europe for hundreds of years.

Muslim scholars also made great achievements in science and math. They developed a decimal system based on Hindu numerals and the concept of zero. This system later spread to Europe. As a result, the symbols we use today are called Arabic numerals.

Muslim astronomers charted planets and stars, measured the size of Earth, and developed precise calendars. Scholars rediscovered an ancient Greek device called an astrolabe (AS troh layb), which is an instrument designed to measure and plot the position of stars. It was later used to find a ship's position at sea.

Muslim scholars also studied geography and history. Muslim travelers visited distant lands and wrote about what they saw. Ibn Khaldun (IHB uhn kahl DOON) wrote a history of the world that tried to explain the rise and fall of dynasties. ☑

The Arts and Literature

Muslims valued the arts as well as learning. Muslim civilization was famous for its decorative arts, such as carpets and colorful tiles. One of the most popular designs was the arabesque (ar uh BEHSK), a pattern of curved shapes and lines resembling flowers or vines.

Muslim architects built striking mosques, shrines, and palaces. Painting, however, was not an important art form in the Islamic world. Islam discouraged art that portrayed human or animal figures, as it was considered a form of idol worship.

The most sacred Muslim art form was calligraphy (kuh LIGH ruh fee), or decorative writing. Passages from the Qur'an were painted in books, carved onto walls, and woven into textiles.

Literature was also highly valued. Islam inspired much religious writing, but Muslim writers also produced folk tales and love stories. A group of spiritual Muslims called Sufis used poetry to express their connection with God. ☑

Check Your Progress

1. What are Arabic numerals?

_____

_____

2. Why was painting not important in the Muslim world?

_____

_____

© Pearson Education, Inc., publishing as Pearson Prentice Hall. All Rights Reserved.

Vocabulary Builder

Inaccurate is an antonym of the word *precise*. What does it mean that Muslim astronomers developed "precise calendars?"

_____

_____

✓ Checkpoint

Name three achievements of Muslim astronomers.

_____

_____

_____

✓ Checkpoint

Name three types of buildings Muslim architecture is known for.

_____

_____

_____

Question to Think About As you read Section 4 in your textbook, keep this question in mind: **How did cultural exchanges and the work of Islamic scholars produce lasting achievements?**

▶ Use this chart to take notes on your reading. Some information has been filled in to get you started.

Muslim Learning	
Scholars studied works from	• • • India
Areas of study	• philosophy • • • • • geography

Muslim Art and Literature		
Examples of decorative arts	• • colorful tiles	
Examples of architecture	**Building**	**Location**
		Jerusalem
	Taj Mahal	
Art form considered most sacred		
Types of literature	• religious writing • •	

Refer to this page to answer the Chapter 4 Focus Question on page 54.

1. The last caliph was killed by the

   A Mongols.   **B** Ottomans.   **C** Persians.

2. What city was the center of a golden age of art, science, and learning during the caliphate?

   A Medina   **B** Damascus   **C** Baghdad

3. The Sharia is a collection of

   A God's laws.   **B** court rulings.   **C** folk tales.

4. The Islamic world was known for its fine

   A dishes.   **B** textiles.   **C** furs.

Directions: Follow the steps to answer this question:

How did Islamic texts and traditions shape Muslim law and society?

Step 1: Recall information: How did Muslims address situations not addressed in the Qur'an or the Sunnah?

_____

_____

_____

Step 2: Analyze: What is the purpose of creating laws based on religion? How does this affect the way people are expected to behave in the society?

_____

_____

_____

Step 3: Complete the topic sentence that follows. Then write two or three sentences that support your topic sentence.

Islamic texts and traditions shaped Muslim law and society by

_____

_____

_____

_____

Now you are ready to answer the Chapter 4 Focus Question: **What were the political, social, economic, and cultural characteristics of Islamic civilization?**

► Complete the following chart to help you answer this question.

Characteristics of Islamic Civilization	
Political	Early Muslim form of government was called a __caliphate__. The _____ family established the first _____ in Islam. After the Mongol invasions, Islamic states were ruled by _____.
Social	The _____ provided rules for personal conduct. The basic duties of all Muslims were known as the _____. The four social classes in the early days of the caliphate: 1. Arab Muslims 3. 2. 4. Men were allowed to have more than one wife. This practice is called _____.
Economic	Strong economy supported _____ growth. Important Islamic trade goods: • textiles • • Banks issued _____ that could be used anywhere in the empire.
Cultural	Famous Muslim scholars: • Ibn Rushd: _philosopher who wanted to integrate faith and reason_ • Ibn Sina: _____ • Ibn Khaldun: _____ The most sacred Muslim art form was _____. Deeply spiritual Muslims called _____ created poetry about God.

Refer to this page to answer the Unit 2 Focus Question on page 55.

What You Have Learned

Chapter 3 Islam, the world's second largest religion, began in the desert of Arabia and spread through conquest and conversion. Muslims follow the teachings of the prophet Muhammad and study the Qur'an and the Sunnah, Islam's sacred texts.

Chapter 4 A government led by caliphs ruled a vast territory that was influenced by Islamic principles. Muslim achievements in trade, science, learning, and the arts contributed to the success of Islamic civilization.

Think Like a Historian

Read the Unit 2 Focus Question: **How can religion have a powerful effect on people's way of life, including their culture and government?**

▶ Use the organizers on this page and the next to collect information to answer this question.

What were the three phases in the spread of Islam? The chart below gives you part of the answer. Review your section and chapter notes. Then fill in the rest of the chart.

The Spread of Islam	
Phase	**How and Where Islam Spread**
Phase 1	Conquests by Arab armies: • Arabian peninsula • South Asia • •
Phase 2	Conquests by non-Arab armies that had embraced Islam: • •
Phase 3	Peaceful spread of Islam by merchants and missionaries: • •

In what ways did Islam affect the lives of early believers? Some of them are listed in this chart. Review your section and chapter notes. Then complete the chart.

Islam as a Way of Life	
Area of Life	**Examples of Influence**
Daily Life	The Five Pillars of Islam • faith • • giving alms • •
Law	•
The Arts	• • •
Learning and Education	• All knowledge is _____ • Where they studied: _____
Education	•
Government	• • •

Civilizations in Sub-Saharan Africa

What You Will Learn

Chapter 5 Sub-Saharan Africa is rich in natural resources. The Ghana Empire rose there, trading gold for salt. The Mali Empire followed Ghana, becoming a center of Islamic learning.

Chapter 6 The Songhai Empire helped spread Islam across West Africa. West African society was based on family and caste, and its oral traditions and art help preserve West Africa's culture.

Focus Your Learning As you study this unit and take notes, you will find the information to answer the questions below. Answering the chapter focus questions will help build your answer to the unit focus question.

Chapter 5 Focus Question
What factors contributed to the rise of empires in West Africa?
(page 58)

Chapter 6 Focus Question
How did Songhai build on the traditions of empires that came before it?
(page 69)

Unit 3 Focus Question
How is a civilization's way of life a product of both people and place?
(page 80)

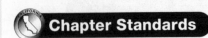
Chapter 5

The Rise of West African Empires

(300–1400)

What You Will Learn

Sub-Saharan Africa is rich in natural resources. The Ghana empire rose there, trading gold for salt. The Mali empire followed the empire of Ghana.

Chapter 5 Focus Question

As you read through this chapter, keep this question in mind: **What factors contributed to the rise of empires in West Africa?**

Section 1

Sub-Saharan Africa

Section 1 Focus Question

How is Africa a continent of great geographic contrasts? To begin answering this question,

- Discover the African landscape.
- Learn about Africa's natural resources.

Section 1 Summary

Africa is a vast continent with many different geographic features. Since ancient times, Africa has been prized for its natural resources.

The African Landscape

Africa is the second-largest continent. Most of Africa is a large **plateau** (pla TOH), or highland area of fairly flat land. Rivers flow across it and fall over waterfalls to a narrow strip of coastal plain. This drop made it difficult to travel by boat from the coast of Africa to its interior. <u>Africa's coastline is smooth, unlike the ragged edges of most continents.</u>

Most of northern Africa, except for the Nile Valley and along the Mediterranean coastline, is covered by the Sahara. The Sahara is the world's largest desert. The Sahara was not always so dry. Thousands of years ago, the land had rivers, trees, and grasslands. Then, about 6,000 years ago, the climate began to get drier.

© Pearson Education, Inc., publishing as Pearson Prentice Hall. All Rights Reserved.

Key Events

About 300	Ancient Ghana is established.
1076	The capture of Ghana's capital by the Almoravids leads to the fall of the empire.
1235	The empire of Mali is established.

Reading Strategy

Read the underlined sentence. The word *unlike* is a clue word. It tells you that something in the sentence is different from something else. Circle the word that describes Africa's coastline, and underline the word that describes other countries' coastlines.

Along the southern edge of the Sahara is a fertile region called the Sahel. Although the Sahel has unpredictable rainfall, farmers are able to grow crops and raise animals there. Still, droughts, or long dry spells, are a threat to those who live in the Sahel.

Sub-Saharan (suhb suh HAR uhn) Africa is the part south of the Sahara. Sub-Saharan lands are divided into vegetation zones. Each zone has its own climate and type of plants. The dry Sahel is in a vegetation zone called the tropical savannah. A savannah (suh VAN uh) is a broad grassland with scattered trees. The African savannah has wet and dry seasons.

South of the savannah, along the Equator, lies the rain forest, a zone of tall trees and climbing vines. The rain forest is hot and wet year round. Thousands of kinds of plants and animals live in this steamy jungle.

The main river of West Africa is the Niger River. People settled along the Niger because it was a reliable water source in a dry land. Farmers grew crops along the river. People fished in lakes and streams that branched off from the river. The Niger also provided a route for trade and travel across West Africa. ✓

Africa's Natural Resources

For thousands of years, many African trade products have come from African natural resources (NACH er uhl REE sors uhs). Natural resources are products of nature that have economic value. Africa has long been rich in minerals. The most prized West African mineral was gold. Other valuable minerals were copper, iron, diamonds, and salt.

Plants and people were other resources. Africans' agricultural wealth was an important for the growth of their trade networks. Also, since ancient times, enslaved Africans were sold across the desert in North Africa or across the Indian Ocean in Asia. ✓

Check Your Progress

1. Why did people settle along the Niger River?

_____

_____

2. What was the most prized West African mineral?

_____

Vocabulary Builder

The word *Sahel* means "shore" in Arabic. Picture the Sahara as a vast sea of sand. How do you think the Sahel got its name?

_____

_____

✓ Checkpoint

Most of Africa is what kind of landform?

_____

✓ Checkpoint

List three kinds of African natural resources.

_____

_____

_____

Question to Think About As you read Section 1 in your textbook and take notes, keep this section focus question in mind: **How is Africa a continent of great geographic contrasts?**

▶ Use these organizers to record key information from the section. Some information has been filled in to get you started.

Geography of the African Continent			
	Where	**Climate**	**Plant and Animal Life**
The Sahara	Covers most of northern Africa	Dry	
The Sahel			Grasslands; supports crops
Tropical Savannah			
Rain Forest			
Other: _____ _____	A reliable source of water in a dry region. Supports farmers and fishers.		

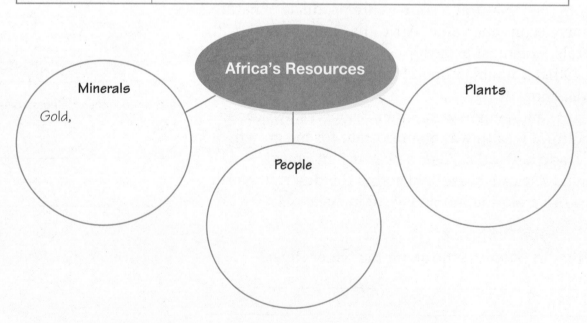

Refer to this page to answer the Chapter 5 Focus Question on page 68.

Section 2

Ghana

Section 2 Focus Question

How did the people of Ghana use their resources and skills to build a wealthy empire? To begin answering this question,

- Find out about the rise of the empire called Ghana.
- Learn about the gold and salt trade.

Section 2 Summary

The development of iron tools and better weapons led to the rise of Ghana. For centuries, Ghana grew wealthy from the trade in gold and salt.

The Rise of Ghana

Ancient West Africans left no written records. So the region's historians have relied mainly on oral history and archaeology. Oral history (OR uhl HIHS tuh ree) is an account of something passed down by word of mouth from one generation to another.

Archaeologists believe that the first Africans to develop ironworking skills were the people of Kush, or Nubia. Ironworking may have spread from there to other parts of Africa. <u>Because iron tools were sharper and stronger than those made of stone, wood, or bone, West Africans could grow more food.</u> As more food became available, the population increased. With a larger population, people needed to organize governments to keep order.

Around A.D. 300, the Soninke people founded a strong kingdom between the Niger and Senegal rivers. The Soninke had iron swords and spears, while their neighbors used wooden clubs. The Soninke kingdom became the empire known as Ghana.

As food supplies increased, not everyone had to grow crops. Some people did other kinds of jobs. The division of jobs and skills in a society is known as labor specialization (LAY buhr spehsh uhl ih ZAY shuhn). Each clan, or group of related families, worked in a certain craft or trade. ✓

Key Events

About 300	Ancient Ghana is established.
1076	The capture of Ghana's capital by the Almoravids leads to the fall of the empire.
1235	The empire of Mali is established.

Reading Strategy

Read the underlined sentence. The word *because* is a clue that the sentence has a cause and an effect. Circle the cause. Draw a box around the effect.

✓ Checkpoint

List what sources historians have relied on to learn about ancient West Africans.

_____

_____

The Gold and Salt Trade

The people of Africa's different regions had different resources and needs. Such differences encouraged trade. By the 700s, North Africans traveled across the Sahara to trade with West Africans.

The trans-Sahara trade was based on two main products: gold and salt. People north of the Sahara needed gold. West Africans had gold, but they needed salt. North African traders brought large blocks of salt to West Africa to trade for gold.

Gold and salt were traded through silent barter. Silent barter was a way of trading without words. Traders from Ghana piled goods at a trading place. Miners came and left gold next to the goods. If the traders wanted more gold, they left without touching the gold or the goods. The miners then left more gold. When both sides were happy, the traders left with their new goods.

Ghana's kings grew rich from this trade. To keep gold prices high, Ghana's rulers ordered that only the king could own nuggets, or chunks of gold. Rulers also taxed trade. This created lots of revenue (REHV uh noo), or income for the government.

Africans also traded other goods. North Africans brought steel swords, copper, and silks to West Africa. They returned with ivory, crafts, precious woods, and enslaved people.

Ghana's rulers welcomed North African traders, but did not adopt their religion, Islam. However, a Muslim religious movement in North Africa began preaching holy war against all non-Muslims. Its members were known as Almoravids. In 1076, an Almoravid army invaded Ghana and captured the capital. The leaders of Ghana converted to Islam. Ghana never returned to normal after the Almoravid invasion. ✓

Check Your Progress

1. Which Africans do historians believe worked with iron first?

_____

2. How did the gold-salt trade affect Ghana's rulers?

_____

© Pearson Education, Inc., publishing as Pearson Prentice Hall. All Rights Reserved.

Vocabulary Builder

You may not know the meaning of the word *barter*, but context clues in the bracketed paragraphs can help you figure it out. Write a definition of *barter* in your own words.

_____

_____

✓ Checkpoint

What did North Africans trade for gold?

_____

Question to Think About As you read Section 2 in your textbook and take notes, keep this section focus question in mind: **How did the people of Ghana use their resources and skills to build a wealthy empire?**

► Use these organizers to record key information from the section. Some information has been filled in to get you started.

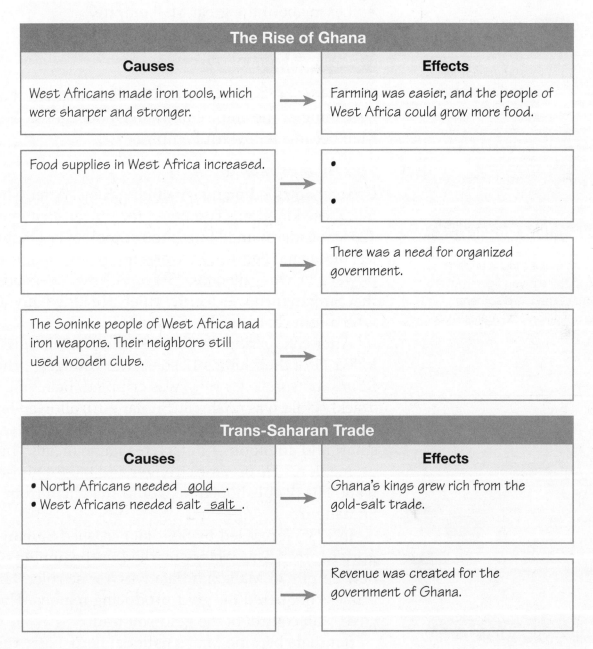

The Rise of Ghana	
Causes	**Effects**
West Africans made iron tools, which were sharper and stronger.	Farming was easier, and the people of West Africa could grow more food.
Food supplies in West Africa increased.	• •
	There was a need for organized government.
The Soninke people of West Africa had iron weapons. Their neighbors still used wooden clubs.	

Trans-Saharan Trade	
Causes	**Effects**
• North Africans needed _gold_ . • West Africans needed salt _salt_ .	Ghana's kings grew rich from the gold-salt trade.
	Revenue was created for the government of Ghana.

Refer to this page to answer the Chapter 5 Focus Question on page 68.

Key Events

About 300	Ancient Ghana is established.
1076	The capture of Ghana's capital by the Almoravids leads to the fall of the empire.
1235	The empire of Mali is established.

Vocabulary Builder

Use context clues in the underlined sentence to help you figure out the meaning of the word *sorcerer*. Write a definition of *sorcerer* in your own words.

_____

_____

✓ Checkpoint

Name the empire that arose after Sundiata's victory.

_____

Section 3 Focus Question

How did Mali become a great empire that reflected the influence of Islam? To begin answering this question,

- Find out how Mali rose to a world power.
- Learn about the great Mali empire.

Section 3 Summary

The defeat of Sumanguru by Sundiata marked the beginning of the empire of Mali. Under Mansa Musa, Mali became a powerful empire.

The Rise of Mali

Ghana had ruled many small kingdoms. After Ghana fell, these kingdoms competed for power. In about 1203, a leader named Sumanguru took over what was left of Ghana. Because he was said to have magical powers, he was called the "Sorcerer King." Legends say that Sumanguru was a cruel ruler. He killed anyone who might challenge his power.

After conquering the Malinke people, Sumanguru killed 11 of their king's 12 sons. The youngest prince, Sundiata (sun DYAH tuh), was crippled. Believing that a sickly child was no threat, Sumanguru allowed him to live. This was a great mistake because Sundiata was smart and ambitious—in fact, his name means "hungering lion." He became stronger and taught himself to walk. His people hoped he would free them from Sumanguru.

In 1235, forces led by Sundiata crushed Sumanguru's forces. This victory marked the beginning of the new empire of Mali. Sundiata was a wise ruler. His armies conquered the gold-producing regions. This gave Mali control of the gold-salt trade.

Sundiata became Mali's national hero. Later rulers struggled to live up to his reputation. Still, they continued to expand the empire. By the 1300s, Mali was about the size of Western Europe. ✓

A Great Empire

Mali had become a world power. It traded with nations in North Africa and southern Europe. Like Ghana, its wealth came from the gold-salt trade. Unlike Ghana, however, Mali adopted the religion of Islam. This **conversion** (kuhn VER zhuhn), or change of religion, led to closer ties between Mali and North Africa. It also influenced Mali's culture.

Mali's most famous Muslim ruler was **Mansa Musa** (MAHN suh MOO suh). The title *Mansa* means "emperor." In 1324, he made a *hajj*, or pilgrimage, to the holy city of Mecca. Pilgrimage is one of the Five Pillars of Islam, the duties of a faithful Muslim. Mansa Musa set off from Mali with a huge camel caravan. He brought many bags of gold dust to pay for the long trip to Mecca.

Mansa Musa reportedly spent and gave away so much gold in Cairo that two unexpected things happened. First, he ran out of gold, and he had to borrow money to finish his hajj. Second, his spending upset the economy of Egypt for years. When the supply of gold suddenly increased in Cairo, gold lost most of its value. The result was **inflation** (ihn FLAY shuhn), or a general rise in prices.

Mansa Musa also spent his wealth at home. Much of it went to encourage Islamic learning. He brought Egyptian scholars, artists, and teachers to Mali. Mansa Musa had great mosques built in Mali. He also built a new palace in Timbuktu. Timbuktu became a center for Islamic **scholarship** (SKAHL uhr shihp), or formal study and learning. North Africans and Middle Easterners came to study there.

Mansa Musa ruled Mali for 25 years. During his reign, he extended Mali's territory north and westward to the Atlantic Ocean. ✓

Check Your Progress

1. Why was Sundiata Mali's national hero?

_____

_____

2. Why did Mansa Musa travel to Mecca?

_____

Reading Strategy

The bracketed paragraph tells some ways Mali and Ghana were alike and different. Circle one way Mali and Ghana were the same. Draw a box around one way they were different.

✓ Checkpoint

List two unexpected things that happened to Mansa Musa in Cairo.

_____

_____

Question to Think About As you read Section 3 in your textbook and take notes, keep this section focus question in mind: **How did Mali become a great empire that reflected the influence of Islam?**

► Use the chart to record key information from the section. Some information has been filled in to get you started.

The Rise of Mali		
	Who	**What**
Sumanguru	• cruel ruler of Ghana called the "Sorcerer King"	• took over what was left of the old Ghana empire in about 1203 • taxed his subjects harshly • killed anyone who challenged his power
Sundiata	• youngest prince of the Malinke people, and the only one not _____ • name means "_____"	• defeated _____ in a great battle in 1235 • began the new empire of _____ • conquered _gold-producing regions_ • became _Mali's national hero_
Mansa Musa	• Mali's most _____ ruler • Mansa means "_____"	• made a pilgrimage to Mecca, a duty of a faithful Muslim • he spent and gave away so much _____ in Cairo that Egypt's _____ was affected for years • encouraged _____; brought scholars, _____ and _____ back from Egypt • established _____ as a center for Islamic scholarship • extended Mali's territory north and westward
Ibn Battuta	•	• described Mali as a _____ whose people followed Islam strictly

Refer to this page to answer the Chapter 5 Focus Question on page 68.

Chapter 5 Assessment

Directions: Circle the letter of the correct answer.

1. The African savannah is
   A a vast desert.
   B a steamy jungle.
   C a broad grassland.

2. What development helped West Africans grow more food?
   A wooden tools   B iron tools   C irrigation

3. What trade did Ghana control?
   A gold-salt   B gold-diamonds   C salt-iron

4. Whose victory marked the beginning of the Mali empire?
   A Mansa Musa   B Sundiata   C Sumanguru

Directions: Follow the steps to answer this question:

What impact did trade have on African empires?

Step 1: Recall information: In the chart, identify each empire's trading partners and the items that were traded.

Ghana	Mali

Step 2: Describe the results of this trade.

_____

_____

_____

Step 3: Read the topic sentence that follows. Then write two or three sentences that support the topic sentence.

Trade had a significant impact on African empires. _____

_____

_____

_____

_____

_____

Chapter 5 Notetaking Study Guide

Now you are ready to answer the Chapter 5 Focus Question: **What factors contributed to the rise of empires in West Africa?**

▶ Fill in the following charts to help you answer this question. Use the notes that you took for each section.

Factors That Contributed to the Rise of Ghana and Mali	
Ghana	**Mali**
↓	↓

Importance of Natural Resources

- Iron: made farming easier, and weapons better
- Niger River:
  - reliable source of water
  -
- Other resources:

Leaders

- Sumanguru: cruel leader, took over what was left of Ghana empire
- Sundiata:
  - defeated <u>Sumanguru</u>
  - began _____
  - Mali's _____
- Mansa Musa:
  -
  -

+

+

Trade

- Trade of natural resources: connected West Africans with Europe
- Trans-Saharan Trade:
  - main goods traded: _____ and _____
  - made kings _____
  - brought _____ influence to West Africa

Exploration and Expansion

- Mansa Musa:
  - brought back Egyptian scholars, teachers, and artists from pilgrimage
  - extended Mali's territory north and _____
- Sundiata:

+

+

Conflict

- How Ghana began:

- Ghana ended when: Almoravids captured the capital

Conflict

- How Mali began:

Refer to this page to answer the Unit 3 Focus Question on page 80.

Chapter 6

West African Civilization (1400s–1591)

What You Will Learn

The Songhai Empire helped spread Islam across West Africa. West African society was based on family and caste, and its oral traditions and art help preserve West Africa's culture.

Chapter 1 Focus Question

As you read this chapter, keep this question in mind: **How did Songhai build on the traditions of empires that came before it?**

Section 1

The Growth of Islam in West Africa

Section 1 Focus Question

How did the Songhai Empire contribute to the spread of Arabic and Islam? To begin answering this question,
- Learn about the growth of the Songhai Empire.
- Find out how the empire helped spread the Arabic language and Islamic scholarship.

Section 1 Summary

Using military force, the Songhai Empire extended its territory. Later, the empire dominated trans-Saharan trade routes. The spread of Islam and Arabic in West Africa benefited scholarship and trade.

The Rise of Songhai

In 1464, the Muslim **Sunni Ali Ber** (SOO nee AH lee ber) became king of **Songhai** (SAWNG hī). Sunni Ali Ber used military power to extend the empire along the Great Bend of the Niger River.

One of Sunni Ali Ber's goals was to conquer Timbuktu. This city was a major trade center that was under the control of the nomadic Tuaregs.

Sunni Ali Ber's army quickly overpowered the Tuaregs. The king allowed his troops to loot the city, and he had many people killed.

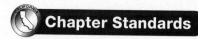**Chapter Standards**

History-Social Science 7.4.2, 7.4.4, 7.4.5

Key Events

1468	Sunni Ali Ber gains control of Songhai.
1493	Askia Muhammad becomes emperor of Songhai.
1591	Moroccan troops capture Timbuktu.

How does the first underlined sentence add meaning to the point being made in the second?

_____

_____

_____

✓ Checkpoint

Name two cities that Ali Ber conquered.

_____

_____

Vocabulary Builder

The word *manuscript* comes from the Latin words *manu*, meaning "hand," and *scriptus*, meaning "written." Use this information and what you read in the summary to write a definition of *manuscript*.

_____

_____

_____

✓ Checkpoint

List the two main ways in which Askia Muhammad helped strengthen Islam within Songhai.

_____

_____

The king's next target was the town of Djenné. <u>This city had never been conquered. After a long siege (seej), Sunni Ali Ber's army took control of the city.</u> A siege is a military plan in which the attacking army cuts off supplies to the defenders. After the surrender, Sunni Ali Ber treated the people with respect.

With the capture of Djenné, Songhai controlled the trans-Saharan trading routes. Over time, Songhai became the largest of West Africa's trading empires. ✓

The Spread of Islam and Arabic

For centuries, Islam influenced life in Songhai. However, many people in nearby lands still practiced their old religions. When the devout Muslim Askia Muhammad (AH skī ah moo HAH muhd) took power, he set out to conquer new lands and spread Islam even farther. He attacked the Mossi kingdom, but it remained independent and did not convert to Islam.

Within Songhai, Askia Muhammad strengthened Islam. He appointed Islamic judges to enforce Songhai's laws. Songhai's scholars learned Arabic, copied old manuscripts, and wrote new books in Arabic. Timbuktu became a leading center of Islamic learning.

Not only scholars used Arabic. Arabic also provided a common language for traders to arrange deals and keep records.

Arabic's Importance to Songhai	
Scholars studied previous Islamic works	Common language, writing benefited trade

In 1591, Moroccan soldiers began invading Songhai. Songhai collapsed and its cities fell to ruins. ✓

Check Your Progress

1. How did Ali Ber treat the people of Djenné?

_____

_____

2. In what way did the spread of Arabic benefit trade?

_____

_____

Question to Think About As you read Section 1 in your textbook and take notes, keep this section focus question in mind: **How did the Songhai Empire contribute to the spread of Arabic and Islam?**

▶ Use the chart to help you record key information. Some of the information has been filled in to get you started.

The Songhai Empire		
Reign of Sunni Ali Ber	Known as what type of leader?	military
	Where did he extend Songhai's empire?	• Along the Niger River's Great Bend
Conquest of Timbuktu	Goods traded at Timbuktu:	_____ and _____
	How did Ali Ber treat those he conquered?	
Conquest of Djenné	What type of military plan was used?	
	How did Ali Ber treat those he conquered?	
	Result of capturing the city:	Songhai dominated the _____
Reign of Askia Muhammad	His goals for empire:	• conquer new land •
	Laws were based on:	
	How he encouraged Islamic studies:	
	Main work of scholars:	• copied old _____ • wrote new books _____
	Effect of spread of Arabic on trade:	• • improved record keeping _____
Decline of Songhai	Cities invaded by:	

Refer to this page to answer the Chapter 6 Focus Question on page 79.

West African Society

© Pearson Education, Inc., publishing as Pearson Prentice Hall. All Rights Reserved.

Key Events

1468	Sunni Ali Ber gains control of Songhai.
1493	Askia Muhammad becomes emperor of Songhai.
1591	Moroccan troops capture Timbuktu.

Vocabulary Builder

Ancestor and *ancient* come from the same Latin root *ante*, which means "before." Use this information to observe a similarity in the words' meanings. Write your observation.

_____

_____

_____

Section 2 Focus Question

What were the characteristics of society and the economy in West Africa? To begin answering this question,

- Learn how society was structured in Songhai.
- Find out about life and trade in West African villages and towns.

Section 2 Summary

Societies in West Africa were well-structured. Families were organized into larger groups, and all people had specific social ranks. West Africans lived both in rural villages and bustling cities. In the cities, the economy was based on trade.

Kinship and Castes

In West Africa, people shared a strong sense of family. Large families formed **lineages** (LIHN ee ihjz), or groups of people who are related to a common ancestor. Each lineage was part of a **clan** (KLAN), or larger group of related families, and several closely related clans lived together in a village. Several villages united into larger **ethnic groups** (EHTH nihk groopz), groups that shared a distinct culture, language, and identity.

In West Africa, a person's **caste** (kast), or social rank, was fixed at birth.

West Africa's Caste System

Emperor
- highest-ranking person in the social structure

Nobles
- helped emperor govern country and lead armies

Traders and free people
- ran businesses and farms

Skilled workers
- specialized in certain jobs

Enslaved people

Enslaved people were at the bottom of the social structure. Many slaves came from groups defeated in wars, and others were born as slaves. Slaves often worked as soldiers, farmers, and house servants.

Slaves did have some rights. For example, they could marry, and families could not be separated. Slaves were protected from harsh punishment, and they could earn money. They could earn money and even buy their freedom. ✓

City and Village Life

West African families lived in towns and villages. In urban areas, Arabic was the main language of trade and worship. In rural villages, however, families spoke the languages of their ancestors and worshiped ancient gods.

Village economies were centered on producing food, such as rice, yams, and beans. In the local markets, villagers traded the things they produced for things they needed, such as salt or cloth from distant areas. City economies were based on trade, and in the city markets, people bought goods using cowrie shells or gold coins.

West African emperors supported trade in many ways. Askia Muhammad used his armies to protect trade routes from raiders. He also used a system of weights and measures to make trade fair, and his officials inspected markets to guarantee honest trading.

Cities such Gao, Timbuktu, and Djenné had large populations due to trade. These cities had a steady supply of foods and finely crafted goods. Many stone buildings existed, though most buildings were made of mud and wood. ✓

Check Your Progress

1. How are lineages and clans related?

_____

_____

2. How did West African emperors support trade?

_____

_____

_____

✓ **Checkpoint**

List three rights that slaves had in West Africa.

_____

_____

_____

Reading Strategy

Reread the bracketed paragraph. On what was the village economy based? On what was the city economy based?

_____

_____

_____

✓ **Checkpoint**

Name two forms of money used in West African cities.

_____

_____

Question to Think About As you read Section 2 in your textbook and take notes, keep this section focus question in mind: **What were the characteristics of society and the economy in West Africa?**

▶ Use the chart to help you record key information. Some of the information has been filled in to get you started.

West African Kinship and Clans	
Type of Kinship	**Consists Of**
Family	Parents, children, grandparents, aunts, uncles, cousins
Lineage	
Clan	
Ethnic group	A group sharing the same _____, _____, and _____.
The Caste System	
Caste levels	1. emperor 4. 2. 5. slaves 3.
Slavery	
How people became slaves	• • born into slavery
Usual jobs of slaves	• • • house servants
Rights of slaves	• • could earn money • • could buy their freedom •
Village and City Life	
Languages spoken	Village:
	Cities:
Economy based on:	Villages:
	Cities:

Refer to this page to answer the Chapter 6 Focus Question on page 79.

Storytelling and the Arts of West Africa

Section 3 Focus Question

How were the cultures and traditions of West Africa preserved and spread? To begin answering this question,

- Learn how West African storytellers preserved history.
- Find out about West African achievements in music, dance, and art.

Key Events

1468	Sunni Ali Ber gains control of Songhai.
1493	Askia Muhammad becomes emperor of Songhai.
1591	Moroccan troops capture Timbuktu.

Section 3 Summary

In West Africa, oral traditions were essential to teaching, entertaining, and preserving history. Music, dance, and art were also central to West African culture. Many West African cultural traditions continue today.

The Telling of Tales

Until the arrival of Arab traders, West Africa had no written language. West Africans used oral history, poetry, folk tales, and sayings to teach and entertain.

The masters of the oral tradition were called **griots** (GREE ohz), or professional storytellers and oral historians. Griots served West African kings and nobles. They encouraged leaders to rule justly with their poetry, which was a "kind of preaching." The griots' main job was to pass on their people's history.

Families also shared folk tales at home. Some stories involved heroes and hunters. Others used animals to teach young people right from wrong.

Proverbs (PRAHV erbz), or wise sayings, provided a quick way to pass on wisdom about all parts of life. Many proverbs have been handed down through countless generations. ✓

✓ Checkpoint

List three major types of oral traditions in West Africa.

_____

_____

_____

Music, Dance, and Art

The arts also helped document West Africans' history and culture. Music filled West Africans' lives. It was used to lull babies to sleep, to teach young people responsibilities, and to honor the dead. The most widely used instruments were drums. African

Vocabulary Builder

Look up *artisan* in a dictionary. What is the difference between an artisan and an artist?

_____

_____

_____

✓ Checkpoint

List two reasons why West Africans created art.

_____

_____

Reading Strategy

Reread the bracketed paragraphs. Write the main idea of each of the two paragraphs in this section.

_____

_____

_____

✓ Checkpoint

Name two ways the legacy of the Ghana, Mali, and Songhai empires is still evident in Africa.

_____

_____

drummers created exciting polyrhythmic (pahl ih RIHTH mihk) drum music, in which two or more different rhythms are played at the same time.

Another important art form was dance. Dancers worked out complex movements to match the drummers' polyrhythms. Dancers performed at many types of religious ceremonies and celebrations, such as weddings and funerals.

West Africans created art for many purposes. Art was a way for emperors to show off their wealth and power, and a way for artists to record events and people. Artisans sculpted graceful portraits of kings and queens. Wooden images of ancestors honored the dead, and masks of gods and spirits were worn in religious ceremonies.

The Legacy of Empires

The legacy of the empires of Ghana, Mali, and Songhai is still evident in Africa. Millions speak the languages of Mali and Songhai, griots still sing about kings, and musicians play complex rhythms. Families and castes are still important, and the market and farming are key parts of the economy. Islam is still a major influence, along with traditional religions.

West African culture has spread to other nations as well. Beginning in the 1500s, many West Africans were taken to the Americas as slaves, bringing their traditions with them. ✓

Check Your Progress

1. What was the griots' main job?

_____

_____

2. How did West African traditions spread to the Americas?

_____

_____

_____

Question to Think About As you read Section 3 in your textbook and take notes, keep this section focus question in mind: **How were the cultures and traditions of West Africa preserved and spread?**

▶ Use these charts to help you record key ideas. Some of the information has been filled in to get you started.

West African Oral Tradition		
Type of Tradition	**Used By**	**Purpose**
oral history and poetry	griots	to _____, and urge leaders to rule justly
folk tales	families	
	all people	To transmit wisdom

West African Music and Dance	
Where music and dance were performed	religious ceremonies, funerals, festivals, celebrations, birth, marriage, coming of adulthood
Most widely used instrument	
Music often accompanied by	

West African Art	
Types of art • • plaques and figures • clay figures • •	**What depicted** • portraits of kings and queens • • soldiers • ancestors • gods and spirits

Legacies of West African Empires	
Cultural Legacies	**Social Legacies**
• languages • • complex rhythms in music	• families and _____ • markets and farming • _____ and traditional religions

Refer to this page to answer the Chapter 6 Focus Question on page 79.

Directions: Circle the letter of the correct answer.

1. West Africans' strong oral tradition was a way to
   A convince children to join the army.
   B preserve the written language.
   C preserve culture and history.

2. Which list goes from smallest to largest?
   A clan, lineage, village, ethnic group, family
   B family, clan, lineage, village, ethnic group
   C family, lineage, clan, village, ethnic group

3. Sunni Ali Ber was
   A a military leader.   **B** a griot.   **C** a prophet.

Directions: Follow the steps to answer this question:

What are some benefits and drawbacks to West African culture being oral and not written?

Step 1: Recall information: Name four oral traditions of West African cultures.

Oral Traditions of West African Cultures	
1.	3.
2.	4.

Step 2: Write some specific details about how these oral traditions were passed on.

_____

_____

Step 3: Read the topic sentence that follows. Then, write two or three more sentences that support this topic sentence.

There are both benefits and drawbacks to West African traditions being oral and not written. _____

_____

_____

_____

_____

Now you are ready to answer the Chapter 6 Focus Question: **How did Songhai build on the traditions of empires that came before it?**

▶ Complete the following charts to help you answer this question.

Songhai Rulers, Society, and Culture	
Ruler	**Contribution to Songhai Empire**
Sunni Ali Ber	Captured important trade cities of _____ and _____ .
Askia Muhammad	Strengthened Islam and the _____ language.

Songhai Society	Songhai Culture
Society divided into: • lineages • •	_____ are people that preserve oral traditions.
Caste system: • Emperor • • • •	Arts: Drummers created _____ music. Artists created sculptures and made _____ of gods and spirits.
Urban life: People spoke _____ and believed in _____ . **Village life:** People spoke _____ and believed in _____ .	People still speak languages of Ghana, _____ , and _____ . Families and _____ are still important.

Refer to this page to answer the Unit 3 Focus Question on page 80.

Unit 3 Pulling It Together Activity

Chapter 5 Sub-Saharan Africa is rich in natural resources. The Ghana Empire rose there, trading gold for salt. The Mali Empire followed Ghana, becoming a center of Islamic learning.

Chapter 6 The Songhai Empire helped spread Islam across West Africa. West African society was based on family and caste, and its oral traditions and art help preserve West Africa's culture.

Think Like a Historian

Read the Unit 3 Focus Question: **How is a civilization's way of life a product of both people and place?**

▶ Use the organizers on this page and the next to collect information to answer this question.

How did geography affect the growth of empires? The chart below gives you part of the answer. Review your section and chapter notes. Then fill in the rest of the chart.

Influence of Geography on Civilization in West Africa	
Geographical Feature	**Influence on Civilization**
Few natural harbors and unusual topography	•
Sahara	• • Traders traveled by _____ caravan.
Sahel	
Niger River	• •
Natural resources	•

How did people affect the growth of civilization? The chart below gives you part of the answer. Review your section and chapter notes. Then complete the chart.

Influence of People on Civilization in West Africa	
Aspect of Human Life	**Influence on Civilization**
Ironworking in West Africa	• sharper tools and weapons • increased food production • •
Trans-Saharan trade	• • • North African merchants spread _____ along trade routes. •
Taxes and control of gold supply	•
Leadership	•
Kinship and caste	•
Oral tradition	•

Civilizations in the Americas

What You Will Learn

Chapter 7 Maya civilization developed in the area of the Americas known as Mesoamerica. The Mayas had a rich culture with a social order based on commoners and nobles, and complex systems of government, religion, writing, and math. The Mayas were also skilled artists and architects.

Chapter 8 The Inca Empire was influenced by the geography of South America. The Incas had a sophisticated society that made achievements in government, engineering, and art.

Chapter 9 In the 1300s, the Aztecs settled in the Valley of Mexico. By 1440, they had built a powerful empire. Tribute and human sacrifice were at the core of Aztec government and religion. The Aztecs were talented architects and artists.

Focus Your Learning As you study this unit and take notes, you will find the information to answer the questions below. Answering the chapter focus questions will help build your answer to the unit focus question.

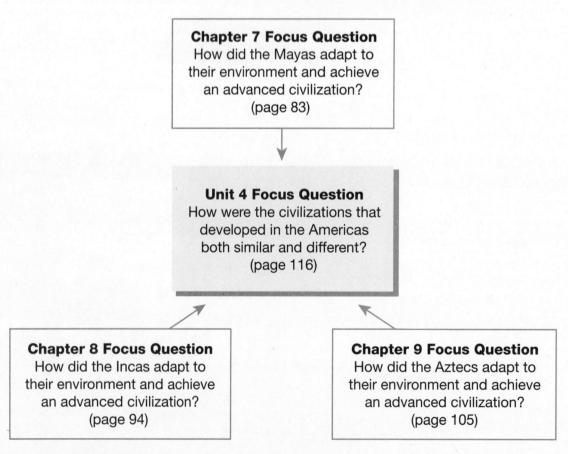

Chapter 7 Focus Question
How did the Mayas adapt to their environment and achieve an advanced civilization?
(page 83)

Unit 4 Focus Question
How were the civilizations that developed in the Americas both similar and different?
(page 116)

Chapter 8 Focus Question
How did the Incas adapt to their environment and achieve an advanced civilization?
(page 94)

Chapter 9 Focus Question
How did the Aztecs adapt to their environment and achieve an advanced civilization?
(page 105)

Chapter Standards

History-Social Science 7.7.1, 7.7.2, 7.7.4, 7.7.5

What You Will Learn

Maya civilization developed in the area of the Americas known as Mesoamerica. They had a rich culture with a social order based on commoners and nobles, and complex systems of government, religion, writing and math. The Mayas were also skilled artists and architects.

Chapter 7 Focus Question

As you read through the sections in this chapter, keep this question in mind: **How did the Mayas adapt to their environment and achieve an advanced civilization?**

Section 1

The Rise of the Mayas

Section 1 Focus Question

How did geography influence the history of Maya civilization? To begin answering this question,
- Explore the setting of Mesoamerica.
- Learn about the rediscovery of Maya civilization.

Key Events

A.D. 300s   Mayas begin building elaborate cities.

A.D. 615   King Pacal comes to power in Palenque.

A.D. 900s   Maya civilization revives in the Yucatán.

A.D. 1500s   Spanish conquest brings Maya civilization to an end.

Section 1 Summary

The Mayas developed an advanced civilization in a part of the Americas called Mesoamerica. Maya civilization disappeared after Spain conquered Mexico. Its ruins lay hidden for 300 years.

The Mesoamerican Setting

Mesoamerica (mehs oh uh MEHR ih kuh) is an area extending from central Mexico into northern Central America. It was the birthplace of a few advanced cultures. The Mayas might be the most advanced of these cultures.

The Maya homeland contained lowlands and highlands. Some of the mountains in the highlands were active volcanoes. Ash from the volcanoes' eruptions made the highland soil fertile and rich. The climate of the highlands was cool, and they had both wet and dry seasons. The lowlands were hot and flat, and they were covered with a rain forest.

It was hard to settle the rain forest. The soil was thin and fragile. So, the Mayas developed a farming method called **slash-and-burn agriculture** (slash and bern AG rih kuhl cher). In this technique, farmers cleared land by cutting down the forest. They burned the fallen trees and plants for fertilizer. When the soil wore out, farmers cleared new fields. ☑

Maya Civilization

All memory of the Mayas was lost for centuries. The American explorer John L. Stephens (STEE vehns) played a key role in rediscovering Maya civilization. In 1839, he and British artist Frederick Catherwood (CATH er wud) went to Central America to find out if rumors about hidden ancient ruins were true. They found ancient sites buried under jungle growth.

Scholars divide Maya civilization into three main periods: Pre-Classic, Classic, and Post-Classic. During the Pre-Classic period, 1800 B.C. to A.D. 250, the Mayas developed important skills. The Classic Maya period lasted from A.D. 250 to 900. By then the Mayas had built many cities. They also had formed complex societies. A large Maya city usually had stone pyramids, temples, and palaces.

Maya civilization collapsed near the start of the Post-Classic period. Scholars think the collapse may have been caused by war, food shortages, disease, or natural disasters including drought (drowt). Drought is a prolonged period of little or no rainfall.

Maya civilization ended after Spain conquered Mexico in the early 1500s. ☑

Check Your Progress

1. Why was slash-and-burn agriculture necessary?

_____

_____

2. Why did John L. Stephens and Frederick Catherwood go to Central America in 1839?

_____

_____

✓ Checkpoint

Describe the lowlands.

_____

_____

_____

Reading Strategy

Reread the bracketed paragraph. Which period has more details, Pre-Classic or Classic? Circle the details.

_____

✓ Checkpoint

List three reasons why scholars believe Maya civilization fell.

_____

_____

_____

Question to Think About As you read Section 1 in your textbook and take notes, keep this focus question in mind: **How did geography influence the history of Maya civilization?**

▶ Use this chart to record key information from the section. Some of the information has been filled in to get you started.

Maya Civilization		
Geography of Maya homeland	**Highlands:** in the south, forested mountains and valleys, active volcanoes, fertile and rich soil, cool climate with wet and dry seasons	
	Lowlands:	
Rain forest agriculture	**Problems with rain forest environment:** **Farming technique:**	
Rediscovery of Maya civilization	**Who rediscovered:** • • **When:**	**What they found:**
Periods of Maya civilization	Period	Years
	Pre-Classic	1800 B.C.– A.D. 250
Characteristics of Maya cities	**Buildings:** hundreds in core area (pyramids, temples, palaces), built of stone **Where people lived:**	
Maya Civilization ends	**Reasons for decline:** **What event marked the ending:** **When it ended:**	

Refer to this page to answer the Chapter 7 Focus Question on page 93.

Key Events

A.D. 300s	Mayas begin building elaborate cities.
A.D. 615	King Pacal comes to power in Palenque.
A.D. 900s	Maya civilization revives in the Yucatán.
A.D. 1500s	Spanish conquest brings Maya civilization to an end.

Vocabulary Builder

The word *aristocrat* comes from the Greek root *aristos*, which means "best." Using context clues in the summary, write a short definition of *aristocrat*.

_____

_____

Section 2 Focus Question

How were the roles and responsibilities of nobles and commoners different in Maya society? To begin to answer this question,

- Find out about the Mayas' life.
- Learn about the importance of gods and rulers in Maya civilization.

Section 2 Summary

The Mayas developed a complex society of commoners and nobles. The Mayas' great emphasis on religion was reflected in many ways.

Life Among the Mayas

In the Pre-Classic period, Mayas lived in farming villages led by chiefs. By the Classic period, however, Mayas had a complex class structure of nobles and commoners. God-kings headed society.

Nobles were people who were born into powerful families. The noble class included the king, top officials, and priests. Lower-ranking nobles and higher-ranking officials formed a kind of middle class. These people might be soldiers, scribes, artisans, or artists.

Most Mayans were peasant farmers who lived on lands outside the city. Men worked in the fields and hunted. They also maintained village buildings. Women raised the children, and tended livestock and gardens. Women also devoted time to weaving and making pottery.

The Mayas' basic social unit was the extended family (ehks TEHN dihd FAM ih lee), a grouping of several related families that lived together. Extended families lived in a cluster of simple houses.

On days of major ceremonies, Mayas living outside the city came into town. They saw great Maya buildings and the homes of nobles in the city. Traders from the coast brought salt, dried fish, shells, stingrays, and pearls to sell to the inlanders. People used beads, beans, and feathers as currency.

For entertainment, Mayas might attend a ballgame. In a ballgame, players scored points by swatting a hard rubber ball. Injuries were common and sometimes players were killed. The ballgame was considered a sacred ritual. Victory showed the king's ability to please the gods. ✓

Gods and Rulers

Each major Maya city had a king. Usually, the ruling family passed down the kingship from a father to his son. Maya kings increased their power through warfare. They fought for captives and for control of trade routes and land.

The Mayas never built true empires. However, some created **spheres of influence** (sfeers uhv IHN floo ehns), or areas strongly influenced or dominated by a particular ruler or government. Maya rulers also formed **alliances** (uh LI uhn sehs) to increase their power. An alliance is an agreement between people or states to cooperate to achieve a common goal.

The Mayas were a deeply religious people who worshiped many gods. Most of these gods represented natural events. Kings were believed to be descended from the gods. Important rituals often involved the spilling of blood. The Mayas also believed in human sacrifice, which they thought helped to keep the universe in balance.

Festivals also were important to Maya society. Their many festivals featured elaborate costumes, music, ritual dancing, plays, and storytelling. ✓

Check Your Progress

1. Which groups were considered part of the Maya middle class?

_____

_____

2. How were Maya kings related to the gods?

_____

_____

Name the basic social unit of Maya society.

_____

Reading Strategy

Reread the text under the heading "Gods and Rulers." Bracket the paragraphs that discuss gods, and write "gods" next to them. Do the same for the paragraphs about rulers.

✓ **Checkpoint**

List two reasons why Maya kings fought.

_____

_____

Question to Think About As you read Section 2 in your textbook and take notes, keep this question in mind: **How were the roles and responsibilities of nobles and commoners different in Maya society?**

▶ Use this chart to record key information from the section. Some of the information has been filled in to get you started.

Maya Society		
Social groups of the Classic Period	• commoners •	
Which people formed a kind of middle class?	• •	
Work done by peasant farmers	**Men**	**Women**
	• worked fields • •	• raised children • • •
Basic social unit in Maya society		
Goods brought by sea traders		
Currency used	• • •	
Gods and Rulers		
Why the ballgame was considered sacred	A victory on the court indicated a king's ability to please the gods	
Kings ruled over	Individual cities	
How kings increased their power	• alliances •	
Purposes of wars	• • •	
Gods represented natural events such as	• • •	

Refer to this page to answer the Chapter 7 Focus Question on page 93.

Maya Achievements

Section 3 Focus Question

How did Mayas demonstrate their knowledge and skills in art, architecture, mathematics, and astronomy? To begin answering this question,

- Learn about the Mayas' complex writing and mathematical systems.
- Find out about the splendid art and architecture of Maya's golden age.

Section 3 Summary

The Mayas had advanced writing, calendar, and math systems. Surviving buildings and artifacts also reveal the great skill of Maya architects and artists.

Advances in Learning

The Mayas developed the most advanced writing system found in the ancient Americas. Maya writing was based on **hieroglyphs** (HĪ ruh glihfs). Hieroglyphs, or "glyphs," are symbols standing for words, ideas, or sounds. Glyphs could be combined to form any word in the Maya language.

Mayas carved hieroglyphs out of stone, and painted them on walls, pottery, and in books. Scribes used the language to keep records in a **codex** (KOH dehks). A codex is an ancient book that was written by hand. Probably only scribes and an **elite** (ih LEET) of nobles were able to read hieroglyphs. An elite is a small group of highly privileged or skilled people.

Carvings on stone buildings and monuments are nearly all that remains of Maya writing. These carvings mostly tell about great rulers and their deeds. They do not reveal much about daily life.

| Maya Kings Known About from Hieroglyphs ||
Pacal	18 Rabbit
<ul><li>ruled city of Palenque between A.D. 615–683</li><li>expanded city's size and power</li></ul>	<ul><li>ruled Copán at its height</li><li>brought together great artists and architects to create monuments for city</li></ul>

Key Events

A.D. 300s	Mayas begin building elaborate cities.
A.D. 615	King Pacal comes to power in Palenque.
A.D. 900s	Maya civilization revives in the Yucatán.
A.D. 1500s	Spanish conquest brings Maya civilization to an end.

Reading Strategy

Read the topic sentences under the heading *Advances in Learning*. List two of the Mayas' intellectual achievements.

_____

_____

The Mayas were brilliant astronomers. They watched the sun, moon, and planets, and they could predict solar and lunar eclipses without a telescope. Maya astronomers also developed calendars. Calendars enabled Mayas to plan festivals and agricultural activities based on seasonal changes.

Maya mathematicians created an advanced number system also. They understood the concept of zero long before Europeans did. ☑

Artistic Achievements

The Mayas created splendid art and architecture during their golden age. The Mayas are perhaps best known for their beautiful architecture.

Maya cities were built around central areas with pyramids, temples, and palaces. These buildings were made of stone. Mayas did not have wheeled vehicles or work animals. They relied on human labor to haul the stone. Since they did not have metal tools, they had to rely on stone tools to cut the blocks.

Pyramids were the largest buildings in Maya cities. They had temples at their tops, and like other Maya buildings, they were decorated with sculptures, bright paint, and murals.

Artists also created fine pottery. They made jewelry and masks from jade and pearls. Perhaps the Mayas' most striking form of art was the stela (STEE luh). A stela is a carved stone slab or pillar usually created to celebrate an event or a person. ☑

Check Your Progress

1. What do the remaining Maya stone carvings mostly tell about?

_____

_____

2. How were Maya buildings decorated?

_____

_____

Question to Think About As you read Section 3 in your textbook and take notes, keep this question in mind: **How did the Mayas demonstrate their knowledge and skills in art, architecture, mathematics, and astronomy?**

▶ Use these charts to record key information from the section.

Astronomy	Writing	Mathematics

• Made detailed observation about the heavens.
  • Plotted positions of:
 	
• Predicted:
 	
• Used a complex series of _____.
	• Most advanced writing system found in the ancient Americas.
	
	• Based on:
	
	• Preserved mostly in:
	  •
	  •
	• Tells scholars about:
		• Developed an advanced number system.
		
		• Used three symbols one:
		  five:
		  zero:
		
		• Understood _____ _____ long before Europeans.

Intellectual Achievements

Maya Achievements

Artistic Achievements

Visual Arts	Architecture

• Decoration on buildings:
 	
• Artists also created:
  • murals on walls of temples and palaces
  •
  •
 	
• A stela is:
	• Perhaps best known for their beautiful architecture
	
	• Maya cities designed around:
	
	• Building material:
	
	• Largest construction:

Refer to this page to answer the Chapter 7 Focus Question on page 93.

Directions: Circle the letter of the correct answer.

1. Maya civilization ended with
   A a volcano eruption.
   B a civil war.
   C the Spanish conquest of Mexico.

2. The ballgame that Mayas watched for entertainment was also
   A a sacred ritual.
   B a game everyone played once.
   C the way new kings were picked.

3. Which is true of Maya cities?
   A They were built with the help of wheeled vehicles and work animals.
   B All were designed around a central area.
   C Most people lived in the city center.

Directions: Follow the steps to answer this question:

Why do we know more about great Maya rulers and their deeds than Maya daily life?

Step 1: Recall Information: What do most Maya stone carvings tell scholars about?

_____

Step 2: Analyze: What is the advantage to recording something in stone rather than on paper? How does this affect what we know about Maya civilization?

_____

_____

Step 3: Complete the topic sentence that follows. Then write two or three sentences that support your topic sentence.

We know more about great Maya rulers than about Maya daily life because _____

_____

_____

_____

Now you are ready to answer the Chapter 7 Focus Question: **How did the Mayas adapt to their environment and achieve an advanced civilization?**

▶ Complete the following charts to help you answer this question. Use the notes that you took for each section.

Mesoamerican Setting

- Mesoamerica is an area extending from _____ into _____.

- **The highlands:**
  Geography:
  Climate:
  Soil:

- **The lowlands:**
  Geography:
  Climate:
  Soil:

↓

Maya Society

- Slash-and-burn agriculture is _____.
- Maya cities usually had many buildings such as temples, _____, and _____. They were built of _____.
- Mayas had a social structure of _____ and _____, which was led by _____. Most Mayans were _____.
- The basic social unit of Maya civilization was the _____.
- The Maya were deeply religious, and they worshiped _____.

↓

Maya Achievements

- Astronomy: The Maya made detailed observations of the heavens and used a complex system of calendars.
- Writing:

- Mathematics:

- Visual Arts:

- Architecture:

Refer to this page to answer the Unit 4 Focus Question on page 116.

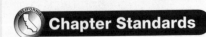
Chapter 8

The Incas (1200–1535)

What You Will Learn

The Inca Empire was influenced by the geography of South America. The Incas had a sophisticated society that made achievements in government, engineering, and art.

Chapter 8 Focus Question

As you read this chapter, keep this question in mind: **How did the Incas adapt to their environment and achieve an advanced civilization?**

Section 1

The Rise of the Incas

Section 1 Focus Question

How did the Incas build an empire? To begin answering this question,

- Find out how the geography of the Andes influenced Inca civilization.
- Learn how the Incas built a large empire.

Section 1 Summary

The Inca civilization emerged in the Andes Mountains of South America around A.D. 1200. The Incas were influenced by geography. They built a great empire.

The World of the Incas

South America is a large continent with many different regions. In the south lie the Pampas (PAM puhz), or the vast grassy plains of Argentina and Uruguay. The Andes Mountains line the western edge of the continent. The Altiplano (ahl tee PLAH noh) is a high plain centered in Bolivia. The cold climate, steep slopes, and high elevation of the Andes make settlement hard for humans. To the east of the slopes lies the Amazon Basin. To the west lies a dry, narrow coastal plain.

Even though the environment was harsh, the first advanced cultures of South America lived in the Andes

Key Events

1200	The Incas settle in the Cuzco Valley.
1300s	The Incas conquer much of the west coast of South America.
1438	Pachacuti becomes the Inca ruler.
1525	Civil war follows Huayna Capac's death.

region. Andean people fished, hunted, and mined. However, agriculture was the key to the growth of civilization in the Andes. Farmers grew a wide range of crops, such as chili peppers, beans, cotton, and potatoes. They also developed techniques to expand farming to hillsides. For example, they cut terraces (TEHR uhs iz), or flat strips of level land, into the slopes to plant with crops. Ancient farm terraces are still evident in the Andes. Farmers also bred livestock such as llamas and alpacas. The llama served as a pack animal and a source of meat. The alpaca served as a source of wool. ✓

The Inca Empire

The Incas built the first great empire of the Andes and of South America. They settled in the valley of Cuzco, in present-day Peru, about 800 years ago. Warrior kings called Sapa Incas led the empire. The greatest of the Sapa Incas, Pachacuti (pah chah KYOO tee), raised a powerful army. He used military force and diplomacy to expand the Inca realm. Diplomacy (duh PLOH muh see) is the management of communication and relationships between peoples or nations. If possible, the Incas tried to conquer through peaceful means. Pachacuti offered protection to those who agreed to join the Inca Empire. He threatened those who resisted. Pachacuti ruled the Inca Empire for more than 30 years and conquered lands in all directions.

The Inca Empire reached its height during the rule of Huayna Capac (WI nah KAH pahk). As the last great Sapa Inca, he took power in 1493. The Inca Empire was prosperous, stable, and peaceful. It covered over 2,500 miles. The empire contained as many as ten million people from a hundred different ethnic groups. After Huayna Capac died, a civil war broke out. Later, Spanish soldiers invaded and conquered the Incas. ✓

Check Your Progress

1. Why were terraces needed to farm in the Andes?

_____

_____

2. What was the Inca Empire like at its height?

_____

_____

✓ Checkpoint

List three reasons why living in the Andes was difficult for humans.

_____

_____

_____

Vocabulary Builder

Part of the word *ethnic* comes from a Latin root meaning "people" or "race." What do you think an "ethnic group" is?

_____

_____

Reading Strategy

The last two sentences of the bracketed paragraph describe a chain of three events. List these events in the order they happened.

_____

_____

_____

✓ Checkpoint

Name two important Sapa Incas.

_____

_____

Question to Think About As you read Section 1 in your textbook and take notes, keep this section focus question in mind: **How did the Incas build a large empire?**

▶ Use these charts to record key information from the section.

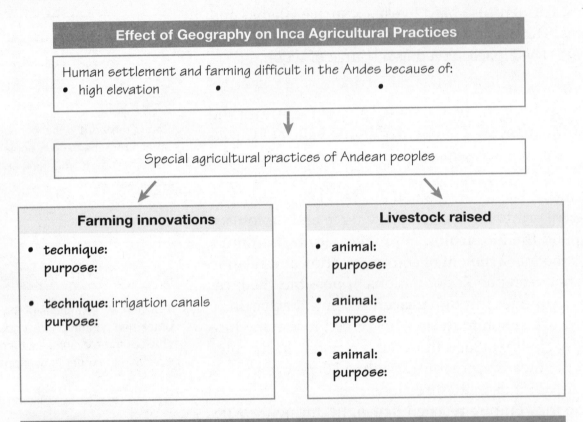

Effect of Geography on Inca Agricultural Practices
Human settlement and farming difficult in the Andes because of: • high elevation   •   •

Special agricultural practices of Andean peoples

Farming innovations	**Livestock raised**

• **technique:**
  purpose:
 	
• **technique:** irrigation canals
  purpose:
	• **animal:**
	  purpose:
	
	• **animal:**
	  purpose:
	
	• **animal:**
	  purpose:

Sapa Incas and Their Contribution to the Inca Empire	
Pachacuti	**Huayna Capac**
Who: greatest Sapa Inca to rule	**Who:** last Sapa Inca to rule
How long:	When:
Contribution to the Inca Empire What: How:	Description of the Inca Empire under his rule:

Refer to this page to answer the Chapter 8 Focus Questions on page 104.

Section 2

Inca Society

Section 2 Focus Question

What were the characteristics of Inca civilization? To begin answering this question,

- Learn how Inca society was organized.
- Find out about Inca religious beliefs.

Section 2 Summary

Inca society was highly organized and controlled. There was no private ownership of land. Incas worshiped many gods and spirits.

Inca Life

The Incas had a strong social structure. The society was divided into two classes, nobles and commoners, and each class had its own hierarchy. A **hierarchy** (HĪ er ahr kee) is a system for ranking members of a group according to their importance. There were three ranks of nobles: nobles by birth, appointed nobles, and curacas (koo RAH kahs). Commoners were divided into twelve categories based on age and gender.

Inca Hierarchy

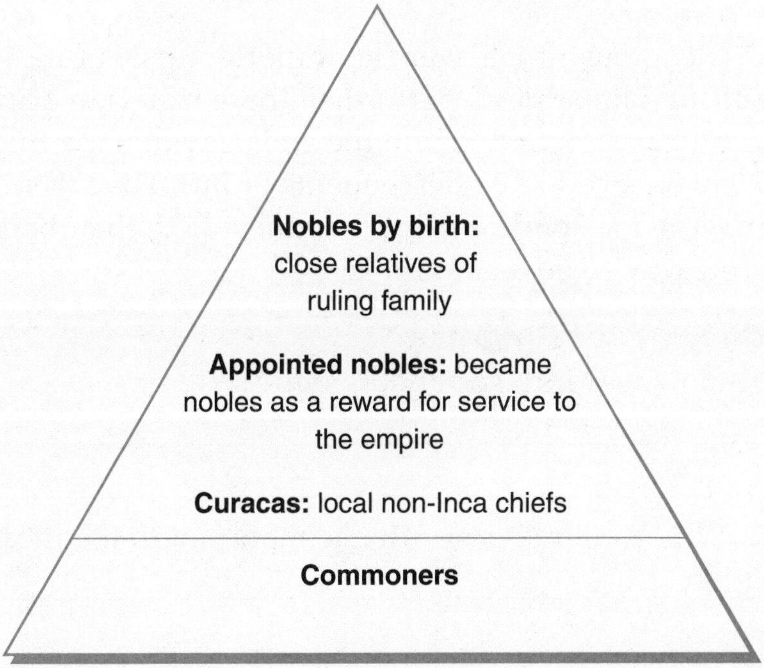
Nobles by birth: close relatives of ruling family
Appointed nobles: became nobles as a reward for service to the empire
Curacas: local non-Inca chiefs
Commoners

Key Events

1200	The Incas settle in the Cuzco Valley.
1300s	The Incas conquer much of the west coast of South America.
1438	Pachacuti becomes the Inca ruler.
1525	Civil war follows Huayna Capac's death.

Reading Strategy

Circle the main idea of the bracketed paragraph. Then, underline two supporting details.

✓ Checkpoint

List the three types of nobles in Inca society.

_____

_____

_____

Vocabulary Builder

This paragraph tells you that Sapa Incas were believed to be descended from Inti. Who does this mean came first, the Sapa Incas or Inti?

_____

_____

✓ Checkpoint

Name two gods the Incas worshiped.

_____

_____

In Inca society, there was no private land or property. Commoners lived in communities called ayllus. An ayllu (Ī loo) was a group of related families that lived in the same location and shared land, food, and resources. All land was considered communal property (kuh MYOON uhl PRAHP er tee). That is, it was owned and managed by the government for public use.

The state divided land into three parts: one for the government, one for the priests and religion, and one for the ayllu. Farmers had to cultivate the lands of the government and the religion before they could farm the ayllu land to sustain their community. Commoners had to supply labor for state projects. This was known as the mita (MEE tah), or labor tax, and included military service.

Most Inca communities produced the goods they needed, so there was little need for money or trade. Inca society ran on the barter system. ✓

Inca Religion

Religion was important to the Incas, but scholars know little about Inca theology (thee AHL uh jee), or religious teachings and practices. Scholars do know that Incas worshiped many gods and nature spirits. Viracocha was the creator god, but the most important god was the sun god, Inti. The Incas believed they were descended from Inti and that they owed him special worship.

Religious rituals were an important part of Inca spiritual life. Priests performed these rituals to bring good harvests and to win the gods' favor. Sapa Incas were believed to be descendents of Inti. They were regarded as living gods. When they died, their bodies were preserved as mummies. ✓

Check Your Progress

1. How was Inca society divided?

_____

_____

2. Why were religious rituals important to the Incas?

_____

_____

Question to Think About As you read Section 2 in your textbook and take notes, keep this question in mind: **What were the characteristics of Inca civilization?**

▶ Use these charts to record key information from the section.

Inca Society
Nobles
Nobles by birth • **who:** close relatives of the ruling family • **privileges:** Held highest positions in government and society, lived in most elaborate houses, ate best food, wore finest clothes.
Nobles by appointment • **who:** • **privileges:** Many of the same privileges as _____.
Curacas • **who:** • **privileges:** Kept their _____ privileges, and enjoyed some benefits of _____ status.
Commoners
• Divided into _____ categories based on their _____ and _____. • living conditions: • obligation to state: Men had to work on state projects and serve in the military.
State/Government

• **owned and managed:**
• **division of land:**
  1. one part for the government
  2.
  3.

Inca Theology
The Inca worshiped many gods and performed rituals to win their favor. • **Viracocha:** the creator god, assisted by moon, stars, and earth • **Inti:** • Inca also worshiped _____.

Refer to this page to answer the Chapter 8 Focus Question on page 104.

Section 3 Focus Question

How did the Incas demonstrate great skills in organization, engineering, and the arts? To begin answering this question,

- Discover how the Incas organized their empire.
- Find out how the Incas excelled at engineering.
- Learn about the crafts of Inca artists.

Section 3 Summary

The Incas created a highly organized government for their empire. They also accomplished much in the fields of engineering and the arts.

Administration of the Empire

The Incas could not have ruled their empire without good **administration** (ad mihn ihs TRAY shuhn). Administration is the management of a government or business. The Inca government was centered in Cuzco. The empire was split into quarters, and each quarter had a governor who was a noble by birth. These officials made up the supreme council and reported directly to the emperor.

Below this level, the administration was based on multiples of ten. Each village was divided into groups of ten families, and each group was governed by the head of one family. The local group leaders reported to a curaca, or a local chief who was responsible for 100 families. The top curacas reported to Inca nobles who, in turn, reported to governors in Cuzco.

<u>The Incas also tried to unify their empire in other ways.</u> They forced conquered peoples to use the Inca language, Quechua. Government officials used an army of messengers to speed reports across the empire. These messengers carried a **quipu** (KEE pu). A quipu was made out of knotted strings. It was a way to count and keep records. The Incas used quipus to record numbers of people or goods. Every year, officials took a **census** (SEHN suhs), or population survey, which the government used to organize its citizens.

© Pearson Education, Inc., publishing as Pearson Prentice Hall. All Rights Reserved.

Key Events

1200	The Incas settle in the Cuzco Valley.
1300s	The Incas conquer much of the west coast of South America.
1438	Pachacuti becomes the Inca ruler.
1525	Civil war follows Huayna Capac's death.

Vocabulary Builder

Reread the underlined sentence. Circle the word that the phrase "bring together" could replace.

With their efficient administration, the Incas created a form of what today we would call a **welfare state** (WEHL fair stayt). This is a government that is responsible for the well-being of its citizens. The government watched over its people and would help them in times of need. The Incas lived under strict controls. Officials visited towns and villages, inspecting homes and fields. People had to wear identifying clothing. But by honoring government rules, citizens could be assured of a secure place in society. ✓

Master Builders

The Incas also excelled in architecture and engineering. Inca cities such as Cuzco were marvels of stone architecture. Buildings were made out of large stone blocks that did not need mortar or cement to hold them together. Many of these structures still stand today.

The Incas engineered a vast road system that stretched more than 15,000 miles across the empire. This system tied the empire together physically, ensuring that soldiers and messengers could travel easily from one place to another. ✓

Arts and Crafts

Inca artists used gold and silver to craft fine objects such as jewelry, dishes, statues, and wall decorations. Incas also wove fine textiles out of cotton, alpaca, and vicuña. These textiles were more valuable to the Incas than the metal work. Today, descendants of the Incas still make beautiful textiles using ancient methods and designs. ✓

Check Your Progress

1. What is one way the Inca government tried to unify its empire?

_____

_____

2. How was the Inca Empire physically tied together?

_____

_____

✓ **Checkpoint**

Name the city in which Inca government was centered.

_____

Reading Strategy

Reread the bracketed paragraph. How does the second sentence relate to the first sentence?

_____

_____

_____

✓ **Checkpoint**

Name a city where Incas showed their skill in architecture and engineering.

_____

✓ **Checkpoint**

List two things Incas made with gold and silver.

_____

_____

Question to Think About As you read Section 3 in your textbook and take notes, keep this question in mind: **How did the Incas demonstrate great skills in organization, engineering, and the arts?**

▶ Use these charts to record key information from the section. Some of the information has been filled in to get you started.

Administration of the Inca Empire	
Method	**Effect of Method**
Organized government	Chain of command was orderly.
Quechua	
Messengers	
Quipu	Government could keep detailed records.
Census	
Establishment of welfare state	

Inca Achievements	
Engineering	**Arts**
• **Architecture:** Incas built structures out of large stones held together without mortar or cement.	• **Metals** types: silver, gold
• **Road System** length:	used to make:
effect:	• **Textiles** types of fiber:
	used to make:

Refer to this page to answer the Chapter 8 Focus Question on page 104.

Directions: Circle the letter of the correct answer.

1. One example of how the Andes' rugged geography was influential is that
   A it prevented the Inca from building empires.
   B it made breeding animals difficult.
   C it encouraged the Inca to invent farming methods like terracing.

2. Which of the following best describes Inca society?
   A Everyone had the same privileges.
   B Property was private.
   C Property was communal.

3. Which of the following best describes the Inca Empire?
   A It had a highly organized government and social structure.
   B It was fragmented.
   C Its administration provided no support or aid for its citizens.

4. The Incas excelled at
   A creating trade partnerships with other Andean cultures.
   B engineering, architecture, and the arts.
   C inventing a system of writing.

Directions: Follow the steps to answer this question:

Did the advantages of living in the Inca welfare state outweigh the disadvantages?

Step 1: Recall information: How was the Inca Empiare like a welfare state?

_____

Step 2: List the advantages and disadvantages of this system for citizens of the empire.

Advantages	Disadvantages

Step 3: Write a topic sentence that states your opinion on this question: Did the advantages of living in the Inca welfare state outweigh the disadvantages? Support your opinion with details.

_____

_____

_____

Chapter 8 Notetaking Study Guide

Now you are ready to answer the Chapter 8 Focus Question: **How did the Incas adapt to their environment and achieve an advanced civilization?**

▶ Complete the following charts to help you answer this question.

Inca Setting
• Human settlement hard because: • high elevation   • steep slopes   •   • Farming innovation method: terraces   purpose: allows crops to be planted on slopes • Raising livestock animal: llama   animal: purpose: pack animal and meat   purpose:

Inca Society		
Social Classes	**Theology**	**Administrative Methods**

Nobles:
 	
• by birth
 	
• by appointment
 	
•
 	
Commoners:
• divided by _____
  and _____
	Worshiped_____ gods:
	
	• Viracocha
	
	•
	
	•
	
	Performed _____ to win gods' favor.
		• Organized government
		  Effect: chain of command was orderly
		
		• Quechua
		  Effect: language unites
		
		• Census
		  Effect:
		
		• Welfare state
		  Effect:

Inca Achievements	
Engineering	**Arts**
• Architecture: built large structures out of stone without mortar or cement • Road system:	• Metal: • Textiles:

Refer to this page to answer the Unit 4 Focus Question on page 116.

Chapter 9

The Aztecs (1325–1519)

Chapter Standards

History-Social Science 7.7.1, 7.7.2, 7.7.4

What You Will Learn

In the 1300s, the Aztecs settled in the Valley of Mexico. By 1440, they had built an empire. Tribute and human sacrifice were at the core of Aztec government and religion. The Aztecs were talented architects and artists.

Chapter 9 Focus Question

As you read this chapter, keep this question in mind: **How did the Aztecs adapt to their environment and achieve an advanced civilization?**

Section 1

The Rise of the Aztecs

Section 1 Focus Question

How did geography influence the development of Aztec civilization? To begin to answer this question,
- Find out about the Aztec world.
- Learn about the Aztec Empire.

Section 1 Summary

The Aztecs settled in the highlands of central Mexico. As they prosp ered and developed their military strength, they built a large empire.

The Aztec World

Some of the best farmland in Mexico is found in the highland basins of central Mexico. A geographic basin (BAY sihn) is a bowl-shaped area, often with a lake at the bottom. The Aztecs built their empire here, in a large, high basin called the Valley of Mexico.

Conditions there were favorable for the growth of civilization. The floor of the basin was covered with several large, shallow lakes, the land was fertile, and the climate was mild. Farming people first settled in the area thousands of years ago. Then around A.D. 1200, nomadic groups began migrating into the valley. The last to arrive were the Mexica, who were later called the Aztecs.

Key Events

1325	The Aztecs found Tenochtitlán.
Early 1400s	The Aztecs begin wars of conquest.
1502	Moctezuma becomes the Aztec king.
1519	Spanish invaders enter Tenochtitlán.

Vocabulary Builder

Condition has several meanings, depending on its context. Which of the sentences below uses the meaning found in this sentence: *Conditions there were favorable for the growth of civilization.*

A. I will go, on one condition.

B. The living conditions at college were different from those at home.

C. We must be in top condition for the race.

The Aztecs settled on a small island in the middle of Lake Texcoco in 1325. There they saw an eagle perched on a thorny cactus. According to legend, their chief god had told them to settle in such a place. ✓

The Aztec Empire

The Aztecs called their island settlement Tenochtitlán (tay nahch tee TLAHN). By this time, the Aztecs had gained a reputation as fierce warriors. They often served as mercenaries (MER suh nehr eez), or soldiers-for-hire, in local conflicts. The Aztecs, however, believed they were destined to become powerful in their own right.

The Aztecs' island setting had many advantages. The lake and its marshes were rich sources of food. The edges of the lake were ideal for farming. The Aztecs also created floating gardens called chinampas (chih NAHM pahz) in the lake itself. Chinampas farming allowed the Aztecs to expand the island and feed their growing population. The island setting made travel, transportation, and defense easy.

In the early 1400s, the Aztecs joined forces with two other city-states in a pact called the Triple Alliance. By 1440, they had formed an empire that included most of the Valley of Mexico. They conquered their enemies and were rarely defeated.

Under the Emperor Moctezuma (mahk tuh ZOO muh), the Aztec Empire reached its height. It covered much of present-day central Mexico and part of coastal Guatemala. Around ten million people lived within its borders. By the early 1500s, the Valley of Mexico had become a great urban area of about one million inhabitants. ✓

Reading Strategy

Reread the bracketed text. It mentions three time periods. In the margin, create a time line listing those periods and their importance.

✓ **Checkpoint**

List two advantages of Tenochtitlán's island setting.

_____

_____

Check Your Progress

1. What made the Valley of Mexico favorable for the growth of civilization?

_____

_____

2. What was the Triple Alliance?

_____

_____

Question to Think About As you read Section 1 in your textbook and take notes, keep this section focus question in mind: **How did geography influence the development of Aztec civilization?**

▶ Use these charts to record key information from the section. Some of the information has been filled in to get you started.

The Geography of Mexico		
Major geographical feature of central Mexico	Central Plateau	
Location of best farmlands in central Mexico		
Advantages of farmland in central Mexico	Soil:	Climate: Mild

Arrival of the Aztecs	
Aztecs previously called	the Mexica
Where the Aztecs settled	
Why they settled there, according to legend	
Name of original settlement	Tenochtitlán
Advantages of the island settlement	**Food** • • Shoreline ideal for farming
	Transport
	Defense island easily defended against attack
Chinampas were	

Important Events During the Aztec Empire	
When	**Event**
Early 1400s	Aztecs formed the Triple Alliance with two other city-states
1440	
Late 1400s	
1502	
1519	

Refer to this page to answer the Chapter 9 Focus Question on page 115.

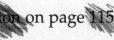

Key Events

1325	The Aztecs found Tenochtitlán.
Early 1400s	The Aztecs begin wars of conquest.
1502	Moctezuma becomes the Aztec king.
1519	Spanish invaders enter Tenochtitlán.

Section 2 Focus Question

What were the characteristics of Aztec civilization? To begin to answer this question,

- Find out about Aztec life.
- Learn about the Aztec government and religion.

Section 2 Summary

The Aztecs were mainly farmers. However, they also frequently went to war to gain tribute and captives for human sacrifices.

Aztec Life

The Aztecs were mainly an agrarian (uh GRAR ee uhn) people. That is, most of their lives were related to farming. They were organized into two main social classes: nobles and commoners. Nobles lived well and served as government officials. Commoners lived more humbly. Although most commoners were farmers, some held respected positions as artisans and traders.

At the lowest level of society were slaves. Some were commoners who had sold themselves into slavery to escape poverty or to avoid punishment. Others were captives taken during war.

Lives of Aztec Nobles, Commoners, and Slaves	
Nobles	• Lived in large homes • Fine, colorful clothes • Best food, including meat
Commoners	• Lived with extended families • Plain, coarse clothing • Plain food (corn, beans, chilis)
Slaves	• Could marry and own property • Children born free

Despite class differences, life for most Aztecs followed similar patterns. All Aztec children went to school for at least a few years. Boys received military training. Girls learned the arts of homemaking. ✓

✓ Checkpoint

List two types of commoners who were respected in Aztec society.

_____

_____

Government and Religion

The Aztecs frequently waged war to win *tribute* (TRIHB yoot), or goods paid as taxes by conquered peoples. Capturing prisoners for human sacrifice was another goal for going to war.

A king led the Aztecs. A group of five royal advisers helped him run the government. Four were military commanders. The fifth was an official much like a *prime minister* (prīm MIHN ihs ter), or a chief official appointed by the ruler of a country. Beneath the royal advisers were lesser officials, such as judges and tax collectors. At the local level, citizens were divided into small districts called *calpulli*, which were led by district chiefs.

Although the Aztecs had a strong ruler, they never had a true central government. Instead, the empire was a loose collection of city-states controlled by the Aztecs, but ruled by local chiefs. The Aztecs kept control through the threat of military force.

The Aztecs believed monarchs ruled with the blessings of the gods. They also believed that the gods gave them life and controlled everything on Earth. They worshiped hundreds of gods. Huitzilopochtli (weet suh loh POHCH tlee) was considered the most important god because he brought success in battle and kept the sun in the sky. The Aztecs believed he needed human blood to remain strong. As a result, the Aztecs killed thousands of victims every year.

Sacrifice was also used to scare conquered peoples so they would be easier to control. Still, revolts were common, which led to a constant cycle of war, sacrifice, and tribute. ✓

Check Your Progress

1. How did most Aztecs make their living?

_____

_____

2. Why did the Aztecs conduct human sacrifices?

_____

_____

Vocabulary Builder

What noun, related to the word *adviser*, completes the following sentence?

The adviser gave _____ to the king to stop the war.

Reading Strategy

Reread the bracketed paragraph. Underline the four levels of Aztec leadership described in the paragraph. Then number them from 1 (most powerful) to 4 (least powerful).

✓ Checkpoint

Name the Aztecs' most important god.

_____

Question to Think About As you read Section 2 in your textbook and take notes, keep this section focus question in mind: **What were the characteristics of Aztec civilization?**

▶ Use this chart to record key information from the section. Some of the information has been filled in to get you started.

Aztec Life and Society			
	Homes	Clothing	Food
Nobles	Large, two-story houses	Fine cotton with colorful designs	Best food, including meat
Commoners			
Most common occupation			
How people became slaves	• • Captives taken during war were sometimes enslaved.		
Rights of slaves	• • • children born free •		
Respected commoners	• •		
Motives for going to war	• tribute •		
Government	No true central government. Instead, empire was a loose collection of _____ that were ruled by _____. The Aztecs maintained control through _____.		
Kings were selected by			
Kingship was passed down from	Father to son or other blood relatives		
Helped king run government	Four _____ One _____		
The Aztecs believed that the gods	• •		
Most important god	Huitzilopochtli		
Aztecs performed human sacrifice for	• religious rituals •		

Refer to this page to answer the Chapter 9 Focus Question on page 115.

Aztec Achievements

Section 3 Focus Question

What were the outstanding achievements of the Aztecs? To begin to answer this question

- Learn about the art and architecture of the Aztecs.
- Find out about the Aztecs' language and literature.

© Pearson Education, Inc., publishing as Pearson Prentice Hall. All Rights Reserved.

Section 3 Summary

The Aztecs created beautiful art and impressive architecture, including a great capital city. They also valued words and language, especially spoken language and poetry.

Art and Architecture

The Aztecs were accomplished artists and architects. They made beautiful objects from gold, feathers, and other natural materials. They also designed and built an extraordinary capital city. Few Aztec structures survived the Spanish conquest. But scholars have used historical accounts and archaeological remains to describe the Aztec capital at its height.

By the early 1500s, around 200,000 people lived in the capital city of Tenochtitlán. The city was divided into four quarters, crossed by avenues and canals. Long causeways connected the island to the lakeshore. A **causeway** (CAWZ way) is a raised road across a body of water.

At the center of the city was a large walled plaza. Dozens of pyramids, temples, and other buildings were scattered around the plaza. The largest structure was a huge, brightly painted pyramid called the Templo Mayor (TEHM plo mī YOR). Two shrines stood at the top of the pyramid. A **shrine** (shrīn) is a place of worship dedicated to a sacred object or person.

The residential districts of the city were spread out around the plaza. Each district had its own small temples and markets. In the markets, many products were available, from food and medicine to live animals and building materials.

Key Events

1325	The Aztecs found Tenochtitlán.
Early 1400s	The Aztecs begin wars of conquest.
1502	Moctezuma becomes the Aztec king.
1519	Spanish invaders enter Tenochtitlán.

Vocabulary Builder

The prefix *extra-* comes from the Latin word meaning "outside" or "beyond." Keeping this in mind, write a definition for the word *extraordinary*.

_____

_____

_____

Reading Strategy

Reread the bracketed paragraph. Circle the main idea. Then, underline two details that support this main idea.

Basic craft goods, such as baskets and pottery, were available in the markets. Luxury goods, however, were sold directly to nobles. Today, collectors view these luxury goods as fine art (fin ahrt), or works that are created mainly to be admired.

Jewelry and mosaics were specialties of the Aztecs. Mosaic artists decorated objects with bits of colorful stones and shells. Jewelers used gold, silver, and semi-precious stones. One of the highest forms of Aztec art was feather work. Fans, headdresses, capes, and shields were created from the feathers of tropical birds. The Aztecs also carved beautiful stone sculptures. ✓

Language and Literature

The Aztecs valued words and language highly. They created beautiful bark-paper books. However, Aztec writing was less advanced than the Maya system, so these books were mainly lists of names and dates. Their writing system was important for record-keeping, but it was the spoken language that mattered most to the Aztecs.

The Aztecs were skilled orators (OR uh terz), or public speakers. Orators performed at public and private gatherings. Their favorite topics were stories from the past and legends of the gods. A great speaker was said to have "flowers on his lips." Even today, the Aztec language, Nahuatl (nah oo AHTL), is known for its beautiful sound.

Poetry was the most popular form of Aztec literature. Even kings composed poetry. The most famous of the royal poets was Nezahualcoyotl, the great ruler of Texcoco. Flowers and the beauty of nature were classic themes of Aztec poetry. ✓

Check Your Progress

1. How did the Aztecs travel within Tenochtitlán?

_____

_____

2. What were some themes of Aztec poetry?

_____

_____

✓ Checkpoint

Name the largest structure in the central walled plaza.

_____

✓ Checkpoint

List two favorite topics of Aztec orators.

_____

_____

Question to Think About As you read Section 3 in your textbook and take notes, keep this question in mind: **What were the outstanding achievements of the Aztecs?**

▶ Use this chart to record key information from the section. Some of the information has been filled in to get you started.

Aztec Achievements	
Aztec building accomplishments: 1. avenues and canals 2. causeways 3. 4. dikes	**Purposes of these projects:** 1. crossed the city 2. 3. brought fresh water to city 4.
Central Plaza in Tenochtitlán • Used for _____ and _____ • Largest building: _____	

Greatest market
• Located in: _____
• Examples of products sold: _____

Forms of Aztec currency: • cacao beans
                              •
                              •
                              •

Aztec fine arts	Type of work: 1. jewelry 2. mosaics 3.	Made from: 1. gold, silver, semiprecious stones 2. 3. feathers of tropical birds

The Aztecs were skilled _____ orators _____. Favorite topics were stories from the past and _____. In this way, Aztec _____ and _____ were passed down from generation to generation.

_____ was the most popular form of Aztec literature. _____ and _____ were classic themes.

Refer to this page to answer the Chapter 9 Focus Question on page 115.

Directions: Circle the letter of the correct answer.

1. Why did the Aztecs develop chinampas?
   A   to cultivate mountainous regions
   B   to irrigate a dry environment
   C   to expand growing areas

2. At its height, the Aztec Empire was ruled by
   A   Nezahualcoyotl.   B   Moctezuma.   C   Quetzalcoatl.

3. Which of the following was an important motive to the Aztecs for going to war?
   A   to spread their religion
   B   to open up trade routes
   C   to take captives

4. What was the most popular form of Aztec literature?
   A   poetry   B   plays   C   folk tales

Directions: Follow the steps to complete this task:
Compare and contrast the lives of nobles and commoners in Aztec society.

Step 1: Recall information: List four details about the lives of nobles. Then, list four details about the lives of commoners.

Lives of Nobles	Lives of Commoners

Step 2: Identify how the lives of nobles and commoners were alike and how they were different.

How Their Lives Were Alike	How Their Lives Were Different

Step 3: Complete the topic sentence that follows. Then, write two or three more sentences that support your topic sentence.

The lives of nobles and commoners in Aztec society were

_____

_____

_____

Chapter 9 Notetaking Study Guide

Now you are ready to answer the Chapter 9 Focus Question: **How did the Aztecs adapt to their environment and achieve an advanced civilizations?**

▶ Fill in the following charts to help you answer this question. Use the notes that you took for each section.

Aztec Setting		
The Aztecs' Environment	**How They Modified It**	**Description**
Tenochtitlán: a small island in the middle of Lake Texcoco	Chinampas	floating gardens that allowed the Aztecs to expand the island and grow more food
	Canals	
	Causeways	
	Aqueducts	
	Dikes	

Aztec Civilization	
Government	**Art and Architecture**
Leader: a king **Advisers:** **Local officials:**	**Types of architectural structures:** pyramids, temples, palaces **Examples of Aztec Art** • **Jewelry:** rings, necklaces • **Mosaic Art:** • **Featherwork:** • **Stone Sculptures:**
Religion	**Language and Literature**
Beliefs about gods: gods gave them life and controlled everything on Earth **Most important god:** **How Aztecs honored the gods:**	**Written texts were mostly:** bark-paper books; mostly lists of names and dates **Orators' favorite topics:** • • **Classic themes of poetry:** • •

Refer to this page to answer the Unit 4 Focus Question on page 116.

Unit 4 Pulling It Together Activity

Chapter 7 Maya civilization developed in the area of the Americas known as Mesoamerica. The Mayas had a rich culture with a social order based on commoners and nobles, and complex systems of government, religion, writing, and math. The Mayas were also skilled artists and architects.

Chapter 8 The Inca Empire was influenced by the geography of South America. The Incas had a sophisticated society that made achievements in government, engineering, and art.

Chapter 9 In the 1300s, the Aztecs settled in the Valley of Mexico. By 1440, they had built a powerful empire. Tribute and human sacrifice were at the core of Aztec government and religion. The Aztecs were talented architects and artists.

Think Like a Historian

Read the Unit 4 Focus Question: **How were the civilizations that developed in the Americas both similar and different?**

▶ Use the organizers on this page and the next to collect information to answer this question.

In what ways were the Maya, Inca, and Aztec civilizations similar? One of them is listed in this chart. Review your section and chapter notes. Then complete the chart.

Similarities Among the Maya, Inca, and Aztec Civilizations	
Characteristics of Civilizations	**How the Maya, Inca, and Aztec Civilizations Were Similar**
Rise and Fall	• The Mayas, Incas, and Aztecs adapted to difficult environments. •
Society and Government	• • • • •
Achievements	• •

Look at the second part of the Unit Focus Question. It asks about the differences among the Maya, Inca, and Aztec civilizations. The chart below gives you part of the answer. Review your section and chapter notes. Then fill in the rest of the chart.

Differences Among the Maya, Inca, and Aztec Civilizations	
Characteristics of Civilizations	**How the Maya, Inca, and Aztec Civilizations Differed**
Rise and Fall	• All rose in different types of geographic regions, with different adaptations. • • •
Society and Government	• • • •
Achievements	• • •

Civilizations in East Asia

Chapter 10 Under the Tang and Song dynasties, China's size, wealth, and political strength grew, and the arts flourished. Daoism, Confucianism, and Buddhism were the three main belief systems.

Chapter 11 The Mongols conquered many parts of Asia, creating a vast empire. The Ming Dynasty then restored Chinese rule. China's ideas, culture, and technological innovations influenced other countries.

Chapter 12 Japan, an island nation, was strongly influenced by Chinese culture. A series of emperors established the Japanese state, and then a group of powerful families gained control. Japan became divided under military rulers, but was reunited by the 1600s.

Chapter 13 Japan adapted cultural influences from its neighbors and created an original culture of its own. Buddhism was an important cultural influence.

Focus Your Learning As you study this unit and take notes, you will find the information to answer the questions below. Answering the chapter focus questions will help build your answer to the unit focus question.

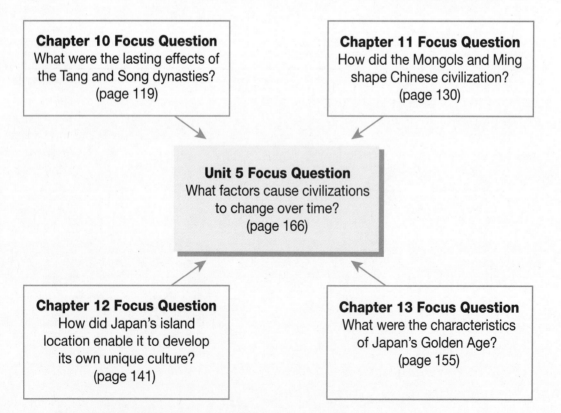

Chapter 10 Focus Question
What were the lasting effects of the Tang and Song dynasties?
(page 119)

Chapter 11 Focus Question
How did the Mongols and Ming shape Chinese civilization?
(page 130)

Unit 5 Focus Question
What factors cause civilizations to change over time?
(page 166)

Chapter 12 Focus Question
How did Japan's island location enable it to develop its own unique culture?
(page 141)

Chapter 13 Focus Question
What were the characteristics of Japan's Golden Age?
(page 155)

Chapter 10

China's Golden Age (618–1279)

 **Chapter Standards**

History-Social Science 7.3.1, 7.3.2, 7.3.3, 7.3.6

What You Will Learn

Under the Tang and Song dynasties, China's size, wealth, and political strength grew, and the arts flourished. Daoism, Confucianism, and Buddhism were the three main belief systems during this time. China also developed new technologies and grew more food.

Chapter 10 Focus Question

As you read through the sections in this chapter, keep this question in mind: **What were the lasting effects of the Tang and Song dynasties?**

Section 1

The Tang and Song Dynasties

Section 1 Focus Question

How did the Tang and Song dynasties strengthen China? To begin answering this question,
- Learn about China under the Tang Dynasty.
- Find out about the Song government.

Section 1 Summary

After the Han fell from power, China was rebuilt under the Tang and Song dynasties. They made the country bigger and built a strong government.

The Splendor of the Tang

The Han Dynasty fell in A.D. 220 and left China divided. In 618, the Tang Dynasty reunited China and ruled for the next 300 years.

Tang Taizong (tahng tī dzuhng) was a military leader who founded the Tang Dynasty. He brought stable government back to China. He revived the country's **bureaucracy** (byoo RAH kruh see). A bureaucracy is a government with many departments and bureaus headed by appointed officials.

Empress Wu (woo) was another strong leader. She was the only woman emperor in Chinese history.

Key Events

618	Tang Dynasty unites China.
906	End of the Tang Dynasty leads to unrest.
960	Song Dynasty begins.
1127	Song Dynasty withdraws from northern China.

Reading Strategy

Reread the bracketed paragraphs. Then underline the subject of each paragraph.

The Tang Dynasty made Changan (chang ahn) their capital city. It was the largest city in the world. It was also a cultural and commercial center. People from all over Asia came to Changan to trade. The imperial palace was built to impress visitors.

The Tang period was a golden age for art, literature, and poetry. Artists created paintings and fine pottery. Architects and sculptors built and decorated great temples. Chinese poets, such as Li Bo (lee boh), wrote poems about subjects such as nature. ☑

The Song Era of Good Government

When the Tang Dynasty collapsed, the Song Dynasty arose and ruled from 960 to 1279. During that time, barbarian tribes threatened the northern borders of China. So the Song turned their attention to the Chinese heartland and southern China.

The Song period was a time of good government. The Song rulers depended on a group of highly educated civil servants to run China's bureaucracy. These civil servants were called scholar-officials (SKAHL ur uh FIHSH uhl). They had to pass special tests, and they had to be honest and efficient. Special rules limited their power. They had to change jobs every three years and could not serve in their home district.

The Song Dynasty developed a merit system (MER iht SIHS tuhm) for their scholar-officials. A merit system is a process for hiring and promoting people based on talent and skills, rather than on wealth or social status.

The good government of the Song led to economic growth and urbanization (er buh nih ZAY shuhn), or the growth of cities. In 1127, the Song moved away from northern China after a barbarian invasion. They made the new capital city in the southern city of Hangzhou (hahng joh). This large port city was a center of trade. ☑

Check Your Progress

1. How did Taizong create a stable government?

_____

2. Under the Song, what was hiring and promoting based on?

_____

✓ Checkpoint

Name the only woman emperor in Chinese history.

_____

Vocabulary Builder

Read the following sentence. Use context clues to help you write your own definition of *efficient*.

Marie decided that the most efficient use of her time was to go to the store on the way home instead of going back out later.

_____

_____

✓ Checkpoint

List two qualifications of scholar-officials.

1. _____

2. _____

Question to Think About As you read Section 1 in your textbook and take notes, keep this section focus question in mind: **How did the Tang and Song dynasties strengthen China?**

► Use this chart to record key information from the section. Some of the information has been filled in to get you started.

	China Under the Tang	China Under the Song
People	Tang Taizong: • founded the Tang Dynasty • reunited China • brought stable government back to China Empress Wu: • • Li Bo: •	
Places	Changan: • • •	Area of focus: Chinese heartland and southern China Hangzhou: • •

Government	Bureaucracy:
	• made up of _____
	  headed by _____
	_____
	Taizong's goal:
		Scholar-officials
		• chosen by _____
		• had to be _____
		  and _____
		• became highest ranking group in Chinese society
		Merit system:

Other	Golden age for _____ and _____ Architects and sculptors designed and decorated _____. Poets wrote about _____.	Good government led to _____, which led to _____. The Southern Song period began in _____, after a _____ invasion.

Refer to this page to answer the Chapter Focus Question on page 129.

Key Events

618	Tang Dynasty unites China.
906	End of the Tang Dynasty leads to unrest.
960	Song Dynasty begins.
1127	Song Dynasty withdraws from northern China.

✓ Checkpoint

What did Daoism begin as?

_____

_____

Religion and Thought in China's Golden Age

Section 2 Focus Question

What is Neo-Confucianism, and how did it influence the Chinese way of life? To begin answering this question,

- Explore Daoist philosophy.
- Find out about Buddhist thought in China.
- Learn about Confucianism.

Section 2 Summary

Daoism, Confucianism, and Buddhism are three belief systems that have played an important role in the development of Chinese culture.

Daoism

Daoism is an ancient Chinese philosophy teaching that all things should follow the Dao. Dao (dow) means the "Way" or the "way of nature." Many Daoists left society to live closer to nature.

Daoism began as a philosophy. But by the Tang period, it had grown into a religion with priests and temples. ✓

Buddhism

Buddhism is a religion based on the teachings of Siddhartha Gautama. He was also known as the Buddha or "the Enlightened One." Gautama taught that life involves suffering. To ease suffering, one must give up worldly desires and seek enlightenment, or perfect wisdom. Those who reach enlightenment enter nirvana (nir VAH nuh), or a state of complete peace.

Buddhism entered China during the Han Dynasty. It gained strength in troubled times. It provided hope for an end to suffering. Two important schools of Buddhist thought in China were the Pure Land and Chan schools. Followers of Pure Land Buddhism worshiped a figure named Amitabha (ah mee TAH buh). They thought that if they performed rituals of devotion they would live in a paradise called the Pure Land after they died. Followers of Chan Buddhism believed that enlightenment could be achieved through being aware and living "in the moment."

By the time of the Tang Dynasty, Buddhism had many followers in China. But some Chinese criticized Buddhism for having no roots in Chinese culture. They also criticized Buddhism for teaching people to leave society and family life. Critics also did not like the wealth and power of Buddhist institutions. The criticism led to persecution. The worst persecution came under Emperor Wuzong (woo dzuhng). He ordered many Buddhist temples destroyed. ✓

Confucianism

<u>Before Buddhism, Confucianism was the main belief system in China.</u> As Buddhism lost strength, Confucianism became the main belief system again. This system was based on the teachings of Confucius, a Chinese teacher and philosopher. Confucius based his philosophy on respect for family and the social order. He also stressed the importance of moral virtue and education. He believed his philosophy would bring peace to China.

Confucianism began as a practical philosophy. But the growth of Buddhism caused Confucian scholars to think about religious questions. By the Song era, a new philosophy was being practiced. It was called Neo-Confucianism. Its followers studied the classic writings of Confucius. But they interpreted them in new ways to answer questions about the meaning of life.

Some followers of Neo-Confucianism sought enlightenment in the Buddhist sense. Others, such as a scholar-official named Zhu Xi (juh shee), said that people should live according to the Dao, or Way. But he defined the Dao as self-improvement and education, instead of the retreat from society. Neo-Confucianism has influenced China from the Song period onward. ✓

Check Your Progress

1. Name one thing about Buddhism that was criticized.

_____

2. What did Confucius believe about his philosophy?

_____

_____

Vocabulary Builder

Reread the bracketed paragraph. Use context clues to help you write a short definition of the word *persecution*.

_____

_____

✓ Checkpoint

List two important schools of Buddhist thought in China.

_____

_____

Reading Strategy

Reread the underlined sentence in the summary. How does it help the summary move from the subject of Buddhism to the subject of Confucianism?

_____

_____

_____

✓ Checkpoint

Name the two things on which Confucius based his philosophy.

_____

_____

Question to Think About As you read Section 2 in your textbook and take notes, keep this section focus question in mind: **What is Neo-Confucianism, and how did it influence the Chinese way of life?**

▶ Use this chart to record key information from the section. Some of the information has been filled in to get you started.

Chinese Belief Systems			
Belief System	**Beginnings**	**Philosophy**	**Effect on Chinese Culture**
Daoism	Began as a philosophy, and grew into a religion.	All things—earth, heaven, and people—should follow the Dao, or the "Way."	Many Daoists withdrew from society to live close to nature.
Buddhism	Based on the teachings of _____ _____, or the _____. Entered China during the _____ _____.	**Gautama taught:** • • **Pure Land:** **Chan:**	**Reasons people opposed Buddhism:** • • •
Confucianism	Based on the teachings of _____. Began as a _____ philosophy.	**Confucius taught:** • respect for the family • • •	• • obedience to people of higher rank • •
Neo-Confucianism	Began because _____ and _____ made Confucian scholars think about _____ questions.	Interpreted classical Confucian writings to answer questions about _____ _____ _____.	Great influence on China from the _____ on.

Refer to this page to answer the Chapter Focus Question on page 129.

Advances in Farming, Technology, and Trade

Section 3 Focus Question

How did developments in agriculture, technology, and commerce influence the economy of China? To begin answering this question,

- Learn about Chinese advances in farming.
- Discover technologies pioneered by the Chinese.
- Find out how trading and industry expanded.

Section 3 Summary

Advances in farming, technology, and trade fueled growth during the Tang and Song eras. China became the world's most advanced economy.

Farming

Under the Tang and Song, the center of agriculture, or farming, shifted to the south. One reason for this was that rice became China's most important crop. Rice crops grew well in the south.

To keep the rice fields wet, the Chinese developed irrigation systems. These systems included pumps and other water-control devices. Rice crops produced a lot of food. As a result, China's population grew quickly.

During this period, China's government changed the land tenure (land TEHN yuhr) system. A land tenure system is the way land is owned. When the Han ruled, the government owned all farmland. All farmers were given equal shares of land. Under the Tang, wealthy families bought much of the good farmland. Most peasants worked as tenant farmers. ✓

Technology

The Chinese made advances in technology during the Tang and Song eras. They engineered and built large ships with watertight compartments and rudders. They also invented the magnetic compass, so they could sail without getting lost.

The Chinese also discovered gunpowder. First, they used it in fireworks. Later they used it to make bombs, rockets, and other weapons. They also made advances in printing.

Key Events

618	Tang Dynasty unites China.
906	End of the Tang Dynasty leads to unrest.
960	Song Dynasty begins.
1127	Song Dynasty withdraws from northern China.

Reading Strategy

Circle the topic sentence and underline two details in the bracketed paragraph.

✓ Checkpoint

Give one reason agriculture shifted to southern China.

_____

_____

Vocabulary Builder

An *engineer* is someone who designs something. What does it mean that the Chinese *engineered* ships?

_____

_____

Inventions in Printing

Block Printing	Movable Type
• Each page carved out of a block of wood	• Each letter carved separately • Pieces could be assembled as needed
↓	↓
Each block was inked and pressed on paper to print.	Lowered cost of books

Lowered cost of books:
↓ Schools expanded.
↓ Literacy (LIHT er uh see), or the ability to read and write, increased.

☑

✓ Checkpoint

Name three key Chinese inventions.

_____

_____

_____

✓ Checkpoint

Name the waterway connecting northern and southern China.

_____

Trade and Industry

Many things helped the growth of trade and industry. For example, more farm production meant more food was available for trade.

A drop in transportation costs also helped trade and industry. This happened in the early 600s after the completion of the Grand Canal, a manmade waterway that connects northern and southern China.

A third factor that helped the growth of trade was the growth of a **money economy** (MUHN ee ih KAHN uh mee). In a money economy, people use money to buy and sell goods. Since coins were so heavy, the Song government made the world's first paper money.

As trade increased, so did industries. Industries made more silk cloth, iron, and **porcelain** (POR suh lihn), a hard white pottery of extremely fine quality. ☑

Check Your Progress

1. What innovation was needed to grow rice?

_____

2. Why was paper currency invented?

_____

Question to Think About As you read Section 3 in your textbook and take notes, keep this section focus question in mind: **How did developments in agriculture, technology, and commerce influence the economy of China?**

▶ Use this organizer to record key information from the section. Some of the information has been filled in to get you started.

Ships and Navigation	**Gunpowder**	**Printing**
• Invention: _____ • Invention:	First use: _____ Other uses: • _____ • _____ • _____	By the 800s, the Chinese had invented _____ _____. _____ led to lowered cost of books, which led to an increase in _____.

Technology

Advances During China's Golden Age

Agriculture   **Trade and Industry**

Southern Rice Farming	**Land Tenure**	**Factors in the Growth of Trade:**
With advanced _____ systems and _____ _____ strains, farmers could plant _____ or _____ crops a year. With more food available, China's population _____.	**Under the Han:** • Chinese government owned _____ _____ • All farmers_____ _____ **Under the Tang:** • wealthy farmers allowed to _____ _____ • peasants worked as _____ _____	**Waterways:** made transportation _____ **Food surplus:** more food available for _____ As trade increased, the _____, _____, and _____ industries expanded.

Refer to this page to answer the Chapter Focus Question on page 129.

Directions: Circle the letter of the correct answer.

1. The Tang Dynasty brought stable government back to China by
   A reviving China's official bureaucracy.
   B establishing the largest city in the world.
   C creating magnificent temples.

2. Confucius believed that his philosophy would
   A make China the most powerful country in the world.
   B help him become the next emperor.
   C restore peace to China.

3. Many of China's agricultural advances were the result of
   A growth in Chinese technology.
   B better farmers.
   C wealthy families.

Directions: Follow the steps to complete this task:

How did the merit system solve problems in the hiring and promotion system?

Step 1: Recall information: What is a merit system?

_____

_____

Step 2: What problems might arise in a system that hires and promotes based on wealth and social status? How could a merit system solve these problems?

_____

_____

_____

Step 3: Complete the topic sentence that follows. Then write two or three additional sentences to support your topic sentence.

The merit system solved problems in the hiring and promotion system by

_____

_____

_____

_____

_____

Now you are ready to answer the Chapter 10 Focus Question: **What were the lasting effects of the Tang and Song dynasties?**

▶ Fill in the following charts to help you answer this question. Use the notes that you took for each section.

Government

Bureaucracy: The Tang created an efficient government.
Scholar-officials: Over time, this group became the _____ _____ class in Chinese society.
Merit system: The _____ created system based on _____ and _____ for hiring and _____ civil servants.

Culture

Golden age for _____ and _____
What was created:
-
-
-
-

Teachings of Belief Systems

Daoism:
   all nature should follow the Dao, or the "Way"
Buddhism:
-
-

Confucianism:
- respect for _____ _____ _____
- stressed importance of _____ _____

Neo-Confucianism:
- answers questions about _____ _____

Lasting Effects of the Tang and Song Dynasties

Technology

Inventions:
- large ships with watertight compartments and rudders
-
-
-

Agriculture

_____ became an important crop.
Advanced _____ systems and new _____ strains of rice increased farm production.
More food led to _____ _____ and a surplus of food for _____.

Trade and Industry

Trade made easy by:
- waterways like _____ _____
-

Industries that expanded:
-
-
-

Refer to this page to answer the Unit 5 Focus Question on page 166.

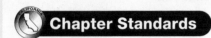

Chapter Standards

History-Social Science 7.3.4, 7.3.5, 7.8.3

Chapter 11

China Under the Mongols and the Ming (1200–1500)

What You Will Learn

The Mongols conquered many parts of Asia, creating a vast empire. The Ming dynasty then restored Chinese rule. China's ideas and culture influenced other East Asian countries, while Chinese technological innovations had an impact on more distant lands.

Chapter 11 Focus Question

As you read through this chapter, keep this question in mind: **How did the Mongols and Ming shape Chinese civilization?**

Section 1

The Mongol Ascendancy

Section 1 Focus Question

How did the Mongol conquest of China mark a new era in Chinese history? To begin answering this question,

- Learn about the Mongol conquests.
- Find out about the Yuan Dynasty.

Section 1 Summary

The Mongols emerged from the plains of central Asia and began to conquer neighboring societies. The Mongols established the Yuan Dynasty in China.

The Mongol Conquests

The Mongols lived on the steppes of the Mongolian plateau, northwest of China. A **steppe** (stehp) is a large, dry, grass-covered plain. Each clan, or tribe, of Mongols was led by a **khan** (kahn), or ruler. In the late 1100s, a leader known as Genghis Khan (GEHNG gihs kahn) built an army and began to conquer rival tribes.

After uniting the Mongols in 1206, Genghis launched successful attacks against his neighbors. He soon conquered most of northern China. His forces then turned west and swept across Central Asia.

Key Events

1206 Mongol tribes unite under Genghis Khan.

1279 Mongols gain control over all of China.

1405 Zheng He makes his first voyage of exploration.

Vocabulary Builder

In the underlined sentence, how would the meaning be changed if the word *rival* were replaced with *allied*?

_____

_____

Keys to Genghis Khan's Success
Genghis was a strong military leader.
He was ruthless in battle.
The Mongols were fierce warriors.
Genghis adopted new types of weapons.
Genghis maintained law and order among the Mongols.

✓

✓ Checkpoint

List two reasons Genghis Khan was a successful military leader.

_____

_____

The Yuan Dynasty

The Mongol ascendancy (uh SEHN dehn see), or rise to a position of power, continued under Genghis Khan's grandson, Kublai Khan (KOO blī kahn). In 1260, Kublai took over northern China. In 1279, he conquered all of China. He declared himself the ruler of a new dynasty, the Yuan.

Kublai kept much of the Song bureaucracy. But under his rule, officials had more power to make their own decisions. The Mongols divided Chinese society into four groups. At the top were the Mongols. Next came other foreigners. Then came the northern Chinese, followed by the southern Chinese.

To limit Chinese influence, the Mongols welcomed foreigners. Many Turks and other Muslims held key positions in the government. Tibetans were encouraged to spread Buddhism in China. The Mongols also allowed Christian missionaries to come to China.

The Mongols supported trade and commerce. They continued the sea trade that began under the Song Dynasty. They also reopened the old Silk Road across Central Asia, which linked China to Europe.

The most famous visitor from Europe was Marco Polo (MAHR koh POH loh). After his return to Europe, Polo published an account of his travels. ✓

Reading Strategy

Reread the bracketed paragraph. Underline the main idea of the paragraph. Circle details that are used to support the main idea.

✓ Checkpoint

Name the four divisions of Chinese society under the Yuan Dynasty.

_____

_____

_____

_____

Check Your Progress

1. Where did the Mongols come from?

_____

2. What is one way the Mongols supported trade?

_____

_____

Question to Think About As you read Section 1 in your textbook and take notes, keep this section focus question in mind: **How did the Mongol conquest of China mark a new era in Chinese history?**

▶ Use these charts to record key information from the section. Some information has been filled in to get you started.

The Rise of the Mongols	
Mongol Society	**Reasons for Genghis Khan's Success**
• lived on the steppes • nomadic people • herded: cattle, _____ • lived in: _____ • led by: _____	• strong military leader • • • • maintained law and order

Chinese Society Under the Yuan Dynasty	
Aspects That Stayed the Same	**Aspects That Changed**
Power • much of the Song bureaucracy left as it was *Society* • rituals: _____ _____ *Trade and Commerce* • continued sea trade	*Power* • Confucian officials: power reduced • civil service examinations: _____ _____ • regional officers: _____ _____ *Society* • foreigners: given high social status _____ • new social order: _____ _____ • merchants:_____ _____ *Trade and Commerce* •

Refer to this page to answer the Chapter 11 Focus Question on page 140.

The Ming Dynasty

Section 2 Focus Question

How did the Ming restore Chinese rule and try to eliminate Mongol influence? To begin answering this question,

- Learn about China under the Ming emperors.
- Find out about foreign relations under the Ming Dynasty.

Section 2 Summary

The Ming Dynasty took control of China as the Mongols' grip on China weakened. Under the Ming, China's foreign policy was based on a tributary system.

Ming Rule

The Mongols' grip on China weakened after Kublai Khan died. In 1368, a new Chinese dynasty called the Ming took control. The Ming Dynasty ruled China for nearly 300 years. The first emperor was a commoner named Hongwu (hawng WOO).

Hongwu and later Ming rulers worked to undo many policies put in place by Mongol emperors. <u>He revived Confucian values and the merit system for choosing officials.</u> Following Confucian traditions, he discouraged trade with other lands.

Under Hongwu, China returned to strong, centralized rule. He tried to rule in the best interests of the people, but over time he became a despot (DEHS puht). A despot is a cruel tyrant. During Hongwu's rule, many people were arrested and executed for treason (TREE zuhn), or disloyal actions against the state.

After Hongwu's death, his son Yongle (yawng LEE) became emperor. He moved the capital from Nanjing to Beijing. He did this to return the capital to China's northern heartland. The move would also strengthen the country's defenses against the Mongols. He also rebuilt the Great Wall along the northern border.

The new capital was designed like a set of boxes, with one inside the other. The outer "box" was a great wall with guard towers and massive gates. Inside,

Key Events

1206	Mongol tribes unite under Genghis Khan.
1279	Mongols gain control over all of China.
1405	Zheng He makes his first voyage of exploration.

Vocabulary Builder

Which of the following could replace the word *revived*, as it is used in the underlined sentence?

A. introduced

B. brought back

C. did away with

✓ **Checkpoint**

Name two changes that Hongwu made to undo Mongol emperors' policies.

_____

_____

Reading Strategy

Underline the definition of *tributary state*. Then circle the sentences that describe the relationship the tributary states had with China.

✓ **Checkpoint**

List two reasons the Ming sponsored great sea voyages.

_____

_____

another wall enclosed the Forbidden City, where the emperor's palace was located. ✓

Foreign Relations Under the Ming

Beijing's design was meant to reinforce the idea of China as the center of the world. This belief is reflected in Ming rulers' foreign policy.

Ming foreign policy was based on the tributary system. Under this system, the Chinese treated nearby lands as tributary states. A tributary state (TRIHB yoo ter ee stayt) is a country that pays tribute in money or goods to a more powerful state.

At its height, the tributary system involved many nations. Tributary states remained independent. Every few years, they sent officials and tribute goods to Beijing to show respect. In return, they received gifts from China. Tribute took the place of trade between China and its neighbors.

In the early 1400s, the Mings sponsored great sea expeditions. They hoped that the voyages would show Chinese power and win more tributary states. The voyages took place long before any European sea-going exploration.

A court official named Zheng He (DZUHNG HEH) led the voyages. On the first voyage, more than 300 ships and 27,000 men set sail. Over the course of the seven voyages, the Chinese sailed to India, the Persian Gulf, and the east coast of Africa.

These voyages were very expensive. They did not earn enough in trade or tribute to repay their costs. In addition, Confucian officials were not interested in overseas ventures. They believed that China already had everything it needed, so they ended the expeditions. China turned inward and reduced contact with lands outside its borders. ✓

Check Your Progress

1. Why did Yongle move the capital to Beijing?

_____

_____

2. What was the design of Beijing intended to reinforce?

_____

Question to Think About As you read Section 2 in your textbook and take notes, keep this question in mind: **How did the Ming restore Chinese rule and try to eliminate Mongol influence?**

▶ Use these charts to record key information from the section. Some information has been filled in to get you started.

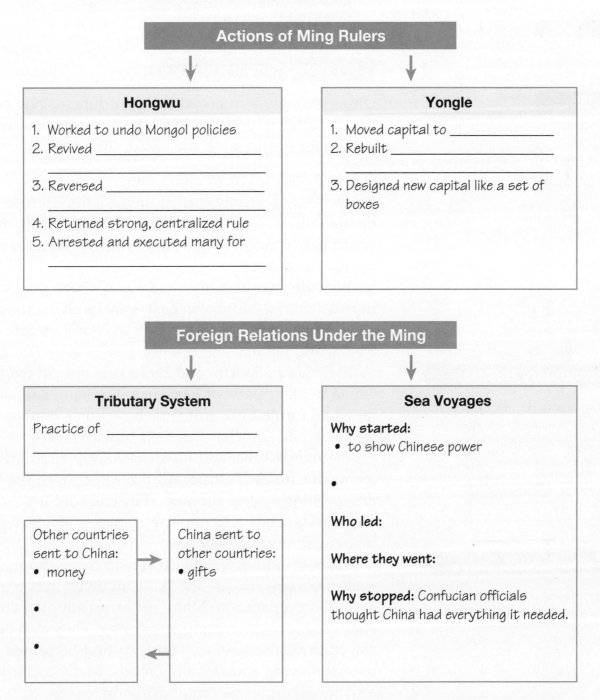

Actions of Ming Rulers

Hongwu

1. Worked to undo Mongol policies
2. Revived _____
   _____
3. Reversed _____
   _____
4. Returned strong, centralized rule
5. Arrested and executed many for
   _____

Yongle

1. Moved capital to _____
2. Rebuilt _____
   _____
3. Designed new capital like a set of boxes

Foreign Relations Under the Ming

Tributary System

Practice of _____
_____

Other countries sent to China:
• money
•
•

China sent to other countries:
• gifts

Sea Voyages

Why started:
• to show Chinese power
•

Who led:

Where they went:

Why stopped: Confucian officials thought China had everything it needed.

Refer to this page to answer the Chapter 11 Focus Question on page 140.

China's Influence on the World

Key Events

1206	Mongol tribes unite under Genghis Khan.
1279	Mongols gain control over all of China.
1405	Zheng He makes his first voyage of exploration.

Vocabulary Builder

Culinary comes from a Latin word meaning "kitchen." How does the term *culinary arts* relate to "kitchen"?

_____

_____

✓ Checkpoint

Name three countries in East Asia that were influenced by China.

_____

_____

_____

Section 3 Focus Question

How did China influence the world? To begin answering this question,

- Learn about how China influenced East Asia.
- Find out about Chinese innovations that had a worldwide impact.

Section 3 Summary

China strongly influenced the governments and cultures of other nations in East Asia. A number of Chinese innovations influenced the rest of the world.

China's Influence in East Asia

As the Ming Dynasty turned inward, the Chinese became more **conservative** (kuhn SER vuh tihv), or resistant to change. China paid little attention to events beyond its borders, but China's influence was still felt in the wider world. China had always been the largest, most advanced country in East Asia. Its civilization had a great impact on smaller countries like Vietnam, Korea, and Japan.

Both Confucianism and Buddhism spread from China to other parts of East Asia. Vietnam, Korea, and Japan all formed governments based on Confucian ideas. Scholar-officials ran their bureaucracies.

Vietnam, Korea, and Japan also adopted many elements of Chinese culture. All three borrowed the Chinese writing system. In time, they changed it to suit their needs. They also imported Chinese styles of painting, music, and architecture.

Chinese culinary arts also spread throughout East Asia. Culinary arts are the skills involved in cooking and food preparation. Many countries adopted chopsticks as tools for cooking and eating. They also borrowed the Chinese **wok**, a large, round-bottomed pan used for frying and steaming foods. Many countries also adopted the custom of drinking tea. ✓

China's Worldwide Impact

Chinese beliefs and customs had less impact on more distant lands. But several Chinese innovations did influence the rest of the world. The most important of these were paper, printing, gunpowder, and the magnetic compass.

Paper first traveled west to Muslim lands. By the 900s, paper had replaced papyrus across the Islamic empire. Next, it spread to Europe.

It is not clear whether printing followed a similar path. What is certain is that paper and printing had an enormous impact on Europe and the rest of the world. Writing and publishing became easier. As a result, more people could learn to read and get an education.

Like paper, gunpowder and the magnetic compass were introduced to Europe via the Muslims. Turkish and European armies used gunpowder. By the 1400s, European sailors were using the compass on long voyages.

The Chinese also developed important inventions for agriculture and construction. Water pumps and the wheelbarrow were widely used in farming and building projects. The Chinese developed a harness that made it easier to control draft animals. A **draft animal** is used to pull a load, such as a wagon or a plow.

Other Chinese inventions helped the growth of industry. Chinese inventors built weaving and spinning machines. They developed desirable trade goods such as silk cloth and porcelain dishes. Their invention of paper money made trade easier.

As China turned inward, however, its technical development stalled. Before long, other parts of the world began to surpass China in the area of technology. ☑

Check Your Progress

1. Why did China have so much influence over other countries of East Asia?

   _____

   _____

2. Why did China's technical development slow down?

   _____

Reading Strategy

What does the title "China's Worldwide Impact" tell you about the text that will follow it? How does this differ from the material under the title "China's Influence in East Asia"?

_____

_____

_____

✓ Checkpoint

List four Chinese innovations that had a worldwide impact.

_____

_____

_____

_____

Question to Think About As you read Section 3 in your textbook and take notes, keep this question in mind: **How did China influence the world?**

▶ Use these charts to record key information from the section. Some information has been filled in to get you started.

China's Influence in East Asia		
Government	**Culinary Arts**	**Culture**
1. based on Confucian ideas	1. chopsticks	1. Chinese writing system
2. _____ for civil servants	2.	2.
	3.	3.
3. _____ ran bureaucracies.		4. architecture

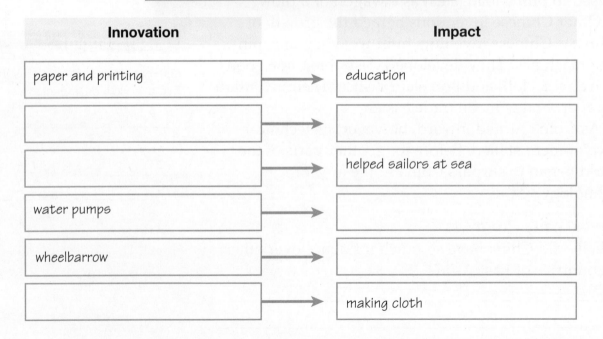

China's Worldwide Impact

Innovation	Impact
paper and printing	education
	helped sailors at sea
water pumps	
wheelbarrow	
	making cloth

Refer to this page to answer the Chapter 11 Focus Question on page 140.

Chapter 11 Assessment

Directions: Circle the letter of the correct answer.

1. Which of the following was a strong leader who united the Mongols?
   A Marco Polo   **B** Genghis Khan   **C** Kublai Khan

2. The Ming Dynasty sponsored great sea expeditions to
   A find a water route to the Americas.
   B show Chinese power and find a water route to Japan.
   C show Chinese power and win more tributary states.

3. The Ming Dynasty took power away from the
   A Song Dynasty.   **B** Mongols.   **C** Italians.

4. Which of the following was NOT a Chinese innovation?
   A electricity   **B** gunpowder   **C** paper

Directions: Follow the steps to complete this task:

Contrast China's influence in East Asia with its impact on the world.

Step 1: Recall information: In the chart, list ways China affected East Asia and then list ways it affected the rest of the world.

Influence on East Asia	Worldwide Impact

Step 2: Contrast China's influence on East Asia with its impact on the whole world. How are they different? Why might they be different?

_____

_____

_____

Step 3: Complete the topic sentence that follows. Then write two or three more sentences that support your topic sentence.

China's influence on East Asia and its worldwide impact are _____

_____

_____

_____

Now you are ready to answer the Chapter 11 Focus Question: **How did the Mongols and Ming shape Chinese civilization?**

▶ Complete the following charts to help you answer this question. Use the notes that you took for each section.

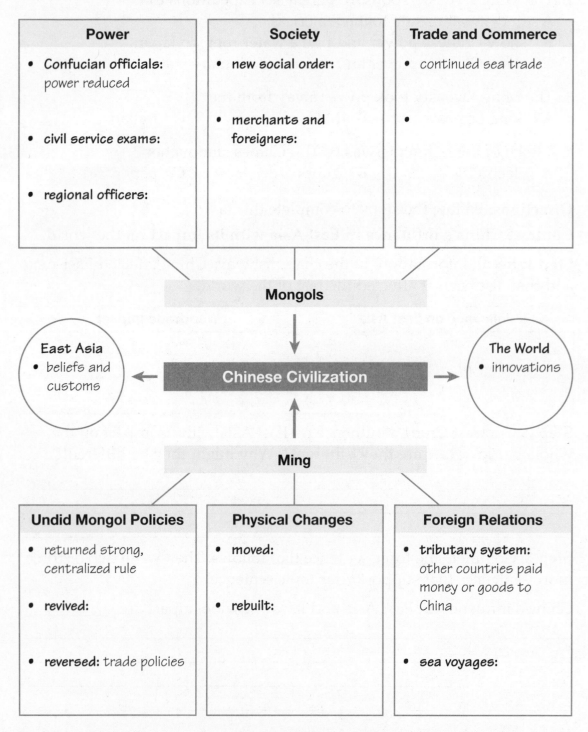

Power	Society	Trade and Commerce
• **Confucian officials:** power reduced	• new social order:	• continued sea trade
• **civil service exams:**	• merchants and foreigners:	•
• **regional officers:**		

Mongols

East Asia
• beliefs and customs

Chinese Civilization

The World
• innovations

Ming

Undid Mongol Policies	Physical Changes	Foreign Relations
• returned strong, centralized rule	• **moved:**	• **tributary system:** other countries paid money or goods to China
• **revived:**	• **rebuilt:**	
• **reversed:** trade policies		• **sea voyages:**

Refer to this page to answer the Unit 5 Focus Question on page 166.

Chapter 12

The Rise of Japan (500–1868)

Chapter Standards

History-Social Science 7.5.1, 7.5.2, 7.5.3, 7.5.6

What You Will Learn

Japan, an island nation, was strongly influenced by Chinese culture. A series of emperors established the Japanese state, and then a group of powerful families gained control. Japan became divided under military rulers, but was reunited by the 1600s.

Chapter 14 Focus Question

As you read through this chapter, keep the following question in mind: **How did Japan's island location enable it to develop its own unique culture?**

Section 1

Land of the Rising Sun

Section 1 Focus Question

How did geography affect the early development of Japanese culture? To begin answering this question,
- Find out about the island geography of Japan.
- Learn about Japan and its neighbors.

Section 1 Summary

Japan is an island nation with a mountainous geography. It was strongly influenced by other Asian cultures.

The Geography of Japan

Japan is an **archipelago** (ahr kuh PEHL uh goh), or chain of islands, to the east of the continent of Asia. In ancient times, the Japanese believed that theirs was the first land to be awakened when the sun rose in the east. They called their country Nippon, which means "land of the rising sun."

Japan consists of four large islands and thousands of smaller ones. The island chain is so long from north to south that it has many different climates. The northernmost part gets heavy snow in winter. The southernmost island is almost tropical.

Key Events

552	Buddhism arrives in Japan.
604	Prince Shotoku gives Japan a constitution.
1192	Feudalism begins under the shoguns.
1600	Tokugawa Ieyasu unites Japan under central rule.

Vocabulary Builder

Early settlers hunted and fished
rather than farmed. What does it
mean that they *survived* by hunting
and fishing?

_____

_____

Reading Strategy

Circle the word in the underlined
sentence that tells you
that the meaning of
the word *proximity* is
being restated. Under-
line the meaning of
proximity.

✓ Checkpoint

List two of Japan's Asian neighbors
that influenced its culture.

_____

_____

Japan is so mountainous that little of the land can be
used for farming. Most people settled on flat plains or
along the coastline.

Japan sits at the boundary between two plates, or
sections, of the earth's outer shell. When one of these
plates moves, earthquakes happen. Japan is part of the
Ring of Fire. This is a region of volcanoes and earthquakes that circle the Pacific Ocean. ✓

Japan and Its Neighbors

Japan's location discouraged frequent contact with the
Asian mainland. The mainland (MAYN land) is the
major land area of a continent.

The first settlers probably came to Japan from the
Asian mainland during the Ice Age. They survived
mainly by hunting and fishing. By 300 B.C., another
group of settlers arrived from Asia. They introduced a
new farming technique—growing rice in irrigated
fields. Rice soon became Japan's main crop.

Though separated by oceans, Asia was the closest
land to Japan. Japanese culture was influenced by this
proximity (prahk SIH mih tee), or closeness in space, to
its Asian neighbors. Over time, contact with the Chinese mainland increased. Around A.D. 500, the Japanese
began to borrow the writing system of their neighbor.
Soon, the Japanese began to write their own language
using Chinese characters.

Japan also developed ties with Korea. In A.D. 552,
Buddhist priests from Korea arrived in Japan. Most
Japanese at the time followed the beliefs of Shinto, the
native religion of Japan. Buddhism, however, appealed
to many Japanese. Over time, it would become an
important part of Japanese culture. ✓

Check Your Progress

1. How did Japan's geography affect where people
   settled?

_____

_____

2. What is one way that mainland Asia influenced
   Japanese culture?

_____

_____

Question to Think About As you read Section 1 in your textbook and take notes, keep this section focus question in mind: **How did geography affect the early development of Japanese culture?**

▶ Use these charts to record key information from the section.

The Geography of Japan	
Geographic Feature	**Effect on Japan and the Japanese Way of Life**
Mountainous landscape	• Little farming possible • People live on flat plains or _____. • People must get their food from _____.
Plate boundary (Ring of Fire)	• •
Country spans great distance north to south	Many different climates • North: • South:
Archipelago (an island nation)	Kept Japan _____ from its neighbors in _____.

Chinese and Korean Influence on Early Japanese Culture			
Language		**Philosophy and Religion**	
How	Japanese borrowed Chinese writing system.	How	
When		When	
Effects	• •	Effects	• •
Settlers			
First settlers	First settlers survived by _____ and _____.		
New settlers	New settlers arrived about _____, and brought new technique of farming _____.		

Refer to this page to answer the Chapter 12 focus question on page 154.

Key Events

552 Buddhism arrives in Japan.

604 Prince Shotoku gives Japan a constitution.

1192 Feudalism begins under the shoguns.

1600 Tokugawa Ieyasu unites Japan under central rule.

Section 2 Focus Question

How did Prince Shotoku unite Japan and set the stage for the development of a strong central government? To begin answering this question,

- Find out about Japan's early history.
- Learn how Prince Shotoku united Japan.

Section 2 Summary

The first rulers of Japan emerged through struggles between local clans. Prince Shotoku brought reform and helped unify the nation.

Japan's Early History

In the 200s, Japan was divided into many local clans. Each clan had its own land and chiefs. Each person in the clan had a certain responsibility. This social organization lasted for hundreds of years.

Under Shinto, each clan worshiped its own kami (KAH mee), or gods and spirits. Kami were found in natural objects such as mountains or trees. People built shrines wherever they felt the power of Kami.

Shinto myths explain how Japan came to be ruled by an emperor. According to legend, the Sun Goddess, and her brother, the Storm God, often argued. Each supported different clans who were fighting to rule Japan. The Sun Goddess won the argument. One of her descendants, Jimmu, became Japan's first emperor in 660 B.C.

Historians think the first emperor appeared much later, around A.D. 200 or 300. About 2,000 years ago, clans were competing for land and power. The winner of this struggle was the Yamato clan who steadily gained power over Japan. Sometimes they went to war against neighboring clans. More often, they tried to win another clan's loyalty through marriage or other ties. Yamato emperors claimed descent from the Sun Goddess. They were thought to be living gods on Earth. ✓

Prince Shotoku Unites Japan

Even after the rise of the Yamato clan, Japan was still not fully united. In 593, **Prince Shotoku** (prihns SHOH

✓ Checkpoint

Name the person from whom the Yamato emperors claimed to be descended.

_____

toh koo) took power. He served as a regent for the empress. A **regent** (REE jihnt) is someone who governs in the name of a ruler who is too young or otherwise unable to rule.

Shotoku undertook the difficult task of uniting Japan under a strong central government. First, he had to reduce the power of clan leaders. To do this he encouraged the spread of Buddhism. Buddhism had recently arrived in Japan from Korea. He hoped that the spread of Buddhism would help the Japanese feel like a single group of people united under one faith.

Shotoku also believed that the Chinese ideas of Confucianism could help unify Japan. The prince gave Japan its first **constitution** (kahn stih TOO shuhn), or plan of government. It is called the Constitution of Seventeen Articles and is based on Confucian and Buddhist thought.

In 607, Prince Shotoku sent official representatives to China to study Chinese arts and government. These experts helped make Japan's government more like that of imperial China.

Other reformers carried on Shotoku's efforts to create a strong central government after his death in 622. In 646, they put forth the Taika Reform. *Taika* means "great change." New laws made everyone a subject of the emperor. Lands and people controlled by clan leaders now belonged to him.

To put forth the reforms, officials issued a new law code for the entire country in 702. The Taiho Code officially made the Yamato clan leader an emperor, the "son of Heaven." The laws spelled out the organization of local government. They also defined crimes and a system of punishments. <u>These laws applied equally to everyone in Japan.</u> ✅

Check Your Progress

1. What are two ways the Yamato clan gained power?

_____

_____

2. How did Prince Shotoku hope that Buddhism would unite Japan?

_____

_____

Reading Strategy

Reread the bracketed paragraph. Underline the topic sentence of the paragraph. Circle two supporting details.

Vocabulary Builder

The word *apply* has several different definitions. Which of the following defines *apply* as it is used in the underlined sentence?

A. to work hard
B. to make a formal request
C. to bring into operation or use

✓ Checkpoint

Name two features of Chinese civilization that Prince Shotoku borrowed.

_____

_____

Question to Think About As you read Section 2 in your textbook and take notes, keep this section focus question in mind: **How did Prince Shotoku unite Japan and set the stage for the development of a strong central government?**

► Use these charts to record key information from the section.

Japan's Early History			
Who/What	**When**	**Why Important**	**The Story**
The Myth of Japan's First Emperor	660 B.C.	• tells how Japan got its first _____ • explains descent from the _____ _____	The _____ won a fight with her _____ _____. Her grandson became the first _____.
Who/What	**When**	**Why Important**	**How Goals Accomplished**
Yamato Clan	A.D. 702	Gained control over Japan from warlike clans	• Going to war • Winning loyalty through marriage and other ties
Prince Shotoku	A.D. 592	United Japan	• Encouraged the spread of _____ • Created first _____ _____
Later reformers	After 622	Made effort to create a strong _____ _____	Put forth _____ _____, which included the _____

Reforms in Early Japanese Government		
Prince Shotoku	**The Constitution of Seventeen Articles**	**The Taiho Code**
Shotoku borrowed ideas for his reforms from _____. Shotoku believed Buddhism and Confucianism could help _____ Japan.	Based on _____ and _____ thought. Gave government ability to raise _____ to support a _____ _____.	Made the leader from the _____ clan the emperor. Defined _____ and established a system of _____ that applied equally to all Japanese.

Refer to this page to answer the Chapter 12 focus question on page 154.

Section 3

The Development of Feudalism

Section 3 Focus Question

Why did the power of the emperor decline and feudal society develop in Japan? To begin answering this question,

- Find out about Japan's two capital cities in the 700s.
- Learn how power shifted from the imperial family to powerful clans.
- Discover a new social order.

Section 3 Summary

Japan had two capitals in the 700s. Over time, the emperor's power faded, and clans gained control. Japan became a feudal society under the shoguns.

Two New Capitals

The Taika Reform called for building a permanent imperial capital for Japan. In 710, the government settled at the new city of Nara, which was modeled after the Chinese capital at Changan.

Buddhist influence dominated the capital. Aristocrats spent generously on Buddhist temples and monasteries. Officials felt threatened by the amount of wealth and political power monks had accumulated, so they moved the government to a new capital. Powerful Buddhist monasteries were not allowed to follow. The new city was named Heian-kyo, or "capital of peace and calm." Later it was called Kyoto, "the capital." ✓

Shifts in Power

In the 800s, the emperor's power began to fade. By about 850, the Fujiwara family ran the country. The emperor had become a "puppet," which means he was not a true ruler. The Fujiwara had gained power by having their sisters and daughters marry princes in the imperial family.

The Fujiwaras' 300-year rule marked a shift in power. Japan remained unified, but the Fujiwara family, not the emperor, was in charge.

Key Events

552	Buddhism arrives in Japan.
604	Prince Shotoku gives Japan a constitution.
1192	Feudalism begins under the shoguns.
1600	Tokugawa Ieyasu unites Japan under central rule.

✓ Checkpoint

Name Japan's two capital cities during the 700s.

_____

_____

© Pearson Education, Inc., publishing as Pearson Prentice Hall. All Rights Reserved.

Vocabulary Builder

Complete the sentence so that the second part clearly shows your understanding of the word *rivalry*.

The Taira-Minamoto rivalry was fierce;

_____

_____

✓ Checkpoint

Name the two rival clans who battled for the Fujiwaras' power.

_____

_____

Reading Strategy

One result, or effect, mentioned in the bracketed paragraph was the development of feudalism. What was its cause?

_____

_____

✓ Checkpoint

What did peasants receive from daimyos in exchange for their labor?

_____

Other clans envied and resented the Fujiwaras' power. Some clan leaders began to raise their own private armies. The most powerful warrior clans were the Taira and Minamoto. They worked together just long enough to drive the Fujiwara from power. Then they turned against each other.

Over long years of war, power shifted between the Taira and Minamoto clans. The fighting reached Kyoto in 1159, when Minamoto forces stormed the palace.

In 1185, the two clans met in a battle at sea. The winner was Minamoto Yoritomo (mih nah MOH toh yoh ree TOH moh). He took the title of shogun (SHOH guhn), or supreme military commander. Yoritomo intended to keep the title permanently, and to rule in the name of the emperor. However, the violent Taira-Minamoto rivalry was not over. ✓

A New Social Order

Life under the shoguns was lawless and violent. Local land-owning lords, or daimyo (DI myoh), took on the job of protecting people. A new social order called feudalism was the result. Feudalism (FYOOD uhl ihzm) is a system in which lords grant people land or other rewards in exchange for military service.

Social Order Under Feudalism	
Emperor	Held highest rank but had no real power
Shogun	Actual ruler of Japan
Daimyo	Large landowners who protected peasants in exchange for labor
Samurai	Highly trained warriors loyal to daimyo
Peasants, Merchants, Artisans	More than three fourths of the population

Check Your Progress

1. How did power shift in Japan in the 800s?

_____

_____

2. List the social ranks in the feudal society in Japan.

_____

_____

Question to Think About As you read Section 3 in your textbook and take notes, keep this section focus question in mind: **Why did the power of the emperor decline and feudal society develop in Japan?**

▶ Use these organizers to record key information from the section.

Two New Capitals

First Capital: Nara

Why built:
Taika Reform called for imperial capital to be built.
What it was like:
- Modeled after the Chinese capital Changan, but did not have _____

  _____
- Dominated by _____

  _____
- Center of _____ and _____

Moved because:
_____
_____
_____
_____
_____
_____

New Capital: Kyoto

First called:

How the nobles spent their days and nights:
-
-
-
-
-

Shifts in Power and a New Social Order

Imperial Family

Fujiwara Family
- Gained power by having _____ and _____ marry _____; Fujiwara leaders became _____
- Emperor became a _____.
- How long they ruled:

Minamoto Yoritomo
- When and how he came to power:

- Title he took:

Life Under the Shoguns

Feudal system: A system in which _____ grant people _____ in exchange for _____.

Refer to this page to answer the Chapter Focus Question on page 154.

Key Events

552	Buddhism arrives in Japan
604	Prince Shotoku gives Japan a constitution.
1192	Feudalism begins under the shoguns.
1600	Tokugawa Ieyasu unites Japan under central rule.

Vocabulary Builder

The word *repel* is made up of the Latin prefix *re* meaning "back" and another word meaning "to drive." What does this tell you about how the samurai had to fight the Mongols?

_____

_____

✓ Checkpoint

Name the two central ideals of the code of bushido.

_____

_____

Section 4 Focus Question

How did the warrior code influence Japanese society and keep Japan from reuniting? To begin answering this question,

- Learn about the way of the warrior.
- Find out about the Mongol invasions of Japan.
- Discover how Japan was finally unified.

Section 4 Summary

Samurai warriors followed a strict code of conduct and helped repel the Mongol invasions. In the 1600s, strong rulers reunited Japan.

The Way of the Warrior

Samurai warriors followed a code called bushido (BOO shee doh), a strict code of conduct that guided the warriors' behavior. Bushido means "the way of the warrior."

Personal honor and loyalty to one's lord formed the heart of this code. Loyalty to one's lord was more important than loyalty to family, religion, or even the emperor. Personal honor was also important. Samurai trained fiercely, fought bravely, and died with honor. The code also required warriors to take pride in their personal appearance. ✓

The Mongol Invasions

During the 1200s, the Mongol ruler, Kublai Khan, controlled all of East Asia except Japan. In 1268, he sent representatives to demand tribute from Japan. The shogun's government sent them away without responding. The Khan then started planning to invade.

In 1274, the Khan sent an armada (ahr MAH duh), or a large fleet of ships, to Japan. The Mongols were terrifying warriors. They used gunpowder weapons, to which the Japanese were not accustomed. Yet the samurai fought bravely and held off the invaders' first attack. That night, a fierce storm arose and destroyed the Mongol ships.

After sending officials to demand tribute again, the Khan launched a second invasion in 1281. Japanese warriors held off the Mongols for nearly two months before a **typhoon** (tī FOON), or violent tropical storm, hit the Japanese coast. Strong winds battered the Mongol ships and many soldiers died.

To the Japanese, the rescue was a miracle. They believed that the kami had sent the typhoon to save them. They called it *kamikaze*, or "wind of the gods." ✓

Japan Is Unified Again

The Mongol defeat did not bring peace to Japan. Clans continued to fight among themselves.

In the 1500s, three ambitious leaders finally ended the constant warfare. The first, **Oda Nobunaga** (OH duh noh boo NAH guh), worked to bring Japan "under a single sword." He did not fully succeed, but he did reduce the warlords' power.

The second leader, **Toyotomi Hideyoshi** (toy oh TOH mee hee day YOH shee), unified Japan in 1590. However, the peace was held together only by personal loyalty. When Hideyoshi died, clans began to quarrel once again.

The third leader, **Tokugawa Ieyasu** (toh koo GAH wah ee ay YAH soo), united the country once more in 1600. He founded a new capital at Edo (present-day Tokyo). He ordered the daimyo to destroy their castles and to spend much time in Edo, where he could watch over them. This finally ended the violence. The Tokugawa family ruled a peaceful, unified Japan until 1868.

Once Japan was at peace, the samurai way of life changed. Many samurai took government jobs, but they remained proud of their fighting skills. Today, the ideals of bushido—bravery and loyalty—continue to influence Japanese culture. ✓

Check Your Progress

1. Why did the Khan decide to invade Japan?

_____

_____

2. How did Tokugawa Ieyasu unite Japan?

_____

_____

✓ Checkpoint

Name the type of weapons the Mongols used in battle that the Japanese had not seen before.

_____

Reading Strategy

Find the symbolic phrase in the bracketed paragraph, and underline it.

✓ Checkpoint

Name three leaders who brought peace and unity to Japan.

_____

_____

_____

Question to Think About: As you read Section 4 in your textbook and take notes, keep this section focus question in mind: **How did the warrior code influence Japanese society and keep Japan from reuniting?**

▶ Use this outline to record key information from the section.

Japan Under the Shoguns

I. The Way of the Warrior

    A. The code of _____, or "the way of the warrior." Two main ideals:

        1. Loyalty to _____

            a. More important than loyalty to one's _____, _____, or _____.

        2. _____

            a. When riding into battle, a samurai shouted out his _____ and _____.

            b. He was careful about his _____. His robe, _____, and _____ reflected his pride.

II. The Mongol Invasions

    A. The first invasion

        1. In 1274, _____ sent a fleet of ships with warriors to Japan to force them to give _____ to China.

        2. The Mongols used _____, which the Japanese had not seen.

        3. It failed because _____.

    B. The second invasion

        1. _____ launched a second invasion in _____.

        2. It failed because _____.

            a. The Japanese thought the _____ had sent the typhoon, and they called it _____, or "_____."

III. Japan Is Unified Again

    A. In the 1500s, three leaders ended the constant warfare.

        1. Oda Nobunaga

            a. Worked to bring Japan "_____"

            b. Reduced power of warlords.

        2. _____

            a. Unified Japan, but only by _____.

        3. _____

            a. Moved capital to _____.

            b. Ordered daimyo to _____ their castles and spend time in Edo.

            c. Ruled a peaceful and _____ Japan, until _____.

Refer to this page to answer the Chapter 12 Focus Question on page 154.

Directions: Circle the letter of the correct answer.

1. Choose the statement that is correct.
   A Japan's location made contact with mainland Asia easy.
   B Japan consists of four tropical islands.
   C Japan is a mountainous archipelago.

2. Which leader *first* undertook the task of uniting Japan under a strong central government?
   A Prince Shotoku   B Tokugawa Ieyasu   C Oda Nobunaga

3. In feudal Japan, the daimyo were
   A warriors loyal to the emperor.
   B landowners.
   C those who worked a lord's land in exchange for protection.

4. Tokugawa Ieyasu was important because
   A he ended a long period of instability and unified Japan.
   B he prevented the Mongols from conquering Japan.
   C he reduced the power of warlords, though he never succeeded in uniting Japan.

Directions: Follow the steps to answer this question:

How did Japan's location influence the development of its culture?

Step 1: Recall information. Where is Japan located?

_____
_____
_____

Step 2: What are some unique features of Japanese culture? What cultural influences come from mainland Asia?

_____
_____
_____

Step 3: Complete the topic sentence that follows. Then write two or three more sentences that support your opinion.

Japan's location influenced the development of its culture by _____
_____
_____
_____

Chapter 12 Notetaking Study Guide

Now you are ready to answer the Chapter 12 Focus Question: **How did Japan's island location enable it to develop its own unique culture?**

▶ Fill in the following organizers to help you answer this question.

The Effect of Japan's Location on Its Development

Proximity

Japan was close enough to _____ _____ and _____ that these countries influenced Japanese culture.

Isolation

Japan was isolated enough as an _____, or chain of islands, that the country formed a unique culture.

Influence of Neighbors

China
- **Writing system:**
  Japanese writing system based on Chinese _____.
- **Confucianism:**
  Shotoku wrote a _____ _____ with the general principles based on _____ and _____ thought.
- **Imperial capital:**
  Based on design of _____ _____, China's capital.
- **Culture:**
  1. architecture
  2. _____ ceremony

Korea
- **Buddhism:**
  Buddhism arrived in Japan in a.d. _____ and became a very important part of Japanese culture.

Unique Development

- **Natural features:**
  1. _____ land influenced where people settled
  2. Natural disasters served as a defense during _____ invasions in 1274 and 1281.

- **Shinto:**
  1. Native _____ of Japan
  2. Means "_____"

- **Government:**
  Unlike China's merit system, power and privilege in Japan was based on _____.

- **Feudal system:**
  1. Emperor: no real power
  2. _____: actual ruler of Japan
  3. _____: large landowners
  4. Samurai: _____
  5. _____: most of the population

- _____
  Code of conduct that guided warriors' behavior

Refer to this page to answer the Unit 5 Focus Question on page 166.

Chapter Standards

History-Social Science 7.5.3, 7.5.4, 7.5.5

What You Will Learn

Japan adapted cultural influences from its neighbors and created an original culture of its own. Buddhism was brought to the country and became an important cultural influence.

Chapter 13 Focus Question

As you read this chapter, keep this question in mind: **What were the characteristics of Japan's Golden Age?**

Section 1

Japan's Cultural Flowering

Section 1 Focus Question

What achievements marked the Golden Age of Japanese culture? To begin answering this question,

* Learn about how the court nobles influenced manners and dress and literature.
* Find out about Japanese art and architecture.
* Read about Noh drama.

Key Events

900	Kana writing is developed.
1000s	*The Tale of Genji* is written.
1200s	Pure Land and Nichiren Buddhism spread throughout the country.

Section 1 Summary

Court nobles influenced the flowering of Japanese culture. New styles of literature, art, architecture, and drama developed. Japan borrowed ideas from China to help create its own unique culture.

Court Life at Heian-kyo

The nobles who surrounded the emperor at Heian-kyo were leaders in the growth of Japanese culture. Nobles had elegant manners and wore elaborate clothing.

Literacy was important in the emperor's court. Nobles learned about proper behavior and good government by reading Buddhist and Confucian writings. Around 900, the Japanese simplified the writing system they had borrowed from China. They created a new set of symbols called kana (KAH nah). Each kana symbol stood for one syllable.

Vocabulary Builder

Literacy is related to the word *literature*. After rereading the bracketed paragraph, what do you think *literacy* means?

_____

_____

_____

_____

Write a question about Japanese architecture. Then, answer your question.

Question:_____

_____ ?

Answer: _____

_____ .

✓ **Checkpoint**

Name the style of art that was distinctly Japanese.

_____

✓ **Checkpoint**

Name three characters that a Noh drama might feature.

_____

_____

_____

The Tale of Genji is regarded as the world's first novel (NAHV uhl). A novel is long and complex fictional story. The novel told of the romantic adventures of a prince named Genji. It was written by a woman named **Murasaki Shikibu** (mur ah SAHK ee SHEE kee boo), who served the empress in the Heian court.

Poems were also popular. The government put out a collection of 1,100 poems called the *Kokinshu* Japanese poets also created haiku (HĪ koo). Haiku is a form of poetry with 17 syllables and three lines. ✓

Art and Architecture

Buddhist monasteries were centers for the arts in Japan. They were decorated with sculptures of Buddha and wall paintings. Some wall paintings showed *mandalas,* or circular designs that symbolized the universe.

Scroll paintings called *Yamato-e* were distinctly Japanese. As a scroll was unrolled, it told a story. Stories were told with pictures and sometimes with words.

The Japanese also borrowed from Chinese architecture. Chinese buildings influenced Japanese temples, palaces, and nobles' homes. Nobles' homes often included several one-story structures built around gardens. Gardens often had teahouses. The tea ceremony was also taken from China. ✓

Noh Drama

Noh theater was created in the 1300s. Noh was a serious and intense style of drama. The plays use colorful costumes, masks, chants, music, and dance to tell a story. They feature gods, warriors, beautiful women, mad people, or ghosts and devils. An evening of Noh drama was made up of several serious plays with funny skits between them. ✓

Check Your Progress

1. How did nobles learn about proper behavior and good government?

_____

2. List three examples of the influence of Chinese culture on Japanese culture.

_____

_____

_____

Question to Think About As you read Section 1 in your textbook and takes notes, keep this section focus question in mind: **What achievements marked the Golden Age of Japanese culture?**

▶ Use this chart to record key information from the section. Some information has been filled in to get you started.

Writing System	Forms of Literature	Architecture
• Simplified during the _____ period	• Poetry Example: _____ _____	• Inspired by _____ _____ architecture
• Characters called _____	• _____ Example: *The Tale of Genji*	• _____ and _____ homes, made up of one-story buildings around a garden.
• Each symbol stood for one _____.		

Japanese Cultural Achievements

Painting and Sculpture	Theater	Ceremony
• Temples often featured _____ and _____ _____.	• New type of drama called _____	• The formal _____ _____ was borrowed from China.
• _____ called _____ told stories with pictures and some-times with words.	• It used costumes, _____, _____, music, and _____.	• Elegant _____ and _____ _____ were expected of those at court.

Refer to this page to answer the Chapter 13 Focus Question on page 165.

The Development of Japanese Buddhism

Key Events

900	Kana writing is developed.
1000s	*The Tale of Genji* is written.
1200s	Pure Land and Nichiren Buddhism spread throughout the country.

Reading Strategy

Reread the underlined sentence. Which word tells you that Shinto and Buddhism are being contrasted?

_____

✓ Checkpoint

From where was Buddhism brought to Japan?

_____

Section 2 Focus Question

How did distinctive forms of Buddhism develop in Japan? To begin answering this question,

- Learn about how Buddhism spread to Japan.
- Find out about the new types of Buddhism that developed in Japan.

Section 2 Summary

Buddhism spread to Japan from Korea. Over time, Buddhism adapted to Japanese culture. New, unique forms of Japanese Buddhism developed, which helped it spread throughout Japanese society.

Buddhism Comes to Japan

In 552, a Korean king sent a group of monks to Japan to spread Buddhism. Many Japanese were slow to adopt Buddhism. They feared it might anger the Shinto gods. They became more frightened when a disease broke out soon after some Japanese adopted the new religion. People feared that the gods were angry.

Over time, their fears faded. <u>Unlike Shinto, Buddhism dealt with questions about life and death.</u> Buddhism taught that humans go through an endless cycle of life and death followed by rebirth into a new life. The cycle could be escaped by reaching enlightenment. At death, an enlightened person enters nirvana. Nirvana is a state of peace and happiness.

These ideas appealed to many Japanese nobles. Emperors and the noble class spread Buddhism by building monasteries. Those who adopted Buddhism also continued some Shinto practices. ✓

New Sects Develop

Buddhism spread and adapted to Japanese culture. Buddhist monks created new sects, or forms, of Buddhism. Each sect taught its own way to enlightenment.

The monk Saicho founded the Tendai sect. It was based on Mahayana Buddhism from China. Mahayana Buddhism taught that all living beings contain part of the universal Buddha. No one is too bad or lowly to be saved. The main Mahayana sutra (SOO truh), was the Lotus Sutra. A sutra is a scripture. The Tendai sect was based on the belief that Buddhism should be open to everyone, not just monks and nuns.

A monk named Kukai founded the Shingon sect. It came from Tantric Buddhism, which began in Tibet and spread to China. This form used secret rituals. Shingon sect members recited mantras (MAHN truhz). A mantra is a sacred word, chant, or sound that is repeated over and over to increase one's spiritual power. Shingon Buddhism appealed mostly to nobles.

Pure Land Buddhism appealed to all classes. It is the most popular sect in Japan today. It was centered around a bodhisattva known as Amida. A bodhisattva is an enlightened being who chose to remain on Earth to help others. This idea came from Mahayana Buddhism. By placing total trust in Amida and repeating his name, followers entered a paradise called the Pure Land upon death.

Nichiren Buddhism originated in Japan. Its founder, Nichiren, claimed that the other sects were based on false teachings. He was especially critical of Pure Land. He taught absolute faith in the Lotus Sutra. People who could not read only had to recite a short phrase based on the sutra to reach enlightenment.

Zen Buddhism came from China. This sect stressed meditation (mehd uh TAY shuhn). Meditation is the emptying of the mind of thoughts in order to achieve spiritual development. This focus on self-control and discipline appealed to the samurai class. It helped them clear their minds of fear before battle. ✓

Check Your Progress

1. How did Buddhism differ from Shinto?

_____

_____

2. Why did Zen Buddhism appeal to the samurai class?

_____

_____

Vocabulary Builder

The verb *originate* contains the word *origin*. The origin is the point where something begins or arises. What do you think *originate* means?

_____

_____

✓ Checkpoint

Name the Buddhist sect that is centered on a being named Amida.

_____

Question to Think About As you read Section 2 in your textbook and takes notes, keep this section focus question in mind: **How did distinctive forms of Buddhism develop in Japan?**

▶ Use this chart to record key information from the section.

Buddhism Comes to Japan
1. How did it spread there?
Buddhism spread to Japan around 552 from Korea. The Korean king sent Buddhist monks.
2. Why did it spread slowly at first?
3. What were Buddhism's main ideas?
4. What happened to Shinto practices after the arrival of Buddhism?

New Buddhist Sects Develop
1. Key facts about Tendai Buddhism:
• Founded by _____
• Based on _____
• Main belief: _____
2. Key facts about Shingon Buddhism:
• Founded by _____
• Based on _____
• Main belief: _____
3. Key facts about Pure Land Buddhism:
• Centered around _____, who ruled a_____ called the Pure Land.
• People can enter the Pure Land by _____.
4. Key facts about Nichiren Buddhism:
• Originated in _____
• Taught that other sects were based on _____
• Taught that enlightenment could come only from _____
5. Key facts about Zen Buddhism:
• The central practice of Zen is _____.
• Its focus on self-control and discipline appealed to _____.

Refer to this page to answer the Chapter 13 Focus Question on page 165.

Section 3
Japanese Society

Section 3 Focus Question

How did Japanese values develop and change? To begin answering this question,

- Learn about the traditional values of Japanese society.
- Find out about how Japanese society changed over time.

Section 3 Summary

All Japanese shared many values based on Shinto, Buddhist, and Confucian beliefs. The establishment of feudalism changed Japan's society.

Traditional Values

Frequent warfare in feudal Japan did not destroy social unity. The emperor was still seen as a living god and keeper of traditional Japanese values.

Family loyalty was the most basic traditional value in Japanese society. Shinto taught families to honor their ancestors. Family interests were seen as more important than personal interests.

The samurai code of bushido was influenced by Buddhism. A belief in reincarnation helped samurai face danger without fear. Reincarnation (ree ihn kahr NAY shun) is the belief that a person is born anew in another body after death.

Japanese society valued harmony and consensus (kuhn SEHN suhs). Consensus is a general agreement among the members of a group or community. Harmony was an important goal of Confucianism. Concern for harmony was also an important influence on Prince Shotoku's Constitution of Seventeen Articles. ✓

A Changing Society

During the golden age of the Heian court, the emperor and his nobles held the highest positions in Japanese society. With the establishment of feudalism, a new aristocracy emerged.

Key Events

900	Kana writing is developed.
1000s	*The Tale of Genji* is written.
1200s	Pure Land and Nichiren Buddhism spread throughout the country.

✓ Checkpoint

List four traditional Japanese values.

_____

_____

_____

_____

Reading Strategy

Underline the main idea of the bracketed paragraph. Circle three details that support the main idea.

Vocabulary Builder

A synonym for *artisan* is *craftsperson*. What does this tell you about the kinds of goods artisans produced?

_____

_____

✓ Checkpoint

List two cultural influences that assigned lower status to women.

_____

_____

In rural (ROOR uhl), or country, areas, local daimyos, or landlords, became important social leaders. They provided protection and kept order among their tenants, or farmers who rented their land. However, farmers ran most of their own affairs. They had village assemblies that made decisions for the community.

Women's role in Japanese society changed. In earlier times, they had held leadership roles. However, Confucianism and Buddhism both assigned women lower status. They were expected to obey their fathers and husbands. The Tendai and Shingon sects did not allow women in their monasteries. Later sects, such as True Land, welcomed women.

In the Heian period education was limited to the aristocracy. Some poor men received an education by entering Buddhist monasteries. Other than those in the emperor's court, women rarely received an education.

Trade increased, which led to economic growth. Towns sprang up. Artisans made goods and merchants bought and sold them.

Trade with China grew as well. At first, Japan exported mostly raw materials. Raw materials (RAW muh TEER ee uhlz) materials are natural products used to make things. As Japan's artisan class grew, Japan made other goods for export, such as swords.

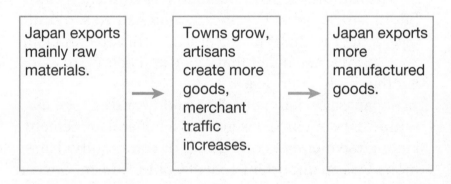

| Japan exports mainly raw materials. | → | Towns grow, artisans create more goods, merchant traffic increases. | → | Japan exports more manufactured goods. |

✓

Check Your Progress

1. How could a Japanese person show family loyalty?

_____

_____

2. What group made decisions for the community in rural areas?

_____

Question to Think About As you read Section 3 in your textbook and take notes, keep this section focus question in mind: **How did Japanese values develop and change?**

▶ Use this chart to record key information from the section. Some information has been filled in to get you started.

Japanese Society	
Traditional Values	**Changes in Japanese Society**
From Shinto • Stressed family loyalty and respect for ancestors. • More concerned with family interests than _____ interests. **From Buddhism** • Helped shape samurai code of _____. • Idea of _____ helped them face danger. **From Confucianism** • Led to desire for order and consensus in society.	**Rural Society** • Most rural people were tenant farmers. • Landlords called _____ kept order. • A _____ made most local decisions. **Women** • Assigned _____ status by Buddhism and Confucianism. **Education** • Limited to the _____, _____ rarely educated. • Some poor educated through monasteries. **Economy** • Towns grew and there were more artisans and merchants. Trade increased. • Japan shifted from exporting _____ to exporting _____ goods.

Refer to this page to answer the Chapter 13 Focus Question on page 165.

Directions: Circle the letter of the correct answer.

1. Which group most influenced the flowering of Japanese culture?
   A   merchants   B   nobles   C   artisans

2. Which was influenced by Chinese culture?
   A   scroll paintings   B   Haiku   C   Buddhist temples

3. Buddhism spread to Japan from
   A   Korea.   B   Russia.   C   India.

4. Which value is associated with Confucianism?
   A   code of bushido   B   consensus   C   respect for women

Directions: Follow the steps to complete this task:

Describe how different forms of Buddhism developed in Japan.

Step 1: Recall information: List the five new Buddhist sects that gained followers in Japan.

Sects of Buddhism in Japan	
1.	4.
2.	5.
3.	

Step 2: Compare the characteristics of Japanese Buddhist sects. What were some of the beliefs and practices? Which sects appealed to nobles? Which appealed to all classes?

_____

_____

_____

Step 3: Complete the topic sentence that follows. Then write two or three more sentences that support your topic sentence.

Buddhism developed into different forms in Japan because

_____

_____

_____

Now you are ready to answer the Chapter 13 Focus Question: **What were the characteristics of Japan's Golden Age?**

► Complete the following charts to help you answer this question. Use the notes that you took for each section.

| Buddhism is first brought to Japan from _____ _____. | Cultural elements borrowed from China:
•

•

• Chinese influence in architecture | Teachings of Shinto, _____, and _____ _____ combine in Japanese society. |

Japan's Golden Age

New Buddhist Sects	**Distinctive Japanese Styles**	**Japanese Society**
• Tendai • • • •	• Kana symbols • Literary forms: _____ _____, and short _____, including _____. • Architecture: Temples and palaces were influenced by _____ architecture. Nobles' homes and palaces were built around _____. • New form of drama: _____	Traditional values: • • • • **Role of women:** Confucian and Buddhist teachings considered women to be _____ _____. **Economic changes:** • Trade _____ • Japan produced more _____ goods.

Refer to this page to answer the Unit 5 Focus Question on page 166.

Chapter 10 Under the Tang and Song dynasties, China's size, wealth, and political strength grew, and the arts flourished. Daoism, Confucianism, and Buddhism were the three main belief systems during this time.

Chapter 11 The Mongols conquered many parts of Asia, creating a vast empire. The Ming Dynasty then restored Chinese rule. China's ideas, culture, and technological innovations influenced other countries.

Chapter 12 Japan, an island nation, was strongly influenced by Chinese culture. A series of emperors established the Japanese state, and then a group of powerful families gained control. Japan became divided under military rulers, but was reunited by the 1600s.

Chapter 13 Japan adapted cultural influences from its neighbors and created an original culture of its own. Buddhism was an important cultural influence.

Think Like a Historian

Read the Unit 5 Focus Question: **What factors cause civilizations to change over time?**

▶ Use the organizers on this page and the next to collect information to answer this question.

What factors led to change over time in China between A.D. 618–A.D. 1500? Some of them are listed in this chart. Review your section and chapter notes. Then complete the chart.

Changes in China Over Time (A.D. 618–A.D. 1500)	
Aspects of Society	**Changes That Took Place**
Government	• efficient government, strong leaders, and the merit system • •
Philosophy and Religion	• Daoism, Confucianism, and Buddhism • •

(continued)

Changes in China Over Time (A.D. 618–A.D. 1500)	
Aspects of Society	**Changes That Took Place**
Agriculture	• rice rose as most important crop; population boomed, increasing trade •
Technology	• gunpowder for weapons • •
Commerce	• a food surplus, the Grand Canal, and a money economy increased trade • •

What factors caused change over time in Japan between A.D. 500–A.D. 1868? The chart below gives you part of the answer. Review your section and chapter notes. Then fill in the rest of the chart.

Changes in Japan Over Time (A.D. 500–A.D. 1868)	
Aspects of Society	**Changes That Took Place**
Influence of Chinese Culture	• Chinese writing system used as basis for new system • •
Government	• Prince Shotoku united Japan. • • • • •
Social System	• clan organization •
Arts	development of unique forms of: • • •
Philosophy and Religion	• Shinto influences • •

Unit 6

Europe in the Middle Ages

What You Will Learn

Chapter 14 After the fall of the Roman Empire, Europe entered a period known as the Middle Ages. During this time, Europe was divided into many small kingdoms, Christianity spread, and feudalism arose.

Chapter 15 Europe witnessed conflicts between kings and popes during the Middle Ages. The Norman Conquest transformed England while the Crusades had significant effects on Europe and Palestine.

Chapter 16 New farming techniques and increased trade helped Europe prosper in the late Middle Ages. Churches and schools thrived. After 1300, however, disease and warfare disrupted the medieval social order.

Focus Your Learning As you study this unit and take notes, you will find the information to answer the questions below. Answering the chapter focus questions will help build your answer to the unit focus question.

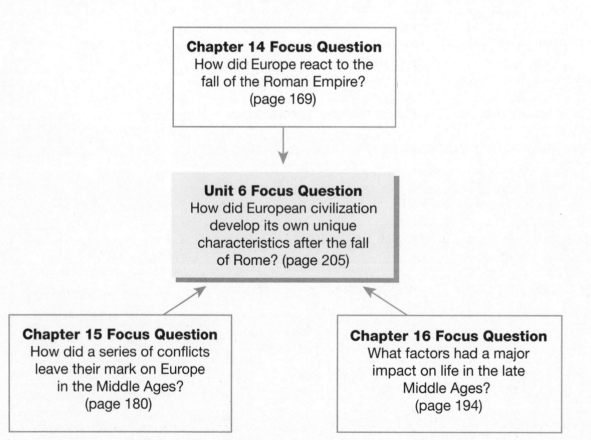

Chapter 14 Focus Question
How did Europe react to the fall of the Roman Empire?
(page 169)

Unit 6 Focus Question
How did European civilization develop its own unique characteristics after the fall of Rome? (page 205)

Chapter 15 Focus Question
How did a series of conflicts leave their mark on Europe in the Middle Ages?
(page 180)

Chapter 16 Focus Question
What factors had a major impact on life in the late Middle Ages?
(page 194)

Chapter 14

A New Civilization in Europe (500–1000)

What You Will Learn

After the fall of the Roman Empire, Europe entered a period known as the Middle Ages. During this time, Europe was divided into many small kingdoms, Christianity spread, and feudalism arose.

Chapter 14 Focus Question

As you read through this chapter, keep this question in mind: **How did Europe react to the fall of the Roman Empire?**

Section 1

Europe in the Early Middle Ages

Section 1 Focus Question

Who came to hold the power once held by the Roman Emperor? To begin answering this question,
- Find out about the geography of Europe.
- Learn about new kingdoms in Europe after the collapse of the Roman Empire.

Section 1 Summary

Europe has attracted many groups of people over time. After the fall of the Roman Empire, Germanic tribes established kingdoms across Europe.

The Geography of Europe

Together Europe and Asia form the Eurasian landmass (LAND mas). A landmass is a large, unbroken area of land. Europe juts out from the western end of this landmass like a huge peninsula.

Europe's topography (tuh PAHG ruh fee), or arrangement of physical features, includes the North European Plain. There are also mountains in the north and south. Westerly winds bring rain and give most of western Europe a warm, moist climate. Mountains block these winds from the countries in the south. So they have hot,

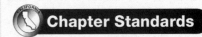

Chapter Standards

History-Social Science 7.6.1, 7.6.2, 7.6.3

Key Events

530	The Franks control France and Germany.
597	Pope Gregory I sends Christian monks to England.
768	Charlemagne becomes king.
900s	Vikings invade northern Europe.

Reading Strategy

The text says Western Europe has a warm, moist climate. What is the reason, or cause, for this kind of climate?

_____

_____

✓ Checkpoint

Name the period in European history between the fall of the Roman Empire and the beginning of the Modern Age.

_____

✓ Checkpoint

Name three important Frankish leaders.

_____

_____

_____

dry, summers and rainy winters. Europe also has many waterways. They serve as trade routes, bring water to farms, and form natural boundaries.

Over time, many people have come through Europe. In the late 300s, Germanic tribes migrated into the Roman Empire. This event marked the start of a new period of European history called the Middle Ages (MIHD uhl AYJ ehz). This is the time between the fall of the Roman Empire, around A.D. 500, and the start of the Modern Age, around A.D. 1500. The term medieval (mee dee EE vuhl) also describes this period. ✓

New Kingdoms in Europe

During the Middle Ages, Germanic tribes divided Europe into kingdoms. By the 530s, the Franks ruled much of present-day France and Germany. Their kingdom broke apart around 700. But in 717, a leader named Charles Martel reunited the Frankish lands. His son Pepin the Short became the first leader of a new dynasty called the Carolingian Dynasty. Pepin's son Charles became one of the most famous rulers of the early Middle Ages. He was known as Charlemagne (SHAR luh mayn), or Charles the Great.

Charlemagne became king in 768. During his long reign, he fought to expand his realm and build a Christian empire. By the year 800, Charlemagne's territory included most of central and western Europe. But the empire did not have a strong government structure. Instead, Charlemagne ruled his empire personally. He also depended on the pope and Roman Catholic Church to support his rule. Within 40 years of Charlemagne's death, quarrels among his grandsons divided the empire. ✓

Check Your Progress

1. What type of climate does Europe have?

_____

_____

2. Who supported Charlemagne's reign?

_____

_____

Question to Think About As you read Section 1 in your textbook and take notes, keep this section focus question in mind: **Who came to hold the power once held by the Roman Emperor?**

► Use these charts to record key information from the section. Some information has been filled in to get you started.

Topography of Europe	
Mountains	Location: _in the north and the south of the continent_ _____ Influence on climate: _____ _____
Rivers	Important rivers: • Rhine • Functions rivers serve: • • •
Plains	Location: _____ Importance of plains: _____ _____

Frankish Leaders	
Leader	**Why He Was Important**
Charles Martel	• reunited _Frankish lands in 717_ _____ • defeated _____
Pepin the Short	• first king of _____
Charlemagne	• wanted to build _____ • defeated _____ • attacks against Spanish Muslims inspired _____ • by 800, empire included _____ • a just ruler who _____

Refer to this page to answer the Chapter 14 Focus Question on page 179.

The Spread of Christianity in Europe

Section 2 Focus Question

How did Christianity spread across Europe? To begin answering this question,

- Learn about rise of religious organizations in Europe.
- Find out about Europe's conversion to Christianity.

Section 2 Summary

After the fall of the Roman Empire, missionaries spread Christianity across Europe. As a result, the Roman Catholic Church gained tremendous power.

The Rise of Religious Orders

After the fall of the Western Roman Empire, the **diffusion** (dih FYOO zhuhn), or spread, of Christianity in Europe began. Among the most important groups that promoted Christian beliefs were the monasteries.

In the early Christian Church, some deeply religious men lived lives of study and prayer. Leading monks founded religious orders. In time, some gathered together in monasteries. **Benedict of Nursia** (BEHN uh dihkt uhv NER see uh) was a monk who had a lasting effect on religious orders. About 529, he founded a monastery that had a series of strict rules, which became the standard for monasteries across Europe. Monks began and ended their days in prayer. During the day, they studied or worked in the monasteries' gardens and workshops. Some cared for the sick or worked copying religious manuscripts.

Religious orders also existed for women. The women, or nuns, lived in convents. Like monks, some spent nearly all of their time in prayer and study. Others took care of the poor and the sick or worked in the convents' gardens. ✔️

The Conversion of Europe

When the Roman Empire collapsed, Christianity had not spread far beyond the Mediterranean area. Priests and monks traveled as missionaries to convert, or

Key Events

530s The Franks control France and Germany.

597 Pope Gregory I sends Christian monks to England.

768 Charlemagne becomes king.

900s Vikings invade northern Europe.

✓ Checkpoint

Name the Italian monk who had a lasting effect on monasteries across Europe.

change from one religion to another, peoples in other parts of Europe.

One famous early missionary was St. Patrick (saynt PA trihk), who set out to convert the people of Ireland. After he gained their trust, many Irish people accepted the Christian faith.

In 597, Pope Gregory I decided to convert England. The king of Kent, in southern England, welcomed the monks Gregory sent. After the king converted to Christianity, many of his subjects followed. Over the next century, most of England became Christian.

In the 700s and 800s, missionaries worked in other parts of Europe. An English monk named Saint Boniface worked to convert pagans in Germany and the Netherlands.

Missionaries brought a message of both fear and hope. The church taught that humans were weak and sinful. This meant that people were likely to break God's laws. Heaven and hell were also key concepts. To reach heaven, Christians had to have faith in Christ, follow his teachings, abandon their sinful ways, and observe the sacraments. Sacraments (SAK ruh mehnts) were the sacred rites of the Church. Sinners would go to hell and suffer forever. For most people in medieval Europe, the Church was the sole source of truth. It controlled almost all areas of thought and teaching and had great power.

Eventually, most Europeans converted to Christianity. They saw themselves as part of Christendom, or the community of Christians spread across Europe. This idea gave people a common identity and a sense of purpose. ✓

Check Your Progress

1. Why did some men and women join religious orders?

_____

_____

2. How did Christianity spread across Europe?

_____

_____

The word *mission* is contained in the word *missionary*. A mission is a self-imposed duty. What does this tell you about how monks felt about spreading the teachings of Christianity?

_____

_____

_____

Reading Strategy

How did Saint Patrick convert the Irish to Christianity? Underline the sentence that answers the question.

✓ Checkpoint

List three people who helped spread Christianity in Europe.

_____

_____

_____

Question to Think About As you read Section 2 in your textbook and take notes, keep this section focus question in mind: **How did Christianity spread across Europe?**

▶ Use these charts to record key information from the section. Some information has been filled in to get you started.

Religious Orders	
Monks	
Activities they performed	• studied • • • •
Vows they took	• poverty • • •
Nuns	
Activities they performed	• prayer and study • • •
Opportunities convent life offered	• study and scholarship •

The Spread and Teachings of Christianity	
St. Patrick	Spread Christianity to ___Ireland___
Pope Gregory I	Spread Christianity to _____
St. Boniface	Spread Christianity to _____
Nature of humans	• •
Heaven and Hell	What heaven was: _____ How to get there: • have faith in Christ • • • What hell was:_____

Refer to this page to answer the Chapter 14 Focus Question on page 179.

The Development of European Feudalism

Section 3 Focus Question

What was feudalism and why did it develop? To begin answering this question,

- Learn about the violent time in European history between 800 and 1000.
- Find out about Europe's feudal society.

Section 3 Summary

Frequent raids by the Vikings led to the development of feudalism in Europe. Under the feudal system, lords offered land in exchange for loyalty.

A Violent Time

Between the years 800 and 1000, invaders threatened Europe. The Magyars, or Hungarians, stormed into central Europe, and Arab raiders attacked from Muslim Spain. The most successful invaders, however, were the Vikings from Scandinavia. Besides loot, they wanted new lands in a better climate. In the 790s, the Vikings began to raid and plunder monasteries in Britain and Ireland. Later, they landed on the French coast. Their settlements in Britain and France brought new ideas into Europe. ✓

A Feudal Society

Viking raids hurried the breakup of Charlemagne's empire. Because the government could not protect people from the Vikings, local nobles took over. This lead to the rise of feudalism.

Europe's feudal system depended on an exchange of land for loyalty. For example, a lord gave a **fief** (feef), or grant of land, to a follower. Those who received the land were called vassals. In return, the vassals agreed to supply the lord with knights, or mounted warriors, in times of trouble.

The king was at the top of feudal society. Below him were powerful nobles and churchmen, who were followed by knights. At the bottom were peasant farmers. **Serfs** (serfs), or peasants who were legally tied to the

Key Events

530s	The Franks control France and Germany.
597	Pope Gregory I sends Christian monks to England.
768	Charlemagne becomes king.
900s	Vikings invade northern Europe.

✓ Checkpoint

List three groups who attacked Europe during the Middle Ages.

_____

_____

_____

Reading Strategy

Reread the bracketed paragraph. Then underline the sentence that explains why Viking raids quickened the breakup of Charlemagne's empire. Circle the word that tells you that this sentence is describing an effect.

lord's land and could not leave it, were the lowest class of peasant farmers.

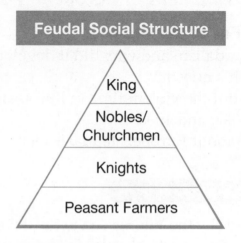

Feudal Social Structure

King

Nobles/
Churchmen

Knights

Peasant Farmers

Side by side with feudalism was an economic system called manorialism. A **manor** (MAN uhr) was the self-sufficient estate of a medieval lord. Its center was the lord's stone house or castle. Around it were a village, a church, and the surrounding fields and forests. The manor produced almost everything the lord, his family, and the villagers needed. The peasants planted and tended the lord's lands, and harvested crops. They were also given strips of land to work themselves. Women spun and wove cloth for clothing, and specialists such as carpenters and a blacksmith lived on the estate.

<u>The role of the lady of the manor was to run the castle and its household.</u> She made sure the manor had enough food, candles, and linens. When the lord was away, she ran the manor. The lord judged minor crimes and settled arguments. He had a staff that helped him run the manor, including a bailiff, who was a sort of business manager, and a reeve, who repaired buildings and oversaw peasants. ✓

Check Your Progress

1. What was the purpose of the Viking invasions?

_____

_____

2. What were the duties of peasant farmers?

_____

_____

© Pearson Education, Inc., publishing as Pearson Prentice Hall. All Rights Reserved.

Vocabulary Builder

Based on context clues from the underlined sentence, write a definition of *role*.

_____

_____

✓ Checkpoint

Name two jobs the lady of the manor performed.

_____

_____

_____

Question to Think About As you read Section 3 in your textbook and take notes, keep this section focus question in mind: **What w[...] [...]udalism and why did it develop?**

▶ Use these charts to record key information from th[...] section. Some information has been filled in to get you started.

Violent Time in Europe
Invaders: <u>Magyars, Arabs, and Vikings</u>
Most successful invaders: _____
From: _____
Nationalities: ___<u>Danish</u>___, _____, an[...] _____
Attacked: _____, _____, and _____
Wanted: _____

A Feudal Society	
Term	**Definition**
Feudalism	a system of government based on the exchange of land for loyalty
Fief	
Vassal	
Knight	
Serf	
Manor	

Feudalism arose in Europe because _____.

Person/Group	Important Roles on a Manor
Peasants	planted and tended lord's lands and harvested crops
Women	
Lady of the manor	
Lord of the manor	
Bailiff	
Reeve	

Refer to this page to answer the Chapter 14 Focus Question on page 179.

Directions: Circle the letter of the correct answer.

1. Charlemagne's empire included most of
   A   central and western Europe.
   B   the Eurasian landmass.
   C   Scandinavia.

2. Who were boldest and most successful invaders during the early Middle Ages?
   A   the Magyars   B   the Arabs   C   the Vikings

3. Which of the following men had a lasting effect on the rules of monastic life?
   A   Benedict of Nursia   B   Pope Gregory I   C   St. Boniface

4. Under feudalism, a lord granted land to a
   A   fief.   B   vassal.   C   knight.

Directions: Follow the steps to answer this question:

How did the spread of Christianity affect Europe during the Middle Ages?

Step 1: Recall information: List three changes that occurred as Christianity spread in Europe during the Middle Ages.

1. _____

2. _____

3. _____

Step 2: Identify how these changes affected European society.

_____

_____

_____

_____

Step 3: Complete the topic sentence that follows. Then write two or three more sentences that support your topic sentence.

The spread of Christianity to Europe during the Middle Ages _____

_____

_____

_____

Now you are ready to answer the Chapter 14 Focus Question: **How did Europe react to the fall of the Roman Empire?**

▶ Complete the following charts to help you answer this question. Use the notes that you took for each section.

New Kingdoms in Europe

Timeline

- Late 300s   Germanic tribes begin to migrate into the Roman Empire.
- 486 _____
- By the 530s _____
- By 700 _____
- 717 _____
- 786 _____
- 800 _____
- 814 _____
- Around 854 _____

Spread of Christianity

Monasteries: places where deeply religious men could dedicate their lives to prayer and study

Role of missionaries: _____
_____

Christendom was _____

Feudalism

Reason feudalism arose in Europe in the Middle Ages: The government could not protect people from the Vikings, so local nobles took over.

Lords gave vassals: _____

Vassals gave lords: _____

Social structure:

1. _____
2. _____
3. _____
4. _____

Economic system that went along with feudalism: _____

Refer to this page to answer the Unit 6 Focus Question on page 205.

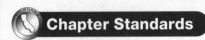
Chapter 15

Medieval Conflicts and Crusades

(700–1500)

What You Will Learn

Europe witnessed conflicts between kings and popes during the Middle Ages. The Norman Conquest transformed England. The Crusades had significant effects on Europe and Palestine.

Chapter 15 Focus Question

As you read this chapter, keep this question in mind: **How did a series of conflicts leave their mark on Europe in the Middle Ages?**

Section 1

Popes and Rulers

Section 1 Focus Question

How did popes try to establish authority over kings? To begin answering this question,

- Learn how Charlemagne and Pope Leo III worked together to rule Christendom.
- Find out about conflicts between Henry IV and Pope Gregory VII.

Section 1 Summary

Kings ruled during the Middle Ages. However, the Christian Church was central to most people's lives. The Pope was the head of the Church. Many times kings and popes had to work together to rule well.

A Study in Cooperation

Charlemagne was the king of a vast area of Europe. But he wanted the greater title of "emperor." According to Roman belief, this gave the ruler a special relationship with God. Charlemagne was a devout Christian. Many of his advisers were members of the clergy. The clergy (KLER jee) is made up of priests and monks who give their lives to serve the Church.

Key Events

800	The pope crowns Charlemagne emperor.
1066	The Normans conquer England.
1215	King John accepts the Magna Carta.
1492	The last Muslim kingdom falls in Spain.

So, when Pope Leo III was threatened by his rivals and had to leave Rome, Charlemagne protected him. Charlemagne later traveled to Rome to further support the pope. On this visit, Leo III made Charlemagne emperor in a special coronation (kor uh NAY shuhn), or crowning ceremony. This strengthened the church's power in Western Europe. ✓

A Study in Conflict

After the collapse of Charlemagne's empire, the German lands to the east were divided among a number of dukes. One duke, known as Otto the Great, was chosen to be king. He formed alliances with other nobles. He then built a small empire. Otto got the pope to crown him as Holy Roman Emperor.

Later, a monk named Hildebrand became Pope Gregory VII (pohp GREHG uh ree thuh SEHV uhnth). Gregory issued, or officially put forth, a list of rules declaring that he had authority over all Church and secular (SEHK yuh luhr), or nonchurch, leaders. He claimed he had the right to choose all bishops and the right to remove emperors from the throne. The emperor at the time, Henry IV, objected to many of Gregory's ideas because they attacked his power and rights.

Henry ignored the pope's rules, and he named his own bishop for the city of Milan, Italy. The pope appointed a rival bishop. Henry tried to remove Gregory as pope. The pope excommunicated Henry. To excommunicate (ehks kuh MYOO nih kayt) is to remove someone from a church or religious group. He also freed Henry's subjects from loyalty to the emperor.

Years after Henry and Gregory died, an agreement called the Concordat of Worms attempted to distribute power between popes and rulers. However, conflict continued for years. ✓

Check Your Progress

1. Why did Charlemagne want the title "emperor"?

_____

_____

2. What were Gregory VII's ideas about his power?

_____

_____

Reading Strategy

Why does the bracketed paragraph begin with the word *so*? What does this word help you understand?

_____

_____

_____

✓ Checkpoint

List two ways that Charlemagne supported Pope Leo III.

_____

_____

Vocabulary Builder

Reread the underlined sentence. The pope's bishop was a "rival bishop" because he competed with the power of Henry's bishop. Name two rivals in today's society or from history.

_____

_____

✓ Checkpoint

List two actions Henry IV took to challenge Pope Gregory VII's authority.

_____

_____

Questions to Think About As you read Section 1 in your textbook and take notes, keep this section focus question in mind: **How did a series of conflicts leave their mark on Europe in the Middle Ages?**

▶ Use these charts to record key information from the section. Some information has been filled in to get you started.

Charlemagne and Pope Leo III		
	Charlemagne	**Pope Leo III**
How they supported each other	• Helped _Pope Leo III_ when rivals in _____ threatened him. • Visited the pope in _____ to show further _____.	Crowned _____ emperor on Christmas Day, 800 in a special _____.
What they believed	• _____ had made him emperor. • It was _____ duty to help him do God's work on Earth.	• The _Church_ had made Charlemagne emperor. • It was the emperor's duty to assist the _____ in doing God's work on Earth.

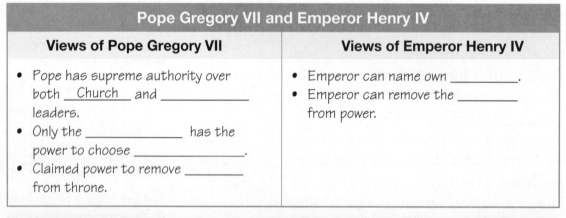

Pope Gregory VII and Emperor Henry IV	
Views of Pope Gregory VII	**Views of Emperor Henry IV**
• Pope has supreme authority over both _Church_ and _____ leaders. • Only the _____ has the power to choose _____. • Claimed power to remove _____ from throne.	• Emperor can name own _____. • Emperor can remove the _____ from power.

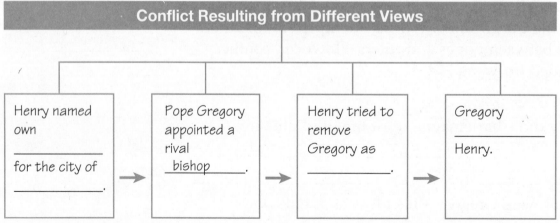

Conflict Resulting from Different Views

Henry named own _____ for the city of _____.	→	Pope Gregory appointed a rival _bishop_ _____.	→	Henry tried to remove Gregory as _____.	→	Gregory _____ Henry.

Refer to this page to answer the Chapter 15 Focus Question on page 193.

Kings, Nobles, and the Magna Carta

Section 2 Focus Question

How did the Norman Conquest set in motion a chain of events that changed English rule and law? To begin answering this question,

- Learn about the Norman conquest.
- Find out about limits placed on royal power.

Section 2 Summary

The Normans were the descendants of Vikings who lived in Normandy, an area in France. They invaded England in 1066, and brought much change to English law and ways of life.

The Norman Conquest

During the Viking expansion, raiders called the Normans settled in Normandy. In time, <u>they</u> wanted to rule England as well. Edward the Confessor, the Anglo-Saxon king, supposedly promised the English crown to Harold Godwin. But William, duke of Normandy, claimed that Edward had already promised the crown to <u>him</u>. Harold became king. But in September 1066, the Normans invaded. They defeated King Harold and the English army at the battle of Hastings. The Norman leader became known as **William the Conqueror** (WIHL yuhm thuh KAHN ker er). On Christmas Day, <u>he</u> was crowned King of England.

William introduced a strong feudal system in England. He divided large shares of English land among about 180 Norman barons. These Norman nobles soon became very wealthy and powerful. French and Latin became the languages of law, culture, and government. ✓

Limits on Royal Power

The Norman kings of England depended on their barons for money and soldiers. In return, the barons made demands on the king. This led to a power struggle between the barons and the kings.

In 1199, **King John** was crowned. As a descendant of William the Conqueror, John claimed to rule Normandy.

Key Events

800	The pope crowns Charlemagne emperor.
1066	The Normans conquer England.
1215	King John accepts the Magna Carta.
1492	The last Muslim kingdom falls in Spain.

Reading Strategy

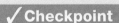

Three pronouns are underlined in the bracketed paragraph. Circle the nouns to which they refer, and connect each pair with a line.

✓Checkpoint

Name the languages of law, culture, and government under the Normans.

_____

_____

The text states, "In 1215, the barons forced King John to sign a document called the Magna Carta." Other examples of documents are the U.S. Constitution and a report card. Write a definition of *document*.

_____

_____

✓ Checkpoint

In the Magna Carta, what does the phrase "the law of the land" refer to?

_____

_____

However, claiming an area and ruling it are not the same thing. By 1204, John had lost control over most of his French lands. To get them back, he needed an army. To raise that army, he needed money. To get that money, he had to raise taxes. This angered the barons.

In 1215, the barons forced King John to sign a document called the Magna Carta. In the Magna Carta, King John agreed to recognize the rights of barons. He promised not to collect more taxes unless a council made up of barons agreed. Also, he promised to recognize the right to a trial by jury in court.

The Magna Carta made it clear that even a king was not above the law of the land. When the Magna Carta makes reference to "the law of the land," it is refering to English **common law** (KAHM uhn law). Common law is a body of law that has grown from custom and judges' decisions instead of laws passed by a government.

An important idea to come from English common law is habeas corpus. **Habeas corpus** (HAY bee uhs COR puhs) refers to a court order to bring an arrested person before a judge or court. A **writ** (riht) is a court order. If a jailer receives a writ of habeas corpus, he must either release the prisoner, or show good cause to keep him in jail. This became an important part of American law. Ideas in the Magna Carta such as rule of law, trial by jury, and the rights of people to have a voice in law have also influenced American government.

The Magna Carta also produced the English Parliament. A **parliament** (PAHR luh muhnt) is a gathering of representatives who make laws. Eventually, the English Parliament became a law-making body that met on a regular basis and was divided into two houses. The House of Lords represented nobles. The House of Commons represented town leaders and knights. ✓

Check Your Progress

1. Who led each side in the battle of Hastings?

_____

_____

2. Name two important limits on the king's power that came from the Magna Carta.

_____

_____

Question to Think About As you read Section 2 in your textbook and take notes, keep this section focus question in mind: **How did the Norman conquest set in motion a chain of events that changed English rule and law?**

► Use these charts to record key information from the section. Some information has been filled in to get you started.

The Norman Conquest

England in 1066

- After Edward the Confessor died, these three men claimed the English throne: <u>Harold, William,</u> and <u>the Norwegian king.</u>
- _____ became king.

The Battle of Hastings

- Fought between the _____ and the _____.
- _____ won.
- _____ was crowned after fighting his way across England.
- _____ rule in England ended.

England after 1066

- King _____ introduced a strong _____ system and divided local landowner's land among _____.
- <u>French</u> and <u>Latin</u> became the language of law, culture, and government.

Limits on Royal Power

The Magna Carta

- King John decided to reclaim _____.
- He had to form a(n) _____, which meant he had to raise ___<u>taxes</u>___.
- Rebellious barons forced King John to sign the _____.
- In this document, King John:
  - agreed to recognize _____
  - promised he would not _____
  - promised he would not _____
- The Magna Carta made clear that even a king must _____.

English Law

- Common law is based on _____ and <u>judges' decisions</u> rather than laws passed by a(n) _____.
- English common law is a mix of these three types of law: _____ _____
- _____ is the law-making body in England. It is divided into the following two houses: _____.

Refer to this page to answer the Chapter 15 Focus Question on page 193.

Religious Crusades

Key Events

800	The pope crowns Charlemagne emperor.
1066	The Normans conquer England.
1215	King John accepts the Magna Carta.
1492	The ~~last~~ Muslim kingdom ~~in~~ Spain.

Section 3 Focus Question

What were the causes and effects of the Crusades?
To begin answering this question,

- Learn about the Crusades against the Muslims.
- Learn about the effects of the Crusades on religious persecutions, trade, and everyday life in Europe.

Section 3 Summary

In 1076, Muslims captured the Christian Holy Land in Palestine. The pope called on Christians in western Europe to take back these lands in organized military campaigns called crusades.

Crusades Against Muslims

During medieval times some Christians became pilgrims. A **pilgrim** (PIHL gruhm) is a religious person who travels to a holy place or shrine. For a long time Muslim rulers allowed Christian pilgrims to visit holy places like Jerusalem in Palestine in peace. However, when the Seljuk Turks conquered Jerusalem in 1071, there was frequent harassment of Christian pilgrims. The Seljuks marched on Constantinople.

The Byzantine emperor asked Pope Urban II for help. The pope called for a **crusade** (kroo SAYD), or a Christian religious war, to free the Holy Land from the Turks. He saw this as an opportunity to make real his claim of authority over all Christendom—even over an emperor. Many people answered the pope's call. By 1099, armies of knights had captured Jerusalem. They also established four crusader states in the Holy Land.

Pope Urban linked the idea of holy war with the idea of pilgrimage. The pope argued that since Jesus was every Christian's Lord, his vassals should defend his lands and holy places. Crusaders made many sacrifices to make the long and dangerous trip.

Europeans launched three more Crusades. However, none was as successful as the first. Even though the Second Crusade had powerful backing, it failed.

Reading Strategy

Reread the bracketed paragraph on this page and the next page. Underline the main idea and circle supporting details.

Part of the reason was because Crusaders were often cruel to Muslims. So, the local population in Palestine did not support Crusaders. The Third Crusade failed also. The Fourth Crusade disgraced the idea of a crusade. Its soldiers captured and looted the rich Byzantine capital city of Constantinople. The pope was furious.

In 1212, the so-called Children's Crusade attracted poor people of all ages. Many were sold as slaves. In 1291, Muslims from Egypt retook the last crusader state.

The Crusades changed Europe forever. People who had spent their entire lives in their villages saw new people, different lands, and other ways of life. They returned home with spices, silk, and other rare goods to trade. To meet demands for these goods, European traders began trading with Asia. This inspired further exploration of the world. ☑

Religious Persecutions

The Crusades inspired religious fervor against Muslims. This turned into attacks on all non-Christians. Jews who would not convert to Christianity were often killed. They were forced to leave England in 1290, and France in 1306. Even groups of Christians who believed in various heresies were attacked, fined, or exiled. A heresy (HEHR uh see) is a belief that is not allowed by official Church doctrine.

Pope Gregory IX created the Inquisition in the 1200s. The Inquisition (ihn kwuh ZIHSH uhn) was a church court designed to investigate and judge heretics. If accused heretics did not change their beliefs, they faced punishments. These ranged from whippings to imprisonment. Death even resulted for those who would not confess to their "errors" in belief. ☑

Check Your Progress

1. What opportunity did Pope Urban II see for himself in calling for the crusades?

_____

_____

2. What was the Inquisition?

_____

_____

✓ Checkpoint

List the two ideas that Pope Urban linked.

_____

_____

Vocabulary Builder

The word *heretics* is underlined in your text. Use the definition of the key term *heresy* and context clues to write a definition of *heretic*.

_____

_____

✓ Checkpoint

Name two countries in Europe that expelled Jews in the Middle Ages.

_____

_____

Question to Think About As you read Section 3 in your textbook and take notes, keep this section focus question in mind: **What were the causes and effects of the Crusades?**

▶ Use these charts to record key information from the section. Some information has been filled in to get you started.

Crusades Against Muslims	
Causes and Main Events of the Crusades	**Effects of the Crusades**
Seljuk _____Turks_____ conquered Jerusalem in the year_____, harrassing Christian pilgrims and _____ _____.	Pope called for _____, or Christian religious _____, to free the Holy Land.
Crusaders formed well-organized armies of _____Knights_____.	They conquered _____ and other lands called crusader _____.
Crusaders gained no su⁀⁀ort from local population in _____.	Europeans mounted _____ more crusades, but they failed.
Crusaders returned home with _____, _____ and other rare goods to trade.	Everyone wanted these things, inspiring further _____ and _____.

Religious Persecutions	
Main Idea	**Supporting Details**
Religious fervor of the Crusades inspired persecution in Europe.	• Jews from _____ and _____. • Even Christian _____ or _____.
Pope Gregory IX created the Inquisition in the 1200s.	• This Inquisition • If heretics did

Refer to this page to answer the Chapter Focus Question on page 193.

Christians and Muslims in Spain

Section 4 Focus Question

How did the rise and fall of Muslim rule alter life in Spain? To begin answering this question,

- Find out about life in Spain under Muslim rule.
- Learn how the Christians recaptured Spain and what happened afterward.

Section 4 Summary

Spain did well under Muslim rule. Later, Christians inspired by the spirit of the Crusades recaptured the Spanish peninsula.

Spain Under Muslim Rule

Spanish Muslims were known as Moors. Moorish Spain became one of the most advanced medieval civilizations in Europe.

The Muslim capital of Córdoba was Europe's largest city in the tenth century. It had mosques, bookshops, public baths, and a great library. Houses had mosaic floors, gardens, and fountains. Traders took goods from Córdoba to markets in Europe. Students from all over the known world flocked to Córdoba to study music, medicine, and philosophy.

By medieval standards, Moorish rulers in Spain were quite tolerant of Jews and Christians. The Qur'an encouraged tolerance, as all three religions worshiped one God. Christians outnumbered the Muslims. So forcing them to convert would have been impossible. Non-Muslims only had to follow certain rules and pay a special tax. Later, Muslim rulers imposed strict new rules. ✓

The Reconquista

<u>The decline of Muslim rule in Spain began in about 1002 with a civil war. This led to the powerful Córdoba caliphate being split up into smaller, weaker kingdoms.</u> At the same time, the Christian kingdoms in northern Spain were united by Christian fervor after the Crusades. The pope encouraged them to win back Spain for

Key Events

800	The pope crowns Charlemagne emperor.
1066	The Normans conquer England.
1215	King John accepts the Magna Carta.
1492	The last Muslim kingdom falls in Spain.

Vocabulary Builder

Use the context clues in the bracketed paragraph to write a definition of *tolerant*.

_____

_____

✓ Checkpoint

List three subjects students came to Córdoba to study.

_____

_____

_____

Reading Strategy

There is a cause and an effect in the underlined text. Put brackets around the cause and circle the effect.

Christendom. The movement to drive the Muslims out of Spain was called the Reconquista (ray kohn KEES tah).

The Reconquista was successful. By the middle of the thirteenth century only Granada was still in Moorish hands.

Key Events in the Reconquista	
Year	Event
1085	City of Toledo captured
1139	Portugal became seperate kingdom
1236	Córdoba fell

In 1469, Isabella (ihz uh BEL uh), queen of Castile-León, married Ferdinand (FERD ihn and), king of Aragon. This marriage was important because it united Spain's largest kingdoms. It also formed the basis for a Spanish state. Ferdinand and Isabella focused on conquering Granada. Granada fell in 1492. This delighted the pope.

Isabella and Ferdinand wanted to make Spain a Catholic society. They brought in a Dominican monk named Torquemada (tor kuh MAH duh) to head the Spanish Inquisition. Jews and Muslims were terrorized and tortured.

By 1502, all Jews and Muslims had been ordered to leave Spain and Portugal. The loss of these two groups did great harm to Spain's culture and economy. An economy is the system by which a country's money and goods are produced and used. ✓

Check Your Progress

1. Why were early Moorish rulers in Spain tolerant of Judaism and Christianity?

_____

_____

_____

2. Why was Isabella and Ferdinand's marriage important?

_____

_____

✓ **Checkpoint**

Name the movement by Christian kingdoms to drive the Muslims out of Spain.

_____

Questions to Think About As you read Section 4 in your textbook and take notes, keep this section focus question in mind: **How did the rise and fall of Muslim rule alter life in Spain?**

▶ Use these organizers to record key information from the section. Some information has been filled in to get you started.

Spain Under Muslim Rule	
Moorish Culture	**Multicultural Society**
1. Muslims in Spain known as: _____ _____	1. Students flocked to _____ to study _____, _____, and _____. with Muslim and _____ scholars.
2. Heartland of Moorish culture: _____Southern Spain_____	
3. Muslim capital in tenth century: _____	2. Famous philosophers of the Middle Ages who lived in Córdoba: • _____ • _____
4. The capital city had: • ___mosques___ • _____ • _____ • ___public baths___	
5. Houses in the capital city had: • _____ • _____ • _____	3. Muslim rulers tolerant of: ___Jews___ ___and Christians___ because: _____ _____
6. Masterpieces of Islamic architecture: • _____ • _____	4. Non-Muslims only had to: • _____ • _____

The Reconquista
I. Beginnings of the Reconquista   A. Decline of Muslim rule began in the year ___1002___ with a civil war.   B. The _____ encouraged Christians to win Spain back from the _____. This movement was called the _____.   **II. Military Campaigns**   A. 1085: Capture of _____   B. 1139: _____   C. 1236: _____   **III. Unification of Spain**   A. Marriage of ___Isabella___ and ___Ferdinand___ unifies Spain's largest _____ kingdoms.   **IV. Religious Persecutions**   A. Muslims and _____ tortured by the Spanish _____.

Refer to this page to answer the Chapter Focus Question on page 193.

Directions: Circle the letter of the correct answer.

1. Who was the strong secular leader who clashed with Pope Gregory VII?
   A Charlemagne   B Otto the Great   C Henry IV

2. The Magna Carta limited the king's right to
   A conquer Normandy.
   B collect taxes.
   C expel the Jews.

3. One of the results of the Crusades was
   A to inspire further exploration of the world.
   B to force the Turks to move to Africa.
   C the torture of Christians during the Spanish Inquisition.

4. What was the Reconquista?
   A a church court designed to investigate and judge heretics
   B a movement to drive the Muslims out of Spain
   C the union of Spain's largest kingdoms

Directions: Follow the steps to answer this question:

How did the fall of Muslim rule change religious life in Spain?

Step 1: Recall: In the chart, list characteristics of religious life under Muslim rule and then under Christian rule.

Life in Muslim Spain	Life in Christian Spain

Step 2: Analyze effects: How did religious life change after the end of Muslim rule?

_____

_____

Step 3: Complete the topic sentence that follows. Then write two or three more sentences that support your topic sentence.

The end of Muslim rule affected Spanish religious life _____

_____

_____

_____

Now you are ready to answer the Chapter 15 Focus Question: **How did a series of conflicts leave their mark on Europe in the Middle Ages?**

▶ Fill in the following chart to help you answer this question. Use the notes that you took for each section.

The Effects of Conflict on Europe in the Middle Ages	
Conflict	**Effects**
1. Conflict between Leaders Pope Gregory III vs. _____ _____ • Gregory believed: _____ _____ • _____ believed: _____	• After a power struggle, Henry tried to remove Gregory as _____, and Gregory _____ Henry. • Years after Gregory and Henry died, an agreement called the _____ attempted to distribute power between _____ and _____.
2. Conflict between Cultures The _____ vs. the English • Fought over:	• Normans introduced _____ system to England. • _____ rule in England ended.
3. Conflict between Classes _____ vs. the barons • _____ angered the barons.	• Barons forced the _____ to sign the _____, which limited _____ power.
4. Religious Conflicts _____ vs. Muslims and Jews. • Goal of Crusades: to win back the Christian Holy Land from Muslims. • Goal of the Reconquista:	• Both the Crusades and the _____ resulted in religious _____ against _____, Jews, and Christian _____. • The Inquisition was a _____ _____ _____.

Refer to this page to answer the Unit 6 Focus Question on page 205.

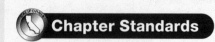
Key Events

1000s	Towns and long-distance trade expand.
1225	Thomas Aquinas is born.
1347	The Black Death strikes Europe.

Chapter 16

A Changing Medieval World (1000–1450)

What You Will Learn

New farming techniques and increased trade helped Europe prosper in the latter Middle Ages. Churches and schools thrived. After 1300, however, disease and warfare disrupted the medieval social order.

Chapter Focus Question

As you read through the sections in this chapter, keep this question in mind: **What factors had a major impact on life in the late Middle Ages?**

Section 1

The Revival of Trade and Towns

Section 1 Focus Question

What caused the revival of trade and towns? To begin answering this question,

- Learn about the farming techniques that improved food production in the Middle Ages.
- Find out how trade became specialized and wealth increased.

Section 1 Summary

Europeans were able to grow much more food in the Middle Ages. Better farming led to a population growth as well as a major increase in trade.

New Ways of Farming

In the Middle Ages, farmers began using iron plows. They also began using horses instead of oxen. Horses could work more quickly, and ate less feed. This allowed farmers to farm more land.

Farmers developed a system of crop rotation (krahp roh TAY shuhn), or changing the use of fields over time. Under the three-field system (three feeld SIHS tuhm) of crop rotation, two fields were each year planted and one was left fallow (FAL oh), or unplanted.

Three-field crop rotation		
Field 1	**Field 2**	**Field 3**
Spring crops planted	Summer crops planted	Fallow for one year
increased the amount of land planted each year		protected farmers from starvation if one crop failed

More food meant that people were healthier. Also, they could feed more children. From 1000 to 1300, Europe's population nearly doubled. ✓

The Growth of Trade and Towns

In the early Middle Ages, peasants made most of the things they needed. But as population and wealth increased, demand for trade goods did too.

The demand for goods encouraged specialization. Long-distance trade also arose. Some areas could specialize in crops that grew best locally, <u>such as</u> French grapes for wine. Some places became famous for certain products. Flanders in northern Europe produced fine woolen cloth. Italian traders imported Asian trade goods, <u>such as</u> spices and perfumes.

As trade increased, Italian bankers created a banking system that included letters of credit. These made trade safer by allowing merchants to travel without carrying large bags of gold coins.

The number of craftworkers in towns increased. Artisans with the same skills often banded together to form **guilds** (gihldz). Guilds were groups of people performing the same craft, usually in the same city, who joined together for their common good. The guilds regulated the quality of goods produced. They set prices and controlled where and to whom goods could be sold. ✓

Check Your Progress

1. How did the three-field system of crop rotation protect against starvation?

_____

2. How did letters of credit make trade safer?

_____

✓ Checkpoint

Name the draft animal that helped farmers produce more food.

_____

Reading Strategy

The underlined words in this paragraph are signal words. They tell you that specific examples will follow. Circle the three items the signal words refer to.

Vocabulary Builder

To *regulate* means to bring under control according to rules. How does this idea apply to the work of the guilds?

_____

_____

✓ Checkpoint

List two items that Italian traders imported.

_____

_____

Question to Think About As you read Section 1 in your textbook and take notes, keep this section focus question in mind: **What caused the revival of trade and towns?**

▶ Use this chart to record key information from the section. Some information has been filled in to get you started.

Farming Improvements in the Middle Ages		
Improvement	**Reasons For Change**	**Combined Effects**
horses instead of oxen	• worked faster • ate less • allowed farmers to cultivate more land	1. food supply in Europe increased
iron plow	• • could cultivate more land	2.
three-field system of crop rotation	• • • protected farmers against starvation	3. 4.

Growth of Trade and Towns	
Surplus crops used for:	
Increase in population and trade led to:	Demand for trade goods encouraged: 1. 2.
Example of crop specialization: • France: grapes for wine	Italian bankers created a system of banking that included:
The revival of trade led to growth of:	An increase in the number of skilled craft-workers led to:
A guild is: a group of people practicing the same craft, usually in the same city, who have joined together for heir common good	
To prevent unfair practices, the guild:	

Refer to this page to answer the Chapter 16 Focus Question on page 204.

Section 2

An Age of Faith

Section 2 Focus Question

How did the Church influence society and culture in the Middle Ages? To begin answering this question,

- Learn how people in the Middle Ages expressed their devotion to God.
- Find out how the Church supported the growth of learning.

Key Events

1000s   Towns and long-distance trade expand.

1225   Thomas Aquinas is born.

1347   The Black Death strikes Europe.

Section 2 Summary

Religion was very important in the Middle Ages. New religious orders were started and great cathedrals were built. The first universities attracted some of the best minds in Europe.

Forms of Devotion

In the Middle Ages, new religious orders were formed out of devotion to God. Many were mendicant (MEHN dih kuhnt) orders. Members of these orders lived on donations and worked in the community, rather than living in monasteries.

One of the best-known of these orders was founded by St. Francis of Assisi (saynt FRAN sihs uhv uh SEE zee). As a young man, Francis was wealthy and spoiled. Later, he felt called to live as Jesus had lived. St. Francis was a friend to all living things and attracted many followers.

People also expressed their devotion to God through art and architecture. Europe's growing wealth enabled people to build great cathedrals. A cathedral (kuh THEE druhl) is a major church, headed by a bishop who oversees a region's churches.

A church built in the early Middle Ages had thick walls, narrow windows, and a domed roof supported by thick columns. By the mid-1100s, Europeans were building cathedrals in a new style known as Gothic.

Gothic cathedrals rose high above town. Their outside walls were decorated with stone carvings. Their inside walls were lined with statues and paintings. People who could not read could learn about their

Reading Strategy

Reread the bracketed paragraph. Draw a box around the sentence describing St. Francis's early life. Label it "before." Then draw a box around the text describing his later, religious life. Label that box "after."

Vocabulary Builder

Devotion comes from the Latin word that means "vow," or promise. How is the concept of making a vow reflected in the idea of "devotion to God"?

_____

_____

_____

_____

✓ **Checkpoint**

Name two items inside and outside churches that helped people learn about their religion.

_____

_____

✓ **Checkpoint**

Name two cultures that preserved Greek works.

_____

_____

religion from this art, as well as from stained-glass windows picturing Bible stories.

Great cathedrals first appeared in France. Soon, however, they rose all across Western Europe. ✓

The Growth of Learning

The great cathedrals became the center of another important new movement: the university. Universities (yoo nuh VER suh teez) are schools, or groups of schools, that train scholars at the highest levels. Cathedral schools for training priests grew into universities. The medieval university was not a building or campus. Professors and students made up the university.

Universities held classes in rented rooms or in churches. Books were expensive and were often shared or rented by students. Many works of ancient Greece had been preserved in the Byzantine Empire and the Islamic world. With the growth of trade, copies of these books traveled to Europe. Universities sprung up in such cities as Bologna, Paris, and Oxford. Courses were taught in Latin. The Church had preserved Latin as the language of learning.

One of the greatest medieval scholars was Thomas Aquinas (TAHM uhs uh KWĪ nuhs). Aquinas was impressed by the writings of the Greek philosopher Aristotle. Aristotle stressed the use of human reason to gain knowledge. On the other hand, church scholars believed that faith was the path to truth. Aquinas argued that both faith and reason came from God. He also believed in the idea of natural law (NACH uhr uhl law). This is the idea that there are laws in nature that are basic to both the natural world and human affairs. Aquinas offered a famous proof for the existence of God based on reason and natural law. ✓

Check Your Progress

1. What are two major ways that Europeans of the Middle Ages expressed their devotion to God?

_____

_____

2. What made up the medieval university?

_____

_____

Question to Think About As you read Section 2 in your textbook and take notes, keep this section focus question in mind: **How did the Church influence society and culture in the Middle Ages?**

► Use these charts to record key information from the section. Some information has been filled in to get you started.

Religious Devotion	
Expressions of European Christians' devotion to God:	1. new religious orders 2.
A mendicant order is: an order whose members lived on donations and worked out in the community, not in monasteries	
St. Francis	Felt called to live: Was a friend of:
A cathedral is:	
Gothic cathedrals first appeared:	
Features of Gothic architecture	1. rise high above town 2. 3. 4.
In the Middle Ages, most art was dedicated to:	
Art helped non-readers: learn about their religion	

The Growth of Learning	
Universities	Began as __cathedral schools__ for training_____. Classes held in _____or _____.
Students studied: works of ancient Greece	
The language of learning:	
St. Thomas Aquinas was deeply impressed by the works of_____.	
Natural law is the idea that there are laws in nature that are basic to both: _____natural world_____ and_____.	
Aquinas' famous proof for the existence of God was based on _____ and _____.	

Refer to this page to answer the Chapter 16 Focus Question on page 204.

The Breakdown of Medieval Society

Key Events

1000s	Towns and long-distance trade expand.
1225	Thomas Aquinas is born.
1347	The Black Death strikes Europe.

Reading Strategy

Reread the bracketed paragraphs. Underline the facts explaining why each side gained the advantage during different phases of the war.

✓ Checkpoint

Name three types of weapons that were introduced during the Hundred Years' War.

_____

_____

_____

Section 3 Focus Question

How did warfare and the plague disrupt life in Europe? To begin answering this question,

- Learn how famine and warfare affected Europe.
- Find out about the effects of the Black Death.

Section 3 Summary

In the early 1300s, Europe suffered from terrible crop failures and warfare. Later, an outbreak of bubonic plague killed a third of Europe's population.

Famine and Warfare

After two centuries of prosperity, Europe faced disaster. From 1315 to 1317, it rained so much that crops were ruined. The years became known as the Great Famine. A famine (FAM ihn) is a serious shortage of food. Many people died of starvation.

Soon after, war broke out. The Hundred Years' War between France and England lasted from 1337 to 1453. It began when King Edward III of England claimed the throne of France.

The English won key battles early on. This was partly because of a new weapon, the longbow. The longbow could pierce French armor. Soon, however, both sides had guns and cannons. Guns shot through armor, and cannons destroyed castle walls.

In France, a young peasant woman known as Joan of Arc (john uhv ahrk) was said to have heard voices from heaven telling her to lead the French army to victory. Her courage in battle inspired the French, who eventually won the war. Joan herself was caught by the English and burned at the stake. ✓

The Black Death

In 1347, Europe was struck by a terrible epidemic (ehp uh DEHM ihk), or widespread outbreak of a disease. The disease was the bubonic plague (byoo BAHN ihk playg). A plague is a deadly infection. The bubonic plague killed about one third of Europeans between 1347 and 1352.

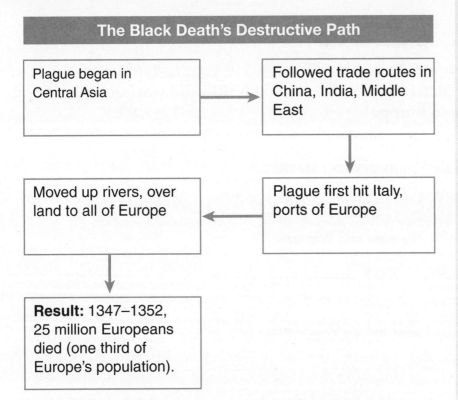

The Black Death's Destructive Path

Plague began in Central Asia	Followed trade routes in China, India, Middle East
Moved up rivers, over land to all of Europe	Plague first hit Italy, ports of Europe

Result: 1347–1352, 25 million Europeans died (one third of Europe's population).

Terrified people looked for someone to blame for their misery. They began to persecute the Jews. Jews were exiled or killed, even though the pope had ordered that they not be killed or forced to convert.

As a result of the plague, too few people were available to cultivate the land. Manor lords became desperate for workers. Serfs now demanded to be paid for their work. Many left manors to work where wages were highest. Peasants across Europe revolted. Although the revolt was put down, the traditional ties between lords and their serfs had been broken.

In old medieval society, everyone had a fixed place. After the Black Death, people were no longer tied to a stable social and spiritual community. They began to act on their own as individuals. People of the Middle Ages began to enter the Modern Age. ✓

Check Your Progress

1. Why did the Hundred Years' War begin?

_____

_____

2. How did the Black Death change society?

_____

_____

© Pearson Education, Inc., publishing as Pearson Prentice Hall. All Rights Reserved.

Vocabulary Builder

The Latin prefix *ex–* means "away." What does it mean that Jews were *exiled*?

_____

_____

_____

✓ Checkpoint

Roughly how many Europeans died during the Black Death?

_____

Question to Think About As you read Section 3 in your textbook and take notes, keep this section focus question in mind: **How did warfare and the plague disrupt life in Europe?**

▶ Use this chart to record key information from the section. Some information has been filled in to get you started.

The Breakdown of Medieval Society	
Famine and Warfare	
Two centuries of prosperity ended by:	1. _Great Famine_ 2. _____
The Hundred Years' War	
New weapons that changed warfare	1. _____ 2. _____ 3. _____
Joan of Arc	What she did: _led the French against the English_ Effect on French: _____
Results of War	Short-term: _____ Long-term: _____
The Black Death	
The epidemic	Name of disease: _____ Began where: _Central Asia_ Route on which it spread: _____ How many killed: _____
Short-term effects	Classes affected: _____ Many people blamed: _____ What became of the land: _____
Later effects	How peasants reacted: _demanded higher wages; revolted_ Ties between lords and their serfs _____

Refer to this page to answer the Chapter 16 Focus Question on page 204.

Directions: Circle the letter of the correct answer.

1. Why did the population of Europe grow rapidly from 1000 to 1300?
   A improvements to medicine
   B trade growth
   C better food production

2. How did guilds protect craftsworkers?
   A They set prices to prevent competition.
   B They forbid those in other cities from having similar businesses.
   C They raised prices regularly.

3. St. Thomas Aquinas emphasized
   A the use of Latin.
   B the value of both faith and reason.
   C vows of poverty.

Directions: Follow the steps to answer this question:

How did the Black Death affect farmers and serfs in Europe?

Step 1: Recall information: Describe the steps of the plague's impact on Europe's working class.

Impact of the Plague	
Europe's population	
Availability of workers	
Demands of the serfs	

Step 2: Describe workers' payment before and after the plague.

Workers' payment before the Plague	
Workers' payment after the Plague	

Step 3: Complete the topic sentence that follows. Then, write two or three more sentences that support your topic sentence.

After the Black Death devastated Europe, life changed for farmers and serfs.

_____

_____

_____

_____

_____

Now you are ready to answer the Chapter 16 Focus Question: **What factors had a major impact on life in the late Middle Ages?**

► Complete the following chart to help you answer this question. Use the notes that you took for each section.

Major Influences on Life in the Late Middle Ages	
Farming	**Trade**
New techniques: 1. using horses rather than oxen 2. Effects of new methods: 1. 2.	More people and wealth led to: **Guilds arose to:** protect the interests of craftspeople
Devotion to God	**Learning**

Expressions of devotion
 	
1.
 	
2.
 	
A mendicant order is: an order whose members lived on donations and worked out in the community, not in monasteries
A cathedral is:
	Universities began as_____
	for training_____.
	
	St. Thomas Aquinas
	
	• impressed by teachings of:
	• Natural law is the idea that:
	• Aquinas' proof for the existence of God was based on:
	
	  •
	
	  •

Famine and Warfare	**The Black Death**
Famine: • cause: heavy rains • effect: **100 Years' War** • fought by: • put an end to: old medieval ways of fighting	Bubonic Plague: • where it began: • how many killed: • classes affected: all • how peasants reacted:

Refer to this page to answer the Unit 6 Focus Question on page 205.

What You Have Learned

Chapter 14 After the fall of the Roman Empire, Europe entered a period known as the Middle Ages. During this time, Europe was divided into many small kingdoms, Christianity spread, and feudalism arose.

Chapter 15 Europe witnessed conflicts between kings and popes during the Middle Ages. The Norman Conquest transformed England while the Crusades had significant effects on Europe and Palestine.

Chapter 16 New farming techniques and increased trade helped Europe prosper in the late Middle Ages. Churches and schools thrived. After 1300, however, disease and warfare disrupted the medieval social order.

Think Like a Historian

Read the Unit 6 Focus Question: **How did European civilization develop its own unique characteristics after the fall of Rome?**

▶ Use the organizers on this page and the next to collect information to answer this question. What changes in European life emerged after the fall of Rome? Review your section and chapter notes. Then complete the chart.

Changes in European Life After the Fall of Rome	
European Life	**Changes After the Fall of Rome**
Conquest and Settlement	• Germanic tribes • •
Spread of Christianity	• the Church benefited from Charlemagne's reign • • •
Government	• no central government • • •
Social Structures	• the Church brought new social roles, obligations, and beliefs •
Art, Literature, and Education	• survived and continued despite Rome's fall • • •

What changes in Europe were caused by conflicts, advancements, and disease? The chart below gives you part of the answer. Review your section and chapter notes. Then fill in the rest of the chart.

Changes in Europe Caused by Conflicts, Advancements, and Disease	
Conflict, Advancements, or Disease	**Changes that Took Place in Europe**
Crusades	Europeans mounted four crusades, motivated by forgiveness of sins and promise of land Effects: • opened Europeans' eyes to the world • • • • •
Conflict in Spain	• Moors: very advanced culture, tolerant of Christians and Jews • •
Technological Advances	• better farming techniques increased food supply and European population • •
Growth of Towns and Trade	• demand for trade goods increased • • •
Disease	• Black Death killed millions • • •
Famine and Warfare	• crops were ruined by heavy rains • •

What You Will Learn

Chapter 17 After the medieval period, Europe moved into the Renaissance. This period saw a new interest in art, literature, and learning.

Chapter 18 The Reformation, a protest against certain practices in the Catholic Church, had far-reaching effects on European society.

Chapter 19 European sailors explored much of the world. Europeans conquered the societies they found in the Americas and set up colonies there.

Chapter 20 A renewed interest in science gave rise to the Scientific Revolution. The growth of science led to a movement called the Enlightenment. Enlightenment ideas spread and sparked the American Revolution. Democracies have expanded and strengthened Enlightenment ideals.

Focus Your Learning As you study this unit and take notes, you will find the information to answer the questions below. Answering the chapter focus questions will help build your answer to the unit focus question.

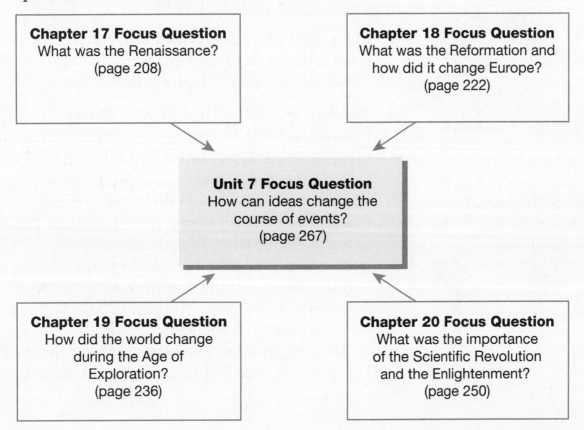

Chapter 17 Focus Question
What was the Renaissance?
(page 208)

Chapter 18 Focus Question
What was the Reformation and how did it change Europe?
(page 222)

Unit 7 Focus Question
How can ideas change the course of events?
(page 267)

Chapter 19 Focus Question
How did the world change during the Age of Exploration?
(page 236)

Chapter 20 Focus Question
What was the importance of the Scientific Revolution and the Enlightenment?
(page 250)

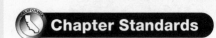

Chapter Standards

History-Social Science 7.8.1, 7.8.2, 7.8.4, 7.8.5

Key Events

1300s	The Renaissance begins in Florence, Italy
1450	Gutenberg develops movable type.
1506	Leonardo da Vinci paints the *Mona Lisa*.
1601	Shakespeare writes *Hamlet*.

Reading Strategy

Reread the bracketed paragraph. Underline the context clues that help you figure out the meaning of the word *urban*.

Chapter 17

The Renaissance (1300–1650)

What You Will Learn

After the medieval period, Europe moved into the Renaissance. This period saw a new interest in art, literature, and learning.

Chapter 17 Focus Question

As you read this chapter, keep the following question in mind: **What was the Renaissance?**

Section 1

The Origins of the Renaissance

Section 1 Focus Question

What economic and social conditions gave rise to the Renaissance? To begin answering this question,

- Learn about the breakdown of feudal order.
- Find out about the birthplace of the Renaissance.

Section 1 Summary

In the 1300s, Europe's feudal order gave way to the economic and cultural changes of the Renaissance. The Renaissance began in wealthy Italian cities.

The Breakdown of the Feudal Order

During the 1300s, the old feudal order in Europe began to break down. Trade and industry began to grow. This weakened the manor system of feudal society.

Urban growth marked this economic expansion. Peasants and nobles alike left their manors. They went to towns for a chance to make money.

In Italian cities, the nobility from the country married into the mercantile middle class. They formed a new urban aristocracy. Mercantile (MER kuhn tǐl) means related to commerce or trade.

Thriving trade and cities also led to cultural shifts. For centuries, learning had been based in the Catholic

Church. Now secular subjects such as law, medicine, philosophy, and science became more popular.

Around 1300, these trends came together in Italy. This began what scholars call the Renaissance. This was a cultural revival that swept through Europe between the fourteenth and sixteenth centuries. The term *Renaissance* is French for "rebirth." This revival was marked by a greater interest in the classical cultures of ancient Greece and Rome. ✓

Birthplace of the Renaissance

In Italy, the feudal order never defined the structure of life as it did in other parts of Europe. This may help explain why Italy was the birthplace of the Renaissance.

By the 1300s, Italy was divided among a number of city-states. These city-states were located on the Mediterranean Sea. They were a natural crossroads between northern Europe, the Middle East, and Africa. The city-states became wealthy and led medieval Europe in commercial growth.

The growth of trade and commerce also promoted a free flow of ideas. As the newly rich merchants and bankers gained status, they became patrons of art and learning. A patron (PAY truhn) is someone who gives money or other support to a person or group.

The Renaissance began in the city of Florence, a wealthy center of banking. One of the most powerful families was the Medici family. The Medicis were great patrons of the arts. In the 1400s, Lorenzo de' Medici (MEH deh chee) spent generously on artistic and architectural projects. Other wealthy Florentines, guilds, and civic groups also sponsored artistic projects. As a result, Florence became a showcase of Renaissance art and architecture. ✓

Check Your Progress

1. How did the rise of the mercantile class contribute to the breakdown of the feudal order?

_____

_____

2. In which city did the Renaissance begin?

_____

Vocabulary Builder

The word *secular* comes from a Latin word meaning "the present world." How does this meaning relate to learning and culture in the Renaissance?

_____

_____

✓ Checkpoint

Name two economic or cultural changes that marked the beginning of the Renaissance.

_____

_____

✓ Checkpoint

Name the Florentine family whose members were great patrons of the arts in the 1400s.

_____

© Pearson Education, Inc., publishing as Pearson Prentice Hall. All Rights Reserved.

Question to Think About As you read Section 1 in your textbook and take notes, keep this section focus question in mind: **What economic and social conditions gave rise to the Renaissance?**

► Use these charts to record key information from the section. Some of the information has been filled in to get you started.

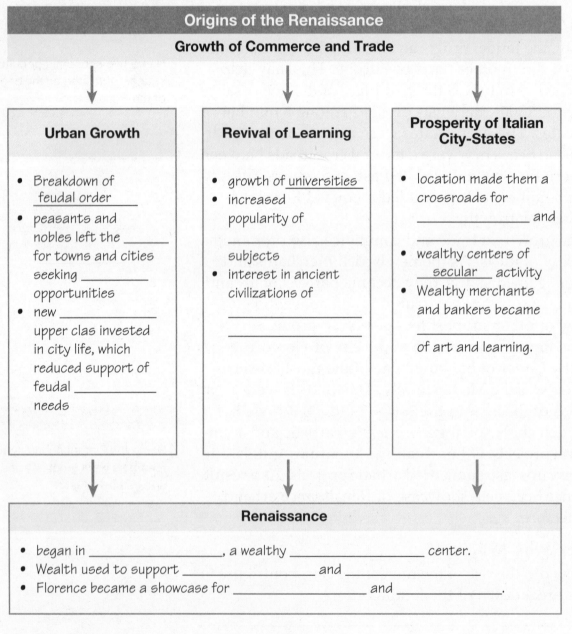

Origins of the Renaissance
Growth of Commerce and Trade

Urban Growth

- Breakdown of _feudal order_
- peasants and nobles left the _____ for towns and cities seeking _____ opportunities
- new _____ upper clas invested in city life, which reduced support of feudal _____ needs

Revival of Learning

- growth of _universities_
- increased popularity of _____ subjects
- interest in ancient civilizations of _____ _____

Prosperity of Italian City-States

- location made them a crossroads for _____ and _____
- wealthy centers of _secular_ activity
- Wealthy merchants and bankers became _____ of art and learning.

Renaissance

- began in _____, a wealthy _____ center.
- Wealth used to support _____ and _____
- Florence became a showcase for _____ and _____.

Refer to this page to answer the Chapter 17 Focus Question on page 221.

New Ways of Viewing the World

Section 2 Focus Question

How did the Renaissance reflect new ways of thinking? To begin answering this question,

- Find out about the "new learning" of the Renaissance.
- Learn how Renaissance art took a new direction.

Section 2 Summary

Renaissance thinkers looked to classical culture for a deeper understanding of human life. This was reflected in the art of the Italian Renaissance.

The "New Learning"

The rediscovery of Greek and Roman culture inspired the Renaissance. <u>Scholars call this revival of interest the "new learning."</u> The new learning suggested that human beings are worth studying as much as God and issues of faith. It also led to important new ideas: humanism, secularism, and individualism.

Humanism (HYOO muh nihz uhm)	Cultural movement of the Renaissance based on the study of classical works
Secularism (SEHK yuh ler ihz uhm)	View that religion need not be the center of education or other human affairs
Individualism (ihn duh VIHJ oo uhl ihz uhm)	Belief in the importance of the individual, as opposed to the larger community

Humanism valued learning as a means for self-improvement. The medieval focus on human sinfulness gave way to a belief in human excellence.

Secularism viewed life as an opportunity for enjoyment. This contrasted with the medieval belief that life was a painful pilgrimage to heaven. Secularism was reflected in the period's writing. Authors wrote to entertain or to inform rather than to promote religion. *The Decameron* by Giovanni Boccaccio was written in the **vernacular** (ver NAK yoo ler), or everyday spoken

Key Events

1300s	The Renaissance begins in Florence, Italy
1450	Gutenberg develops movable type.
1506	Leonardo da Vinci paints the *Mona Lisa*.
1601	Shakespeare writes *Hamlet*.

Vocabulary Builder

The word *revival* is made up of the prefix *re-* meaning "back" and a root meaning "to live." Write a definition for *revival* as it is used in the underlined sentence.

_____

_____

_____

language. *The Prince*, by Niccolò Machiavelli (mahk ee uh VEHL ee), described the realities of politics.

Individualism reflected the idea that the individual should be the judge of what was good or important. It also encouraged artists to seek recognition for their work. This was very different from the typical attitude of the medieval period. The artists who made most medieval art are unknown. Renaissance thinkers thought creativity brought glory to an individual. ☑

New Directions in Art

Renaissance art reflected these new ideas. <u>Most medieval art dealt with religious themes. Much Renaissance art did as well. But many artists wove in secular themes</u>. More and more, Renaissance art was not religious at all. Greek and Roman mythology were popular themes. Individual portraits, self-portraits, landscapes, and scenes of daily life became common.

Medieval art was stiff and unrealistic. But Renaissance art was realistic and showed the living world, including human emotions. New materials made this realism possible. Oil paints were developed in the 1400s. They produced softer shades and a richer blending of tones than the medieval tempera paints.

Renaissance artists took inspiration from Greek and Roman ideas about art and beauty. The ideas of harmony, proportion, or balance between parts, and mathematical ratio were important in creating beautiful works of art. ☑

Check Your Progress

1. What was the "new learning"?

_____

_____

_____

2. How did new paints help change art?

_____

_____

_____

✓ Checkpoint

Name three key Renaissance ideas.

_____

_____

_____

Reading Strategy

Reread the underlined sentences. Circle the word that tells you how Renaissance art was different from medieval art.

✓ Checkpoint

List four categories of paintings that became common during the Renaissance.

_____

_____

_____

_____

Question to Think About As you read Section 2 in your textbook and take notes, keep this section focus question in mind: **How did the Renaissance reflect new ways of thinking?**

▶ Complete these charts to record key information from the section. Some information has been filled in to get you started.

Renaissance Ideas		
Humanism	**Secularism**	**Individualism**
What it was: A cultural movement based on the study of classical works.	What it was: _____ _____ _____	What it was: _____ _____ _____
Why it was important: • emphasized human potential to _____ _____ • considered learning a means of _____ _____ _____	Why it was important: • changed medieval view that _____ _____ • considered life an _____ _____ _____	Why it was important: • believed that the individual_____ _____ _____ • encouraged artists and writers to _____ _____ _____ _____

Changes in Art	
Medieval Art	**Renaissance Art**
Content: • only _____ subjects Style: • _____ • _____ Material: • _____ • _____	Content: • secular themes reflected Renaissance ideas • subjects from Greek and Roman mythology Style: • _____ • _____ • _____ Material: • _____ that rendered soft shades and rich tones

Refer to this page to answer the Chapter 17 Focus Question on page 221.

Key Events

1300s	The Renaissance begins in Florence, Italy
1450	Gutenberg develops movable type.
1506	Leonardo da Vinci paints the *Mona Lisa*.
1601	Shakespeare writes *Hamlet*.

Reading Strategy

Why is this part of the summary titled "The Renaissance Moves North"? Was it really the Renaissance itself that left Italy?

_____

_____

Vocabulary Builder

The words *wisdom*, *sense*, and *logic* are antonyms of the word *folly*. Based on this and clues the text gives you about Erasmus's book, what would be a synonym of *folly*?

_____

_____

✓ Checkpoint

Name three northern European scholars who used "new learning" to bring about reforms.

_____

_____

_____

Section 3 Focus Question

Where and how did the ideas of the Renaissance spread? To begin answering this question,

- Learn about the Renaissance thinkers of northern Europe.
- Find out how Renaissance ideas spread.

Section 3 Summary

Northern Renaissance thinkers such as More, Erasmus, and Rabelais promoted change. Advances in printing and literacy spread Renaissance ideas.

The Renaissance Moves North

Scholars throughout Europe were drawn to Italy by the brilliance of the "new learning." They took the ideas of the Renaissance back to their home countries.

As the ideas spread, northern Europe became an important center of humanist scholarship. Northern scholars wanted to use the new learning to bring about reforms in the Church and society.

Thomas More (mor) was an English scholar best known for his book called *Utopia*. Utopia was the name More gave to his ideal society. This imaginary society was governed only by reason. Today, utopia (yoo TOH pee uh) means an ideal imaginary place. More's picture of Utopia showed the corruption of the Church and the governments of his time.

Another famous reformer was a Dutch scholar named Desiderius Erasmus (ee RAZ muhs). He believed that Church should use the life and lessons of Christ as its model. He claimed that the Church had abandoned Christian morality. Erasmus's most famous book was *The Praise of Folly*. It used satire to criticize the Church. A satire (SA tïr) is a piece of writing that attacks vice or folly through ridicule or sarcasm.

The French humanist François Rabelais (RAB uh lay) wrote the book *Gargantua and Pantagruel*. In this work, Rabelais pointed out the absurdity of much of traditional religion, education, and politics. ✓

The Dissemination of Ideas

Two new developments helped promote the dissemination, or spread, of humanist ideas: advances in printing and the expansion of literacy.

In the 1200s, the idea of block printing traveled from China to Europe. But this method was time-consuming and expensive. Other technologies advanced the art of making books in the 1300s. Europeans learned how to make paper out of linen rags and developed a useful oily ink. These improvements set the stage for a communications revolution.

In 1450, a German printer named Johann Gutenberg (GOOT uhn berg) invented movable metal type. The letters of this type could be rearranged and reused to form lines and then pages of text. The first book Gutenberg published was the Bible. Printing presses spread through Europe and by 1500, six million books had been printed.

With the invention of printing, the literacy rate in Europe began to rise. Most people wanted to read works in addition to the Bible. Printers began to publish works on medicine, travel, and other subjects. Governments used print to communicate with their subjects.

As the number of books increased, so did efforts to censor them. Censor (SEHN ser) means to remove material from published works or to prevent their publication. At first, the Church burned books it thought were offensive. It later required that all books get the Church's approval before publication. These measures were generally not effective.

The development of printing has been called a revolution as radical as the development of writing itself. It changed history forever. ✓

Check Your Progress

1. What did More, Erasmus and Rabelais aim to do through their writings?

_____

_____

2. What two developments promoted the spread of humanist ideas in the Renaissance?

_____

_____

✓ Checkpoint

How many books had been printed by 1500?

_____

Question to Think About As you read Section 3 in your textbook and take notes, keep this section focus question in mind: **Where and how did the ideas of the Renaissance spread?**

▶ Use this organizer to record key information from the section. Some of the information has been filled in to get you started.

The Spread of Renaissance Ideas			
Reformer	**Where from**	**What he wrote**	**Why important**
More	England	Utopia	revealed corruption of church and governments
Erasmus			
Rabelais		France	

Development of Movable Type

Who: Johann Gutenberg _____

When: _____

Why important:
- made printing much _____ and _____
- made books _____
- printing spread across _____
- increased _____ and helped spread _____ ideas
- Church increased efforts to _____ what people read

Dissemination of Ideas

Refer to this page to answer the Chapter 17 Focus Question on page 221.

Section 4

The Renaissance Legacy

Section 4 Focus Question

Who were important artists of the Renaissance and what was their legacy? To begin answering this question,

- Learn about the accomplishments of Renaissance architects and artists.
- Read about the literary legacy of the Renaissance.

Section 4 Summary

The Renaissance left an artistic, architectural, and literary legacy for modern society.

Architectural and Artistic Legacy

The Renaissance left an architectural and artistic legacy for modern society. Renaissance architects studied buildings of classical Greece and Rome. The column, the round arch, and the dome became popular features. Renaissance architects followed the principles of classical mathematics. They aimed to create beauty through harmony and proportion.

Filippo Brunelleschi was an early Renaissance architect. He long studied ancient Roman buildings. He wanted to understand their proportions. Using this knowledge, Brunelleschi built the dome of the cathedral of Santa Maria del Fiore. He also discovered the rules of **linear perspective** (LIHN ee er per SPEHK tihv). This is a mathematical system for representing three-dimensional space on a flat surface. This made it possible for paintings to look more realistic.

Another great figure was **Leonardo da Vinci** (lee uh NAR doh duh VIHN chee). He was an artist, writer, musician, scientist, and inventor. He is best known for two paintings, *The Last Supper* and the *Mona Lisa*. In the second work, Leonardo used a technique he invented called *sfumato*. Sfumato softens outlines and shadows. This produces an effect of distance. Leonardo also completed studies of human anatomy. Anatomy is the study of the body's structure. These studies greatly contributed to the world's scientific knowledge.

Key Events

1300s	The Renaissance begins in Florence, Italy
1450	Gutenberg develops movable type.
1506	Leonardo da Vinci paints the *Mona Lisa*.
1601	Shakespeare writes *Hamlet*.

Reading Strategy

The underlined sentence is the topic of this section of text. Underline three other sentences in this section that support this main idea.

✓ **Checkpoint**

Name three important Renaissance artists or architects.

_____

_____

_____

Vocabulary Builder

Reread the underlined sentence. How would its meaning be changed if the word *endure* were replaced with the phrase *are forgotten*?

_____

_____

✓ **Checkpoint**

Name three great writers of the Renaissance.

_____

_____

_____

Another Renaissance genius was Michelangelo Buonarroti, known simply as Michelangelo (mī kuhl AN juh loh). He was a painter, sculptor, architect, and poet. Michelangelo's most famous work is his painting on the ceiling of the Sistine Chapel. This masterpiece shows the stories of Creation and of Noah. The artist was often called the "divine Michelangelo." This means that his creations were godlike in their magnificence. ✓

The Literary Legacy

The Renaissance also left a strong literary legacy. Dante (DAHN tay) Alighieri was an Italian writer born in the late 1200s. His long poem *The Divine Comedy* describes an imaginary journey through heaven and hell. Dante wrote in Italian rather than in Latin. His writing in the vernacular helped shape Italian as a written language.

William Shakespeare (SHAYK spir) was born 300 years after Dante in England. He is generally considered the world's greatest playwright. His work had a great impact on the development of English. <u>Many expressions from Shakespeare's plays, sonnets, and other poetry endure today</u>. A sonnet (SAHN iht) is a poem of fourteen lines with a fixed rhyming pattern. Shakespeare's work is also famous for its deep understanding of humanity that is universal and timeless.

Miguel de Cervantes (ser VAHN teez) was a Spanish writer who lived around the same time as Shakespeare. His most famous novel is *Don Quixote*. Cervantes was a key figure in the growth of Spanish literature. He also played a role in the development of the novel. ✓

Check Your Progress

1. What features of architecture did Renaissance artists borrow from ancient Rome and Greece?

_____

_____

2. What was significant about Dante writing in the vernacular?

_____

_____

_____

Question to Think About As you read Section 4 in your textbook and take notes, keep this section focus question in mind: **Who were important artists of the Renaissance and what was their legacy?**

▶ Use these charts to record key information from the section. Some information has been filled in to get you started.

Renaissance Architectural and Artistic Legacy		
Artist	**Important work(s)**	**Other notable facts**
Brunelleschi	• Dome of the cathedral of Santa Maria del Fiore	Discovered rules of linear perspective
Leonardo da Vinci	• •	• artist, _____, _____, _____, and _____ • painting technique: _____ • studied _____
Michelangelo	• Sistine Chapel	• painter, _____, _____, and _____ • mastery of _____ and _____
Renaissance Architecture		
• modeled works on classical architecture of <u>Greece</u> and _____ • used _____ and _____ to create beauty • Important features: <u>column</u> , _____, _____		

Renaissance Writers				
Writer	**When**	**Where**	**Works**	**Why important**
Dante	Late 1200s	Italy	• *The Divine Comedy*	Wrote in vernacular; helped shape Italian as a written language
Shakespeare			• 37 plays • sonnets and other poetry	• shaped the development of the _____ • his work shows a deep understanding of _____
Cervantes			•	• key role in the development of _____ • key figure in the growth of the _____

Refer to this page to answer the Chapter 17 Focus Question on page 221.

Directions: Circle the letter of the correct answer.

1. The Italian city-states were
   A   all well-positioned port cities.
   B   located at a natural crossroads on the Mediterranean.
   C   located inland.

2. One humanist scholar and reformer from northern Europe was
   A   Johann Gutenberg.
   B   Shakespeare.
   C   Thomas More.

3. Which of the following is a well-known Renaissance architect?
   A   Filippo Brunelleschi
   B   Niccolò Machiavelli
   C   Dante Alighieri

Directions: Follow the steps to answer this question: **What made the art of the Renaissance different from the art of the Middle Ages?**

Step 1: Recall: Identify the key ideas of Renaissance learning and art.

_____

_____

Step 2: Describe how these ideas differed from those of the Middle Ages.

Renaissance Ideas	How It Differed From Medieval Ideas

Step 3: Complete the topic sentence that follows. Then write two or three more sentences that support your opinion.

The art of the Renaissance was different from the art of Middle Ages because _____

_____

_____

_____

Now you are ready to answer the Chapter 17 Focus Question: **What was the Renaissance?**

▶ Fill in the following charts to help you answer this question. Use the notes that you took for each section.

The Renaissance

Origins of the Renaissance

- People migrated from __manors__ to towns.
- _____ subjects became more popular.
- People rediscovered the culture of ancient _____ and _____.
- Italian _____ became centers of _____ activity.
- _____ became a major banking center.

New Ideas of the Renaissance	The Spread of Ideas	Artistic Legacy
- **Humanism:** <u>Cultural movement based on the study of classical works</u> - **Secularism:** _____ _____ _____ - **Individualism:** _____ _____ _____ - **Art:** • Less focus on _____ • New emphasis on _____	- Northern Europe became a center for _____ of the Church and society. - Books criticized the _____ of the Church. - With the invention of movable type, the _____ rate rose. - Church's reaction to increase in printed books: • _____ • _____	- **Architecture:** • focused on _____ and _____ - **Art:** • _____ was a multitalented genius who invented the technique of _____. • _____'s figures seemed very real because of his mastery of _____. - **Literature:** • Dante: poetry shaped Italian as a _____ • Shakespeare: experimented with _____ and _____ • Cervantes: played a key role in development of the _____

Refer to this page to answer the Unit 7 Focus Question on page 267.

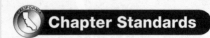
Chapter 18

The Reformation (1517–1688)

What You Will Learn

The Reformation, a protest against certain practices in the Catholic Church, had far-reaching effects on European society.

Chapter 18 Focus Question

As you read the section in this chapter, keep this question in mind: **What was the Reformation and how did it change Europe?**

Section 1

The Origins of the Reformation

Section 1 Focus Question

How did the leaders of the Reformation challenge the Catholic Church? To begin to answer this question,

- Find out about Martin Luther's challenges to the Church.
- Learn about the spread of Protestant ideas.

Section 1 Summary

The Reformation began as a protest against abuses in the Catholic Church. The Protestant movement grew and spread through much of Europe.

Luther Challenges the Church

The Reformation (rehf uhr MAY shuhn) was a movement that began in the 1500s to reform the Catholic Church.

In 1509, a German monk named Martin Luther (LOO thuhr) visited Rome. He was shocked by what he saw. Church officials seemed to care more about wealth and power than saving souls. The Church sold indulgences (ihn DUHL juhns sez). These were pardons for sins. This angered Luther the most. He wrote a list of theses, or arguments, against indulgences, and posted the list on

Key Events

1517	Luther posts his 95 Theses.
1598	Catholic Church becomes official church of France.
1648	Treaty of Westphalia ends the Thirty Years' War.
1688	Glorious Revolution takes place in England.

a church door. Copies of the theses quickly spread across Europe.

Martin Luther's 95 Theses
• Challenged Church authority
• Stressed spiritual, inward nature of faith
• Said that God gives salvation as a gift to all Christians
• Stated that salvation cannot be bought

In the city of Worms, Luther was called to trial before an assembly, or diet. Luther refused to take back his criticism. The Holy Roman Emperor declared Luther an outlaw, but many people in Germany hailed him as a hero. ☑

The Protestant Movement Grows

Protestant sects sprang up all over Europe. John Calvin (KAL vihn) was one of the most important leaders. Like Luther, he believed that salvation came through faith alone. He also believed in predestination (pree dehs tuh NAY shun). This is the idea that God long ago had determined who would gain salvation. In Geneva, Switzerland, Calvin set up a theocracy (thee AHK ruh see), or government ruled by religious leaders.

With the help of the printing press, Protestant ideas spread throughout Europe. In 1534, Martin Luther produced the first Bible in German. He wanted ordinary people to read the Bible for themselves. William Tyndale (TIHN duhl) printed an English Bible, which spread Reformation ideas to England. The Catholic Church officials burned him at the stake for heresy. ☑

Check Your Progress

1. Why was Martin Luther shocked on his visit to Rome?

   _____

   _____

2. Why did Martin Luther produce Bibles in German?

   _____

   _____

Name the Catholic Church practice that angered Martin Luther the most.

_____

Vocabulary Builder

Democracy means government by the people. What do you think the Greek root *theo* means in the word *theocracy*?

_____

Reading Strategy

Circle three Protestant leaders mentioned in this section. Then, underline an accomplishment of each.

✓ Checkpoint

Name the person who helped to bring Reformation ideas to England.

_____

Question to Think About As you read Section 1 in your textbook and take notes, keep this question in mind: **How did the leaders of the Reformation challenge the Catholic Church?**

▶ Use these charts to record key information from the section. Some of the information has been filled in to get you started.

The Origins of the Reformation
Martin Luther
• Noted the following abuses by the Catholic Church on a visit to Rome:
• <u>Clergy more interested in amassing wealth and power than saving souls</u>
• _____
• _____
• _____
• _____
• Luther responded by _____
• This action challenged _____ and stressed
_____.
• The Diet of Worms
• Its purpose: <u>to put Luther on trial for attacking the Church</u>
• Luther's response: _____
• Result: _____
John Calvin
• Published book called <u>The Institutes of Christian Religion</u>
• Its importance: _____
• Calvin's beliefs
• Salvation: _____
• Sole source of religious truth: _____
• "City of God"
• Location: _____
• What Calvin was asked to do: _____
• Results: _____
The Printing Press Helps to Spread Protestant Ideas
• Martin Luther's contribution in 1534: <u>the first translation of the Bible into German</u>
• Importance: _____
• William Tyndale's contribution: _____

Refer to this page to answer the Chapter 18 Focus Question on page 235.

Section 2

The Counter-Reformation

Section 2 Focus Question

How did the Catholic Church respond to the Reformation? To begin to answer this question,
- Learn about the Society of Jesus.
- Find out about the Council of Trent.

Section 2 Summary

Leaders of the Catholic Church began to make reforms. New religious orders gained respect for the Church. However, the Church also fought the spread of Protestantism.

The Society of Jesus

The Catholic Church began to make changes. The movement to strengthen the teachings and structure of the church became known as the Counter-Reformation (KOWNT er rehf uhr MAY shuhn).

During this period, Catholic reformers founded new religious orders. These organizations helped the poor and taught Catholic doctrine. They also led spiritual lives. This won new respect for the Church.

The Society of Jesus was the most influential of these new orders. It was founded by Ignatius Loyola (loi OH luh). Today we call this group the Jesuits (JEHZ oo ihts). Their goal was to defend and spread the Catholic faith worldwide.

Ignatius Loyola ran the Society like a military unit. Members lived under strict rules, and new recruits had to go through years of difficult training.

The Jesuits helped correct some of the abuses of the Church. They helped the sick and the poor. Jesuit missionaries spread the faith to distant lands. They worked in places such as Africa, Asia, and the Americas. One missionary, Francis Xavier, was said to have converted hundreds of thousands of Asians.

The Jesuits also founded schools and universities. They did important work in both religious and secular scholarship. Jesuits also served as advisers to kings and popes. ☑

Key Events

1517	Luther posts his 95 Theses.
1598	Catholic Church becomes official church of France.
1648	Treaty of Westphalia ends the Thirty Years' War.
1688	Glorious Revolution takes place in England.

Vocabulary Builder

Reread the bracketed paragraph. *Convert* can refer to any kind of change. What kind of change is described here?

_____

_____

✓ Checkpoint

Name the movement to strengthen Church teachings and structure.

_____

The Council of Trent

In 1545, Pope Paul III called a series of meetings known as the Council of Trent (KOWN suhl uhv trehnt). Their goals were to revive the moral authority of the Catholic Church and to stop the spread of Protestantism. The Council was the peak of the Counter-Reformation.

The Council reaffirmed traditional Catholic doctrines, or teachings. It rejected Luther's view of the Bible. The Council said the Bible was not the only source of truth. It stated that faith alone would not bring salvation. Good works must also be done. Finally, the Council affirmed that people had free will. The Council also made sweeping major reforms, including better training for priests.

The Church enforced the Council's decisions through the Inquisition. The Inquisition was a court set up to find people who were guilty of heresy, or beliefs that disagreed with the Church. Suspects were harshly questioned and often tortured before being put to death.

The Inquisition tried people even for small violations. Protestants living in Catholic lands were among its victims. Some church leaders and nobles fled for their lives. Those unable to escape were burned at the stake for their beliefs.

The Church banned books to stop the spread of Protestant ideas. It published an Index of Forbidden Books. These were books that Catholics were not allowed to read. The list included books by Martin Luther, John Calvin, and William Tyndale. ☑

Check Your Progress

1. How did the Jesuits help education and learning?

_____

_____

_____

2. What were the two main goals of the Council of Trent?

_____

_____

_____

Reading Strategy

Martin Luther taught that Christians reached salvation by studying the Bible. Underline the two sentences that describe the Council's teachings about salvation.

✓ Checkpoint

List three authors whose books were banned by the Inquisition.

_____

_____

_____

Question to Think About As you read Section 2 in your textbook and take notes, keep this section focus question in mind: **How did the Catholic Church respond to the Reformation?**

▶ Use this chart to record key information from the section. Some of the information has been filled in to get you started.

Elements of the Counter-Reformation	

Jesuits	• Formal name: _the Society of Jesus_
	• Founder: _____
	• Main goals:
	  • _defend the Catholic faith_
	  • _____
	• Reached out to people by
	  • _____
	  • _____
	• Sent _missionaries_ to _____, _____, and _____ to spread _____ .
	• The Jesuits founded _____. Some Jesuits served as _____ to popes and kings.

Council of Trent	Goals
	• to revive _the moral authority of the Catholic Church_
	• to stop _____
	Results
	• reaffirmed _traditional Catholic teachings_, including
	  • _____
	  • _____
	  • _____
	• reforms to Catholic practices, including
	  • _____
	  • _____
	  • _____

The Inquisition	• Enforced: _the Council of Trent's decisions_ • A court that tried people for: _____ • Many people found guilty were _____ .
Index of Forbidden Books	• Created to battle _the spread of Protestantism_ • Was a list of _____ • Banned books by _____, _____, and _____ .

Refer to this page to answer the Chapter 18 Focus Question on page 235.

The Division of Christendom

© Pearson Education, Inc., publishing as Pearson Prentice Hall. All Rights Reserved.

Key Events

1517	Luther posts his 95 Theses.
1598	Catholic Church becomes official church of France.
1648	Treaty of Westphalia ends the Thirty Years' War.
1688	Glorious Revolution takes place in England.

Reading Strategy

Reread the paragraph. The last sentence describes an effect: *In 1534, England passed an Act of Supremacy, making the king the head of an independent Church of England.* Underline the cause of this effect.

✓ Checkpoint

Name the law that made King Henry VIII the head of the Church of England.

Section 3 Focus Question

How did religious conflict divide Europe? To begin to answer this question,

- Find out about the spread of Protestantism in northern Europe.
- Learn about Spain's attempts to secure Catholicism in southern Europe.

Section 3 Summary

The Lutheran Church spread quickly in northern Europe. In other areas, religious wars erupted. Spain used its military strength in an attempt to defend Catholicism in Europe.

Protestant Northern Europe

Protestantism grew quickly in northern Europe. In some places, the ideas of Luther and Calvin took hold easily. In others, fighting erupted over religion.

In England, Protestants were exiled or killed. In 1529, however, the pope refused King Henry VIII's (HEHN ree thuh ayth) request for a marriage annulment (uh NUHL muhnt). An annulment is an official action ending a marriage. Henry remarried anyway. In 1534, England passed the Act of Supremacy (soo PREHM uh see). This made the king the head of an independent Church of England.

In southern Germany, the Holy Roman Emperor sided with the Catholic Church. Other German leaders were Protestant. This led to eight years of war. The Peace of Augsburg ended the war in 1555. It allowed each German prince to decide which religion his subjects would follow. ✓

Catholic Southern Europe

Protestantism spread into southern Europe as well. However, the countries of southern Europe remained mostly Catholic. In 1534, the Huguenots, as French Protestants were called, denounced the Catholic Church. Hundreds of Protestants were arrested. Some were burned alive for their views. Civil war broke out between Catholics and Huguenots in 1560. In the worst incident, some 3,000 Huguenots were killed in the St. Bartholomew's Day <u>Massacre</u> in Paris in 1572.

Henry of Navarre, a Huguenot, was the rightful heir to the throne. However, French Catholics did not want a Protestant king. In 1593 Henry became a Catholic. He was crowned Henry IV (HENH ree thuh forth) the next year. In 1598, he issued the Edict of Nantes. An edict (EE dihkt) is an official public order made by a king or another authority. The edict made the Catholic Church the official church of France. It also gave the Huguenots religious freedom.

Philip II (FIHL ihp thuh SEHK uhnd), the Catholic ruler of Spain, used the Inquisition against Protestants and paid for troops to fight them in other countries. In 1555, Philip inherited control of the Netherlands, where many people were Calvinists. The Dutch people rebelled against Spanish control. The rebellion lasted more than 75 years. Finally the northern Netherlands were freed from Spanish control.

Philip was angry that Elizabeth I, queen of England, had aided the Dutch. He wanted to force England back to the Catholic Church. In 1588, he sent an armada (ahr MAH duh), or fleet of ships, to attack England. However, English ships attacked and sank most of the Spanish fleet.

Spain found little success in its efforts to restore Catholicism. It became involved in the Thirty Years' War. In 1618, the Holy Roman Emperor fought against Protestants in what is now the Czech Republic. Other countries joined the conflict. Their armies fought their way across Germany. Finally, in 1648, the Treaty of Westphalia ended the war. The Treaty let people practice their own religion, even if it was different from the king's religion. ✓

Check Your Progress

1. What were two results of the Peace of Augsburg?

_____

_____

2. Against what country did Philip II send his armada?

_____

_____

Look up *massacre*. Explain how i means more than simply "to kill."

_____

_____

_____

_____

✓ Checkpoint

Name the conflict that the Treaty of Westphalia ended.

_____

Question to Think About As you read Section 3 in your textbook and take notes, keep this section focus question in mind: **How did religious conflict divide Europe?**

▶ Use these charts to record key information from the section. Some of the information has been filled in to get you started.

Religious Divisions in Europe			
	Lutheranism	**Calvinism**	**Catholicism**
Countries and regions of countries	• Sweden • • • • northern Germany	• Switzerland • •	• Italy • • •

Political and Religious Conflicts	
Reformation in England	Parliament declared the <u>Church of England</u> to be independent of the Catholic Church. The _____ made the _____ leader of the church.
Religious Warfare in Germany	The Holy Roman Emperor forced the people in some German cities to convert to _____, which led to _____. The Peace of Augsburg allowed _____.
Religious Conflicts in France	French Protestants were known as ___Huguenots____. Major events • 1534: Huguenots denounced the Catholic Church and hundreds were arrested and some were burned alive. • 1560: • 1572: The heir to the French throne, Henry of Navarre, was a _____. He had to convert to _____ to become king. The Edict of Nantes made _____ the official church of France, but allowed _____.
Philip II	Used the _____ against Protestants and financed _____ to fight against Protestants. Sent an _____ to attack England.
The Thirty Years' War	In 1618, the <u>Holy Roman Emperor</u> fought against_____ in _____. Soon _____, _____, and _____ sent troops to fight _____. Soldiers fought their way across _____. In 1648, _____ ended the war.

Refer to this page to answer the Chapter 18 Focus Question on page 235.

The Political Impact of the Reformation

Section 4 Focus Question

How did the Reformation affect the way nations were ruled? To begin to answer this question,

- Learn how monarchs gained new power.
- Find out about other new forms of government in Europe.

© Pearson Education, Inc., publishing as Pearson Prentice Hall. All Rights Reserved.

Section 4 Summary

Rulers gained political power in Europe during this period. New forms of government developed in France and England. In Europe, Protestants tried out new ideas of self-government.

Royal Rulers Increase Their Power

The armies that fought the Thirty Years' War showed the growing power of Europe's secular rulers. In the Middle Ages, wars had been fought by small armies. During the Thirty Years' War, strong kings taxed large areas to equip large armies.

The Thirty Years' War weakened the power of the pope. The pope opposed the Treaty of Westphalia but Europe's monarchs simply ignored him. Kings and queens would now define the religious future of their nations. ✓

New Ways of Governing

As European nations grew in size and power, new kinds of government appeared.

After the religious wars, Europeans wanted stability. In France, political thinkers argued for an **absolute monarchy** (AB suh loot MAHN uhr kee). An absolute monarch had complete power over the government and the people. Absolute monarchs made laws, declared new taxes, and appointed officials. France's absolute monarchs believed that they ruled by the **divine right of kings** (duh VIN rīt uhv kihngz). This theory states that a king's right to rule comes from God.

Key Events

1517	Luther posts his 95 Theses.
1598	Catholic Church becomes official church of France.
1648	Treaty of Westphalia ends the Thirty Years' War.
1688	Glorious Revolution takes place in England.

✓ Checkpoint

Name a figure who lost power as a result of the Thirty Years' War.

_____

Vocabulary Builder

Reread the description of absolute monarchs in this paragraph. What is a word that means the opposite of *absolute*, as it is used here?

_____

These ideas created a powerful leader in France's king Louis XIV (LOO ee thuh FOR TEENTH). He raised taxes for building projects and appointed town and Church officials. He reversed earlier policy and closed Protestant churches.

England, however, had a history of limiting royal power. Parliament gradually gained power. It came into conflict with kings who wanted to raise taxes without its approval. This conflict reached a crisis in 1641. Parliament's troops fought the king's army in the English Civil War. The king was executed. England became a republic until 1660, when the monarchy was restored.

When a new king threatened a return to the Catholic Church, Parliament invited William of Orange, a Dutch prince married to the king's daughter Mary, to become king. Both William and Mary were Protestant. They took the throne. This event is known as the Glorious Revolution. William and Mary agreed to accept the English Bill of Rights. It protected such rights as holding property and worshiping in the religion of one's choice. It also established a **constitutional monarchy** (kahn stuh TOO shuh nuhl MAHN uhr kee). This is a form of government in which a king or queen's power is limited by a constitution.

At the same time, Protestant nations were learning about self-government. In Geneva, Calvinist churches elected their leaders. Protestants began to voice opinions on politics, as well as religion. A German Calvinist, John Althusius, thought his city should rule itself. He was the first to write about **federalism** (FEHD uhr uhl ihz uhm). This is a form of government in which power is shared between local and national levels. Federalist ideas would later influence the Constitution of the United States. ✓

✓ Checkpoint

What concept caused absolute monarchs to believe that they were worthy of such power?

_____

_____

Check Your Progress

1. How did the Thirty Years' War show the growing power of kings?

_____

_____

2. What was the Glorious Revolution?

_____

_____

Question to Think About As you read Section 4 in your textbook and take notes, keep this section focus question in mind: **How did the Reformation affect how nations were ruled?**

▶ Use this chart to record key information from the section. Some of the information has been filled in to get you started.

The Political Impact of the Reformation	
Royal Rulers Increase Their Power	
Changes in Warfare	Warfare in the Middle Ages: <u>small armies supplied by lords fought wars</u> Warfare during the Thirty Years' War: _____ This meant: _____ _____
Growing Power of Secular Rulers	Rulers gained control over <u>religious affairs in their kingdoms</u> Monarchy gained power by _____
New Ways of Governing in Europe	
Absolute Monarchy in France	What absolute monarchy means: _____ _____ French monarchs believed their rule was by <u>divine right</u> Famous French absolute monarch: _____
Constitutional Monarchy in England	Importance of the Magna Carta: _____ _____ Role of Parliament: _____ Major events in history of Constitutional Monarchy in England • 1641: <u>Conflict between Parliament and the king led to the outbreak of the English Civil War.</u> • 1649: _____ • 1660: _____ Glorious Revolution • Parliament's problem: _____ • Parliament's solution: _____ English Bill of Rights • Protected the <u>rights to hold property and worship freely</u> • Recognized _____ • Established _____
Experiments in Self-Government	In Geneva, <u>Protestants</u> elected their own leaders. Protestant leaders encouraged individuals to _____, which led people to voice opinions about _____ and _____ issues.

Refer to this page to answer the Chapter 18 Focus Question on page 235.

Directions: Circle the letter of the correct answer.

1. Martin Luther believed that
   A God had decided long ago who would be saved.
   B the priests in Rome were closest to God.
   C salvation was a gift from God.

2. Which of these aided the spread of Protestantism?
   A the Jesuits
   B the printing press
   C the Spanish Armada

3. Why was the Treaty of Westphalia so significant?
   A It allowed people to practice their own religions.
   B It re-established Catholic power in Germany.
   C Henry IV gave the Huguenots freedom of worship.

Directions: Follow the steps to answer this question:

How did the actions of rulers influence the Reformation?

Step 1: Recall information. Complete the chart below:

Henry VIII of England	1. Wanted the pope to _____ his marriage 2. Parliament passed _____, making him head of _____ 3. This church was _____ of the Catholic Church
Henry IV of France	1. Initially practiced the _____ religion 2. Took throne after he _____ 3. Made declaration called _____, which allowed _____ to worship _____

Step 2: Make Connections: How did each ruler's actions affect the Reformation?

Ruler	Influence on Reformation
Henry VIII of England	
Henry IV of France	

Step 3: Complete the topic sentence that follows. Then, write two or three more sentences that support your topic sentence.

The actions of rulers affected the course of the Reformation by _____

_____

_____

_____

Now you are ready to answer the Chapter 18 Focus Question: **What was the Reformation and how did it change Europe?**

▶ Complete the following graphic organizer to help you answer this question. Use the notes that you took for each section.

The Reformation and Its Effects on Europe
Martin Luther
• Angry at Church corruption, especially the sale of _____, Luther posted his _____ on a church door.
• The Holy Roman Emperor called Luther before a _____, or assembly, in the city of _____.
• Luther was <u>declared an outlaw</u>, but thousands <u>hailed him as a hero</u>.
The Reformation
• Luther's ideas spread quickly, with the help of the _____.
• John Calvin set up a _____ in Geneva.
• William Tyndale carried Reformation ideas to _____, and was executed.
The Counter-Reformation
• Founding of new religious orders, like the <u>Jesuits</u>, which won respect for the Catholic Church by <u>helping the poor</u>, <u>teaching Catholic doctrine</u>, and <u>leading spiritual lives</u>.
• The Council of Trent tried to revive the _____ of the Catholic Church and stop the spread of _____.
• The _____ enforced the Council's rulings using trials, torture, and executions.
Conflicts
• Europe was divided by religion: northern Europe was _____ and southern Europe was _____.
• French Protestants, called _____, fought a civil war against the Catholic majority.
• The _____ involved many countries. Their armies battled in <u>Germany</u>, causing heavy damage.
• The _____ ended the war in 1648 and allowed people to practice their own religion.
Political Changes
• France favored an _____, a ruler with total power.
• The idea that a monarch's power came from God was called _____.
• England's government evolved into a _____.
• John Althusius introduced the idea of _____, which is a form of government in which power is shared between <u>local and national levels</u>.

Refer to this page to answer the Unit 6 Focus Question on page 267.

Key Events

1492	Christopher Columbus crosses the Atlantic.
1520s–1530s	Spanish conquer Aztec and Inca empires.
1607	English found Jamestown colony in North America.
1600s	Europe adopts capitalism and mercantilism.

Vocabulary Builder

Reread the bracketed paragraph. Write a synonym for *modified*.

_____

_____

✓ Checkpoint

Name two types of ocean-going ships.

_____

_____

Chapter 19

The Age of Exploration (1400–1700)

What You Will Learn

European sailors explored much of the world. Europeans conquered the societies they found in the Americas and set up colonies there.

Chapter 19 Focus Question

As you read the sections in this chapter, keep this question in mind: **How did the world change during the Age of Exploration?**

Section 1

The Voyages of Discovery

Section 1 Focus Question

How did advances in technology spur new voyages of discovery? To begin to answer this question,
- Explore the advances in sailing technology.
- Learn about voyages into the unknown.

Section 1 Summary

Europeans set out to find ocean routes to Asia that bypassed the Mediterranean.

Advances in Sailing Technology

In the 1400s, explorers from Portugal and Spain made many voyages to find gold, spices, and Catholic converts. Advances in mapmaking, navigation, and shipbuilding helped explorers on these voyages.

During the Renaissance, mapmakers invented cartography. **Cartography** (kahr TAHG ruh fee) is the science of making maps and globes. Sailors began to use the compass and the astrolabe to navigate the ocean.

New ships were also invented. European shipbuilders modified a ship called a caravel. The caravel was a small ship that was fast and easy to steer. They designed a larger ship called a galleon for long-distance trips. Galleons were fast, and had room for a large crew, supplies, and trade goods. ✓

Voyages Into the Unknown

Portuguese ships led the world in exploration. They sailed down the western coast of Africa. Their goal was to sail south around Africa to Asia. In 1487, Bartolomeu Dias and his crew sailed past the southern tip of Africa. Finally, in 1497, Vasco da Gama (duh GAH muh) sailed all the way to India.

Christopher Columbus (kuh LUHM buhs) was a merchant from Italy. He hoped to sail west across the Atlantic to Asia. With backing from the rulers of Spain, he set sail in 1492. When he landed on an island in what is today the Bahamas, Columbus thought he had reached lands off the coast of China.

An Italian navigator named Amerigo Vespucci (ves POOT chee) believed that the lands Columbus found were part of a "New World." The new lands were eventually named "America," a version of Vespucci's first name.

Ferdinand Magellan (muh JEHL uhn) went on the biggest voyage of discovery in 1519 from Spain. He had five ships and a crew of more than 250. He hoped to find a sea route west across the Atlantic, as Columbus had tried to do. But Magellan knew that a continent stood in his way. He sailed south along the uncharted continent, through a strait, or narrow channel, and into the Pacific Ocean.

He continued west across the Pacific. Many, including Magellan, died during the voyage. Only one ship and 31 crew members made it back to Spain. They had circumnavigated (ser kuhm NAV uh gay ted), or sailed completely around, the world. ✓

Check Your Progress

1. What two things helped sailors navigate the open ocean?

_____

_____

2. What was the achievement of Ferdinand Magellan's crew?

_____

_____

© Pearson Education, Inc., publishing as Pearson Prentice Hall. All Rights Reserved.

Reading Strategy

Reread the bracketed paragraph. Circle the topic sentence.

✓ Checkpoint

For whom was *America* named?

_____

Question to Think About As you read Section 1 in your textbook and take notes, keep this section focus question in mind: **How did advances in technology spur new voyages of discovery?**

► Use these organizers to record key information from the section.

Advances in Sailing Technology

Explorers in the 1400s from _____ and _____ set off on voyages of discovery. These voyages were made possible by advances in:

Cartography

- Cartography is the
  _____
  _____

Navigation

Advances in Navigation
New Tools:
- Compass: showed direction
- _____:
  determined a ship's north-south position based on the stars.

Shipbuilding

New ocean-going ships:
- The _____ was small, fast, and easy to maneuver.
- The _____ was a larger ship, built for long-distance voyages.

Voyages Into the Unknown

1487: Portuguese captain Bartolomeu Dias was the first to sail past
_____
_____
_____.

1497: Portuguese explorer Vasco da Gama made a round-trip voyage from
_____
to _____.

1492: Christopher Columbus set sail with three ships across the Atlantic.
- He believed he had reached islands off the coast of _____.
- He actually landed in _____.

Early 1500s: _____
_____ believed Columbus had discovered part of a "New World."

1519: Ferdinand Magellan hoped to find a sea route west across the Atlantic.
- Magellan sailed south until he reached a strait that led to the _____
  _____.
- Magellan died during the voyage.
- His fleet was the first to _____
  _____.

Refer to this page to answer the Chapter 19 Focus Question on page 249.

Section 2

The Conquest of the Americas

Section 2 Focus Question

How did Spain gain wealth and territory at the expense of the Aztecs and Incas? To begin to answer this question,

- Learn how the Spanish conquered two empires.
- Find out about the impact of Spain's conquest.

Section 2 Summary

The Aztec and Inca empires were large and powerful, but both were quickly defeated by the Spanish.

The Spanish Conquer Two Empires

In the Americas, Spain quickly began colonization (kahl uh nih ZAY shuhn), or the process of taking over territory, creating a new government, and settling towns. The Spanish explorers and soldiers who conquered territory were known as conquistadors (kahn KWIHS tuh dors).

In 1519, Hernán Cortés (kor TEHZ) sailed to Mexico to conquer the rich Aztecs. The Aztecs had a large empire, with Moctezuma (MAWK tay SOO mah) as their leader. Cortés only had about 600 soldiers. However, he made friends with other Mexican peoples. Tens of thousands of native soldiers joined Cortés to fight the Aztecs.

In the battle that broke out, Moctezuma was killed. The Spanish surrounded the Aztec capital city. Soon after, a smallpox epidemic killed many Aztecs. The survivors surrendered in 1521.

Another Spaniard, Francisco Pizarro (pee THAHR roh), heard rumors of another large empire in South America. He led a small group of conquistadors to find the Inca Empire in 1531. A smallpox epidemic had already killed many Incas, including the Inca emperor. After a civil war, Atahualpa (ah tuh WAHL puh) became the new emperor. However, the war had left the empire weak and divided.

Pizarro took advantage of this weakness. He invited Atahualpa to a friendly meeting, and then had him

Key Events

1492	Christopher Columbus crosses the Atlantic.
1520s–1530s	Spanish conquer Aztec and Inca empires.
1607	English found Jamestown colony in North America.
1600s	Europe adopts capitalism and mercantilism.

✓ Checkpoint

Name the Inca emperor who was imprisoned and killed by Pizarro.

_____

Reading Strategy

Reread the bracketed paragraph. Circle the phrase that tells you how often the galleons carried gold and silver bullion from the Americas to Europe.

Vocabulary Builder

Reread the underlined sentence. Circle the word that the phrase *very big* or the word *huge* could replace.

✓ Checkpoint

Under Spanish rule, what became the name of the Aztec territories?

_____

imprisoned and killed. The Inca Empire could not unite without its leader. In 1533, the Spanish captured the Inca capital, Cuzco. ✓

The Impact of Conquest

The Spanish had defeated the Aztec and Inca empires. The former Aztec Empire became the Spanish territory of New Spain. The territory of Peru was established where the Incas had once ruled. These colonies brought great wealth to Spain. But the Aztecs and Incas were devastated. Disease had killed millions of people. Their cultural treasures were destroyed.

The wealth of the Aztecs and Incas was taken to Spain. Each year, a large fleet of galleons carried gold and silver bullion (BOOL yuhn) from the Americas to Europe. Bullion is precious metal melted into bars. Sometimes, pirates attacked the ships. Other galleons sank. Other European countries began to send their own explorers to conquer colonies for themselves.

<u>While Aztec and Inca gold enriched Spain, the loss to Native American culture was monumental.</u> Native art was melted down and lost forever. The cities were torn down, and new cities were built over the ruins. The Spanish attacked native religions by destroying temples, statues of gods, and books. History books were also burned, erasing important information.

The greatest loss was the millions of Aztecs and Incas who died from smallpox. They had no immunity (ih MYOON uh tee), or the ability of the body to fight a disease. The Spanish, on the other hand, had built up a resistance to the disease. These losses weakened the very foundations of Aztec and Inca cultures. ✓

Check Your Progress

1. How did Cortés gather the troops he needed to fight the Aztecs?

_____

_____

2. What caused the largest number of deaths among the Aztecs and Incas?

_____

_____

Question to Think About As you read Section 2 in your textbook and take notes, keep this section focus question in mind: **How did Spain gain wealth and territory at the expense of the Aztecs and Incas?**

▶ Use this organizer to record key information from the section.

The Fall of Two Empires

Aztec Empire

- In 1519, Cortés sailed to _____ to conquer the Aztec Empire.
- _____, the Aztec emperor, was killed.
- The Spanish began a siege of the city.
- A _____ struck, killing many _____.
- Aztecs surrendered in _____.

Inca Empire

- A smallpox epidemic struck the Inca empire, killing _____.
- Civil war broke out.
- _____ became the new emperor.
- _____ imprisoned and then killed Atahualpa.
- In _____ the Inca Empire crumbled and the Spanish emerged as victors.

Wealth of Spain

- The _____ became New Spain, and the Inca Empire became known as _____.
- The colonies brought great wealth to Spain.
- Each year, a fleet of _____ loaded with Inca and Aztec _____ sailed for Spain.

Loss of Culture

- The Spanish melted down Aztec and Inca _____.
- Conquistadors destroyed _____ and stripped _____ of their riches.
- The Spaniards attacked native religions by destroying _____ and killing _____.
- The conquistadors destroyed records of Inca history by burning _____ and _____.

Refer to this page to answer the Chapter 19 Focus Question on page 249.

1492	Christopher Columbus crosses the Atlantic.
1520s–1530s	Spanish conquer Aztec and Inca empires.
1607	English found Jamestown colony in North America.
1600s	Europe adopts capitalism and mercantilism.

Reading Strategy

Reread the bracketed paragraphs. Underline the European powers that had colonies in the Americas. Then draw an arrow from each underlined name to the place in the text that tells where each country had its colonies.

✓ Checkpoint

Name the trading company that was given many powers by the Dutch government.

Section 3 Focus Question

How did the movement of people lead to the spread of plants, animals, and ideas? To begin to answer this question,

- Learn about global empires.
- Read about the Columbian Exchange.

Section 3 Summary

European countries set up empires in the Americas, Africa, and Asia. People, goods, and ideas were transported around the globe.

Global Empires

Portugal and Spain led the world in setting up global empires. But the Netherlands, England, and France were not far behind. Portugal set up trading posts in Africa, India, and East Asia. These posts helped the Portuguese trade freely in the Indian Ocean.

The Dutch developed a trading company called the Dutch East India Company. The Dutch government gave this company many powers. English and French trading companies soon gained control of trading posts in India.

Europeans also set up colonies. Spain led the colonization of the Americas. By 1650, Spanish colonies had more than 500,000 settlers. Portugal colonized Brazil. Sugar plantations in Brazil and a gold rush attracted settlers. The Dutch controlled part of Brazil for a short time. They also settled some Caribbean islands. They used these colonies as bases to raid Spanish ships.

The French established the territory of New France in North America. England founded colonies along the east coast beginning in the early 1600s.

Catholic missionaries worked in the Spanish, Portuguese, and French colonies. Missionaries (MISH uhn er eez) are church members who try to convert people to a particular religion. They worked to convert native populations to Catholicism. ✓

The Columbian Exchange

The voyages made by Columbus linked the Eastern and Western hemispheres. The Eastern Hemisphere means all continents east of the Atlantic Ocean. The Western Hemisphere is made up of the Americas. Plants, animals, ideas, and diseases were exchanged between the Eastern and Western hemispheres. This exchange is called the Columbian Exchange. It brought growth and change to both East and West.

Many plants flowed across the oceans and changed history. For example, maize, or corn, became a major food crop in Europe, Asia, and Africa. Sugar cane was a crop from the Eastern Hemisphere that grew well in Brazil and the Caribbean. Plantation owners bought enslaved people from Africa to work on the sugar plantations.

People were also part of the Columbian Exchange. In addition to Africans, millions of Europeans settled in the Americas. Later, Asians came to the Americas.

Several kinds of animals were brought to the Americas. Horses became a central part of some Native American cultures. Many Native Americans from the Great Plains became expert horsemen.

Not all exchanges had a positive effect. European diseases killed millions of Native Americans. Diseases from the Americas may have also killed many people in the Eastern Hemisphere.

The Columbian Exchange also included a global exchange of beliefs and ideas. As people traveled, they carried their beliefs and religions with them. Thus, many Native Americans and Asians became Christian. Africans and Asians also brought their religions to the Western Hemisphere. ✓

Check Your Progress

1. The Dutch settled on several Caribbean islands. What did these settlements serve as?

_____

2. What was the Columbian Exchange?

_____

_____

© Pearson Education, Inc., publishing as Pearson Prentice Hall. All Rights Reserved.

Vocabulary Builder

The prefix *hemi-* comes from a Greek word meaning "half." Based on this, what do you think the word *hemisphere* means, as applied to Earth?

_____

✓ Checkpoint

Name the animal that became a central part of some Native American cultures.

_____

Question to Think About As you read Section 3 in your textbook and take notes, keep this section focus question in mind: **How did the movement of people lead to the spread of plants, animals, and ideas?**

▶ Use these charts to record key information from the section.

Global Empires

Trading Posts	Colonies	Missionaries
• The Portuguese set up trading posts in _____, _____, and _____. • The Dutch East India Company traded in _____, which _____ the Portuguese. • English and French gained control of trading posts in _____.	• _____ led the rush to colonize the Americas. • Sugar plantations and a _____ brought settlers to Brazil. • The Dutch settled several Caribbean islands that served as _____. • The French claimed land in North America as far south as _____. • The English set up colonies along the _____ of North America.	• Catholic missionaries worked in the Spanish, Portuguese, and French _____. • Missionaries are _____ to a particular religion. • They set up _____, or religious settlements, in areas where _____ lived.

The Columbian Exchange: The exchange of people, other living things, and ideas between _____.

Plants and Animals	Other Exchanges
• Corn was planted across Europe, Africa, and Asia. • _____ came from the Eastern Hemisphere. It grew well in the Caribbean and _____. • Columbus introduced animals such as the _____, which became a central part of some Native American cultures.	• Enslaved Africans, Europeans, and Asians came to the Americas, which have the most _____ societies in the world as a result. • _____ had a deadly effect on both East and West. • Beliefs, faiths, and religions were exchanged. Many Native Americans became _____.

Refer to this page to answer the Chapter 19 Focus Question on page 249.

The Origins of Modern Capitalism

Section 4 Focus Question

How did capitalism and mercantilism develop? To begin to answer this question,

- Learn about the beginnings of capitalism.
- Find out how mercantilism increases a nation's wealth.

© Pearson Education, Inc., publishing as Pearson Prentice Hall. All Rights Reserved.

Section 4 Summary

Overseas trade also helped create a new world economic system. Capitalism and mercantilism changed the way people lived and worked.

The Beginnings of Capitalism

The voyages of discovery brought about a new kind of economy. It was known as capitalism (KAP iht uhl ihz uhm). Capitalism is an economy based on the private ownership of property and the use of property to compete for profits in a market.

One important part of capitalism is a free market. In a free market, sellers compete to supply goods to buyers. Buyers create a demand when they offer bids for goods. This interplay of supply and demand determines prices.

In the 1500s, prices for food and other goods went up. This was called the price revolution.

Causes of the Price Revolution	Effects
Rapid population growth	• More demand for food • Farmers could not meet the demand • Food prices increased
Gold and silver from the Americas	• People had more money to pay for goods and food • Prices increased

Higher prices meant bigger profits for landowners and merchants. These people became rich, and used their money to invest in businesses.

A second major part of capitalism is landownership. The people who own land can grow crops and buy and

Key Events

1492	Christopher Columbus crosses the Atlantic.
1520s–1530s	Spanish conquer Aztec and Inca empires.
1607	English found Jamestown colony in North America.
1600s	Europe adopts capitalism and mercantilism.

Vocabulary Builder

Part of the word *interplay* means "between." What do you think the word *interplay* means in the underlined sentence?

_____

Reread the underlined sentence. It contains a cause and an effect. Identify each on the lines below.

Cause: _____

_____

Effect: _____

_____

✓ Checkpoint

List the two major parts of capitalism.

_____

_____

✓ Checkpoint

Under mercantilism, what did colonies provide to the home country?

_____

sell land for a profit. <u>The price revolution helped landowners because increased prices for crops meant bigger profits.</u>

The price revolution also drove up prices for cloth. English cloth merchants found a way to make cloth more cheaply and earn a bigger profit. They bought raw wool at very low prices. Then, they took the wool to nearby villages. They paid peasant workers to make the wool into cloth. When it was ready, the merchants sold it and earned big profits. The use of workers who work at home with their own equipment is known as **cottage industry** (KAHT ihj IHN duhs tree).

England and the Netherlands were the first European nations to move away from a traditional economy. A **traditional economy** (truh DIHSH uh nuhl ih KAHN uh mee) is an economy in which the exchange of goods is based on custom. In a **market economy** (MAHR kiht ih KAHN uh mee), the price and share of goods are based on competition in a market. ✓

Mercantilism

While capitalism was on the rise, mercantilism developed. **Mercantilism** (MER kuhn tihl ihz uhm) is an economic policy that aims to build a nation's strength through trade. The goal was to bring as much wealth as possible into the country. More trade would mean more money to pay for a strong army and navy.

Mercantilists thought that the best way to increase a nation's wealth was to export more valuable goods than it imported. Mercantilists taxed imports to keep foreign goods out. They also supported industry and farming. They founded colonies to help their trade. Colonies provided raw materials to the home country. The home country made the raw materials into products to sell to other countries. ✓

Check Your Progress

1. In a free market, what determines prices?

_____

_____

2. According to mercantilism, what is the best way for a nation to increase its wealth?

_____

_____

Question to Think About As you read Section 4 in your textbook and take notes, keep this section focus question in mind: **How did capitalism and mercantilism develop?**

▶ Use these charts to record key information from the section.

Free Market Economy	Landownership	Cottage Industry
• Sellers compete to supply goods. • Buyers create _____ _____. • The interplay between supply and demand determines _____ _____. • Market economy replaced _____ _____, the exchange of goods based on custom.	Landowners buy and sell land for _____.	• Cottage industry is an early form of capitalism in which _____ _____ _____ _____. • Merchants bought wool at cheap prices, paid peasants to weave it, and sold it _____ _____.

Capitalism

Capitalism is _____
_____
_____
_____
_____.

Price revolution

- 1500s: Prices for food and goods _____.
- Two causes:
  1. _____
  2. _____
- Benefited _____ and _____.
- Higher prices for crops and goods meant higher profits.

Mercantilism

Definition of mercantilism: _____
_____

- Best way to increase a nation's wealth: a nation should _____ more valuable goods than it _____.
- European nations practiced mercantilism by
  1. taxing imports.
  2. encouraging _____ and _____.
  3. founding colonies to help their trade. Colonies provided
     _____.

Refer to this page to answer the Chapter 19 Focus Question on page 249.

Directions: Circle the letter of the correct answer.

1. Who led the first expedition to sail around the world?
   A Christopher Columbus
   B Ferdinand Magellan
   C Amerigo Vespucci

2. In 1519, Hernán Cortés sailed to Mexico to conquer
   A the Aztecs.   B the Incas.   C the Spanish.

3. The exchange of people, other living things, and ideas between the Eastern and Western Hemispheres is known as
   A colonization.
   B trade.
   C the Columbian Exchange.

4. Two major parts of capitalism are
   A industry and trade.
   B free market and landownership.
   C price revolution and mercantilism.

Directions: Follow the steps to answer this question:

Did the Columbian Exchange have more positive effects or more negative effects?

Step 1: Recall information: List things that were part of the Columbian Exchange.

_____

_____

Step 2: Which parts of the Columbian Exchange were positive? Which were negative?

_____

_____

Step 3: Complete the topic sentence that follows. Then, write two or three more sentences that support your topic sentence.

On the whole, the Columbian Exchange was more _____

_____

_____

_____

Now you are ready to answer the Chapter 19 Focus Question: **How did the world change during the Age of Exploration?**

▶ Complete the following organizers to help you answer this question. Use the notes that you took for each section.

Voyages of Discovery

- Advances in mapmaking, navigation, and shipbuilding made voyages possible.
- Portuguese explorers sailed around _____ and reached _____.
- Columbus sailed west across the _____. He landed on an island in what is today _____.
- Significance of Magellan's expedition: _____
  _____.

European Conquests in the New World

Aztecs:	Incas:
• Conquered by _____	• Conquered by _____

The Spaniards attacked native cultures by destroying temples, killing priests, burning _____, and melting down _____.

Colonization

- _____ took the lead in colonizing the Americas.
- _____ established a colony in Brazil.
- _____ settled several Caribbean islands.
- _____ owned Caribbean islands and claimed large areas of North America.
- _____ set up colonies on the east coast of North America.
- The Columbian Exchange was the movement of humans, animals, _____, and _____ between the Eastern and Western _____.

Economic Changes

Capitalism	Mercantilism
• Based on the private _____ of property and the use of property to compete for profits.	• Promotes _____ as a way to build a nation's _____
• Buyers and sellers compete in a _____.	• Stressed that a nation should _____ more valuable goods than it _____

Refer to this page to answer the Unit 7 Focus Question on page 267.

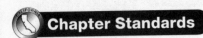
Chapter 20

Revolutions in Thought (1500–1800)

What You Will Learn

A renewed interest in science beginning in the 1500s gave rise to the Scientific Revolution. The growth of science led to a movement called the Enlightenment. Enlightenment ideas spread and eventually sparked the American Revolution. Democracies like the United States have expanded and strengthened Enlightenment ideals.

Chapter 20 Focus Question

As you read through the sections in this chapter, keep the following question in mind: **What was the importance of the Scientific Revolution and the Enlightenment?**

Section 1

The Origins of the Scientific Revolution

Section 1 Focus Question

What were the origins of the Scientific Revolution? To begin answering this question,
- Learn about ancient and medieval science.
- Find out about science during the Renaissance.

Section 1 Summary

Ancient Greek scientific thinking was later blended with Christian beliefs. The Renaissance led to a renewed interest in science.

Ancient and Medieval Science

The ancient Greeks began the study of the natural world, which we call science. The Greeks tried to answer questions about the natural world using logic and reason. They took an approach called rationalism. Rationalism (RASH uhn uhl ih zuhm) is the belief that knowledge can be gained through the use of reason.

Key Events

1543 Copernicus describes a sun-centered universe.

1633 Galileo goes on trial for heresy.

1687 Newton presents his theory of gravity.

In medieval Europe, Thomas Aquinas worked to blend ancient science with Christian teachings. The result was a view that put Earth at the center of the universe. The idea of an Earth-centered universe was based on the writings of the Greek philosopher Aristotle. He divided the universe into lower and higher realms, or areas. Earth makes up the lower realm. The higher realm is made up of the heavenly bodies that move around Earth.

This view of the universe fit well with Christian beliefs. The Church taught that God had put Earth at the center of the universe because it was the home of humankind, God's most important creation. ✓

Science During the Renaissance

During the Renaissance there was a renewed interest in science. One factor, or thing that influences or causes a situation, that inspired this interest was humanism. Renaissance humanists were willing to challenge accepted beliefs, even religious beliefs. They also valued individual scholarship.

A second factor was the Age of Exploration. As they explored distant lands, Europeans discovered that there was more to the world than they had thought.

The third factor was the invention of new scientific tools. For example, the telescope allows people to see distant celestial bodies. The microscope (MĪ kruh skohp), a device that uses a lens to magnify objects, allows people to see very small objects. Two measurement tools were the thermometer, which allows scientists to measure temperatures, and the barometer. A barometer (buh RAH muh ter) is an instrument that measures changes in air pressure. ✓

Check Your Progress

1. How did Aristotle believe the universe was divided?

_____

_____

2. How did humanism contribute to a renewed interest in science?

_____

_____

Reading Strategy

Reread the bracketed paragraph. The second sentence includes both a cause and an effect. Circle the cause. Underline the effect.

✓ Checkpoint

Name the person who tried to blend ancient science with Christian teachings.

_____

Vocabulary Builder

The underlined word, *celestial*, comes from a Latin word meaning "heaven." What does this tell you about what telescopes allow you to see?

_____

_____

✓ Checkpoint

List three factors that helped renew interest in science during the 1500s.

_____

_____

_____

Question to Think About As you read Section 1 in your textbook and take notes, keep this section focus question in mind: **What were the origins of the Scientific Revolution?**

▶ Use these charts to record key information from the section. Some information has been filled in to get you started.

Ancient and Medieval Science	
Ancient Science	**Medieval View of the Universe**
The study of the natural world was begun by the Greeks.	European scholars began to study _____.
Approach based on: Rationalism, which is _____ _____	Thomas Aquinas blended ancient science with Christian teachings. This resulted in a view of the universe that put _____.
Key philosopher: _____	The idea of an Earth-centered universe was based on _Aristotle's writings_____.
After the fall of the Roman empire, Greek learning was preserved in the_____ _____.	This view of universe fit well with Christian beliefs that taught that God _____.

Science During the Renaissance	
Humanism	Why it led to a renewed interest in science: • Humanists were willing to challenge established beliefs. • _____.
Global Exploration	What Europeans discovered: _____ This led Europeans to realize that _____ _____
New Tools for Science	Tool: _telescope_ What it did: _allowed scientists to see planets and stars more clearly_ Tool: _____ What it did: _____ Tool: _____ What it did: _____ Tool: _____ What it did: _____

Refer to this page to answer the Chapter 20 Focus Question on page 266.

Section 2

The Rise of Modern Science

Section 2 Focus Question

How did scientists and philosophers contribute to the rise of modern science? To begin answering this question,

- Learn about scientists' new view of the universe.
- Find out about how science and reason led to the scientific method.

Section 2 Summary

Beginning in the 1500s, scientists challenged the Earth-centered model of the universe. They used many new tools to study the world around them. Later, the ideas of Francis Bacon and René Descartes helped create the scientific method.

A New View of the Universe

The first scientist to challenge the idea that Earth was the center of the universe was the Polish astronomer **Nicolaus Copernicus** (kuh PER nih kuhs). He tracked the movements of the sun, moon, and planets. He learned that the sun, not Earth, was the center of the universe. Copernicus waited years before publishing his work. When he did, many people ridiculed his conclusion.

A German astronomer named **Johannes Kepler** (KEH pler) used mathematics to prove that Earth and other planets move in orbits around the sun. However, he could not explain what kept the planets in orbit.

The Italian mathematician **Galileo** (ga lih LAY oh) **Galilei** used a telescope to study the sky. He observed that not all heavenly objects revolve around Earth. Galileo's views challenged the Church's teaching. The Church believed that human beings were at the center of the universe. Galileo was brought to trial for heresy.

The English mathematician **Isaac Newton** (NOOT uhn) <u>formulated</u> a theory to explain why planets do not fly off into space. He realized that a force called gravity pulls two objects toward each other. Newton described this mathematically in his law of gravity.

Key Events

1543	Copernicus describes a sun-centered universe.
1633	Galileo goes on trial for heresy.
1687	Newton presents his theory of gravity.

Reading Strategy

Reread the bracketed paragraph. It describes a cause and an effect. Underline the cause and circle the effect.

Vocabulary Builder

What word do you see within the underlined word *formulated*? Formulate means to state in a brief or orderly way. How do the meanings of the two words relate?

_____

_____

The law of gravity completed the revolution begun by Copernicus. Most educated people came to accept that Earth was not the center of the universe. They also accepted that the universe was governed by laws that could be described mathematically. ✓

Science and Reason

During this period, two thinkers supported a new way to develop knowledge. They were English philosopher **Francis Bacon** (BAY kuhn) and French philosopher **René Descartes** (day KART). They believed that observing, experimenting, and reasoning should be used to gain knowledge and reach conclusions. This approach led to the development of the **scientific method** (SI uhn TIHF ihk MEHTH uhd).

Steps in the Scientific Method	
Step 1	Identify the research question.
Step 2	Gather information through observation and experimentation.
Step 3	Form a **hypothesis** (hi PAHTH uh sihs), or a possible answer.
Step 4	Test the hypothesis through more observations and experimentation.

✓

Check Your Progress

1. Why did the Catholic Church object to Galileo's discoveries?

_____

_____

2. Why are Francis Bacon and René Descartes important?

_____

_____

Question to Think About As you read Section 2 in your textbook and take notes, keep this section focus question in mind: **How did scientists and philosophers contribute to the rise of modern science?**

▶ Use this organizer to record key information from the section. Some information has been filled in to get you started.

Beginnings of the Scientific Revolution	
Scientist	**Why important**
Copernicus	• the first scientist to challenge the medieval view of the universe • concluded that the _____, not _____, was the center of the universe • showed that _____ moved in predictable orbits
Kepler	• used mathematics to prove that _____ _____
Galileo	• one of the first scientists to use experiments to discover _____ laws of nature • showed that not all heavenly objects _____ and that they were not _____ and _____ • attacked by _____ for his _____ view of the universe
Newton	• called the force that pulls one object to another _____ • described the pull between objects mathematically in his _____ _____

Bacon	Descartes
How to develop knowledge: <u>Use inductive reasoning</u> **How this worked:** 1. Used _____ and _____ to gather facts 2. Draw a general conclusion based on facts	**How to develop knowledge:** 1. doubt everything except ideas that were <u>true beyond doubt</u> 2. from basic truths, use _____ _____ and _____ to show the _____ of other things

↓   ↓

The Scientific Method	
1. <u>identify a research question</u>	3. _____
2. _____	4. _____

Refer to this page to answer the Chapter 20 Focus Question on page 266.

Key Events

1543 — Copernicus describes a sun-centered universe.

1633 — Galileo goes on trial for heresy.

1687 — Newton presents his theory of gravity.

Vocabulary Builder

The word *balance* has different meanings in different contexts. Which meaning does it have in the underlined sentence?

a. to put in a steady position
b. to limit
c. to put equal proportions of ingredients into something

Reading Strategy

Ask and answer a question about the idea of a social contract.

Question: _____

_____?

Answer: _____

_____

Section 3 Focus Question

How did the Enlightenment affect people's ideas about government, economics and society? To begin answering this question,

- Learn about political thought during the Enlightenment.
- Find out about social and economic thought during the Enlightenment.

Section 3 Summary

Enlightenment thinkers developed new ideas about good government. They examined ways to improve society and create stronger economies.

Political Thought

In the 1700s, an intellectual movement known as the Enlightenment emphasized the use of reason in the study of human society. Enlightenment thinkers believed that natural laws governed human affairs. People tried to know and apply these laws to create a perfect society.

The English philosopher **John Locke** (lahk) reasoned that people are born with natural rights. **Natural rights** (NACH uhr uhl rīts) are rights which no government can take away. These are the rights to life, liberty, and personal property. Locke argued that people formed governments to protect their natural rights. If a government did not do so, people had the right to fight back and form a new government.

The French philosopher **Montesquieu** (MAHN tuhs kyoo) focused on ways to promote liberty and prevent rulers from becoming despots. His ideal government was composed of three branches. Each branch could balance the powers of the other two. This would keep any one branch from becoming powerful enough to take away people's freedom.

The French philosopher Jean Jacques Rousseau revived the idea known as the **social contract** (SOH shuhl KAHN trakt). This was an unwritten agreement between people and their government. Long ago, people formed governments to protect themselves. They did this by entering into a social contract. People agreed to give up complete freedom to do anything they wanted. In return, rulers would protect people's natural rights. Rousseau believed that people had often lost their liberty by giving power to governments that did not promote the general good. He felt that the only governments with the right to exist were ones based on the will of the people. ✓

✓ **Checkpoint**

List Locke's three natural rights.

_____

_____

_____

Social and Economic Thought

The Enlightenment was also a time of new thinking about the structure of human society and economic systems. A French writer known as Voltaire had a strong sense of social justice. He saw the damage caused by religious wars. As a result, he wrote about the need for religious tolerance.

The English writer Mary Wollstonecraft called for improvement of the rights of women. She believed that men and women were equal in their ability to reason. Wollstonecraft called for the education of women, so they would be able to take their place in society as the equals of men.

The Scottish writer Adam Smith applied reason to economic questions. In his book *The Wealth of Nations*, he said that the way for a nation to become wealthy was to allow free trade. Smith argued that an economy works best when people are allowed to make their own economic decisions. This concept is called *laissez faire*. **Laissez faire** (leh say FAYR) is the policy that the economy should be free from government regulation. ✓

✓ **Checkpoint**

Name two Enlightenment philosophers who examined ways to improve society.

_____

_____

Check Your Progress

1. What was the purpose of government according to John Locke?

_____

_____

2. What social improvements did Mary Wollstonecraft promote?

_____

_____

Question to Think About As you read Section 3 in your textbook and take notes, keep this question in mind: **How did the Enlightenment affect people's ideas about government, economics, and society?**

► Use these charts to record key information from the section. Some information has been filled in to get you started.

Political Thought During the Enlightenment	
Philosopher	**Ideas About Government**
Locke	• Governments were formed to protect people's natural rights. If a government does not live up to that purpose, people can <u>create a new government</u>. • People are born with the ability to control their _____. • The natural rights are the rights to _____, _____, and _____.
Montesquieu	• A balanced government is the only way to prevent rulers from becoming _____. • three branches of ideal government: _____, _____, and _____ • The division of power among branches <u>limits</u> the _____ of any one branch.
Rousseau	• revived the idea of a social contract, an unwritten agreement between _____ and their <u>governments</u> about the _____ and <u>duties</u> of each • Society existed because its members agreed to live together for _____. • Only governments based on the will of the people have the right to rule.

Social and Economic Thought During the Enlightenment	
Writer	**Ideas About Improving Society/Economy**
Voltaire	• wrote about religion and the need for <u>tolerance</u>
Wollstonecraft	• Men and women are <u>equal</u> in their ability to reason. • Women should be _____ so that they could be _____ in society.
Smith	• applied <u>reason</u> to economic questions • a nation became wealthy through _____ • promoted the policy of _____: the economy should be free of _____

Refer to this page to answer the Chapter 20 Focus question on page 266.

The Influence of Enlightenment Ideas

Section 4 Focus Question

How were the American colonies affected by their roots
in English history and the Enlightenment? To begin
answering this question,

- Learn about the roots of American democracy.
- Find out about the American Revolution.

Section 4 Summary

English colonies were established in America, with
governments based on English law and Enlightenment
ideas. Later, American colonists rebelled and declared
their independence.

The Roots of American Democracy

The United States began as thirteen separate English
colonies. One thing they shared was ideas about political rights and good government, which were rooted in
English history and the Enlightenment.

The English people had long struggled to protect
their rights from rulers. Their first victory came in 1215.
That year, King John accepted the Magna Carta, or
"Great Charter." This established the idea that even a
king must respect English law.

The next victory was the development of Parliament. Representatives met regularly to advise the monarch. But what if the monarch refused to take their
advice? That question was finally settled in the Glorious Revolution of 1689, when King James II was forced
from his throne. The new rulers had to sign the English
Bill of Rights before being crowned.

The English Bill of Rights stated that Parliament
alone had the power to make laws and levy taxes. It
guaranteed the right of the English people to elect
members of Parliament. It also placed limits on the
power of the monarch.

The thirteen colonial governments in America were
based on the English government. But they were also
influenced by Enlightenment ideas. Most important
was the idea that government should be based on the
will of the people.

Key Events	
1543	Copernicus describes a sun-centered universe.
1633	Galileo goes on trial for heresy.
1687	Newton presents his theory of gravity.

Circle the word in the underlined sentence that tells you that the definition of *legislature* is being stated.

✓ Checkpoint

Name one guarantee in the English Bill of Rights.

_____

_____

_____

Vocabulary Builder

A militia is an army of citizen volunteers who train to fight during emergencies. Think of another word that is related to *militia*. How do the meanings of the two words relate?

_____

_____

✓ Checkpoint

Name the document in which the colonists stated that they wanted to separate from Great Britain.

_____

Each colony had its own elected legislature (LEHJ ihs lay chuhr), or lawmaking body. Like Parliament, this body had the power to pass laws and levy taxes. An executive branch and a judicial branch balanced the power of the legislature. A governor headed the executive branch. He had the power to veto (VEE tow), or reject, any law passed by the legislature. ✓

The American Revolution

Beginning in 1764, Parliament placed a series of taxes on the colonies. For example, the Stamp Act taxed everything that was printed in the colonies. This enraged the colonists. They argued that because colonists did not elect members of Parliament, that body had no right to tax them.

The crisis came to a head in 1775, when fighting broke out between British troops and colonial militias. Then, in 1776, colonial delegates announced their separation from Great Britain in the Declaration of Independence. Enlightenment ideas shaped this document. It began with the idea that people were born with certain natural rights. It also said that governments get their right to rule from the people. It stated that a government's main job is to protect people's rights. When it does not do so, people have the right to replace it. Finally, the Declaration explained how the British monarch had abused the colonists' rights. ✓

Check Your Progress

1. In the colonies, on what were ideas about good government based?

_____

_____

2. Why did the Stamp Act anger the colonists?

_____

_____

Question to Think About As you read Section 4 in your textbook and take notes, keep this section focus question in mind: **How were the American colonies affected by their roots in English history and the Enlightenment?**

▶ Use these charts to record key information from the section. Some information has been filled in to get you started.

History of the English People's Struggle to Protect Their Rights		
Magna Carta	**Development of Parliament**	**English Bill of Rights**
When: 1215	What it was •	When
Why important: • King and nobles must respect English law • •	Why important: • •	Why important: • Parliament alone had the power to make laws and levy taxes. • •

How Enlightenment Ideas Influenced English Colonies in North America	
Colonial Governments	• Government should be based on the will of the people • Structure: three branches of government (executive, legislative, and judicial) that balance each others' powers • No _____ without _____
Declaration of Independence	• People have ___natural___ rights. • The right to rule comes from _____. • The main job of government is to protect _____ _____. • When government fails, people have the right to replace _____.

Refer to this page to answer the Chapter 20 Focus Question on page 266.

Key Events

1543	Copernicus describes a sun-centered universe.
1633	Galileo goes on trial for heresy.
1687	Newton presents his theory of gravity.

Reading Strategy

Reread the bracketed paragraph. Circle the words that show the main idea. Underline the sentences that explain the main idea.

Section 5 Focus Question

How have ideas from the past shaped the present? To begin answering this question,

- Learn about the enduring ideas, beliefs, and values of the United States.
- Find out about enduring institutions in the United States.

Section 5 Summary

Ideas from the Scientific Revolution and the Enlightenment influence our lives today. Ancient religious and political institutions are still important.

Enduring Ideas, Beliefs, and Values

The United States was the first country founded on ideas of the Scientific Revolution and the Enlightenment. The Founders of our country would recognize many of the ideas, beliefs, and values that shape life today in our nation and around the world.

The Founders would discover that their idea of natural rights has endured and grown. Today, we call these rights **human rights** (HYOO muhn ṝts). These are the rights every person should have. The Founders defined these basic rights as "life, liberty, and the pursuit of happiness." Many people today would add other rights, such as the rights to privacy and a decent standard of living. **Standard of living** (STAN derd uhv LIV ihng) is the level of wealth and comfort that a person or group has.

The Founders would see that freedom is still valued in the United States. They believed that people should be free to choose their own form of government. They thought that people should follow their own religion and express their ideas freely. These freedoms are protected in the United States Constitution and the Bill of Rights.

The Founders would be surprised to see how the meaning of equality has changed since the nation's beginning. At that time, many groups lacked many rights that white men enjoyed. For example, women, African Americans, and Native Americans had few rights. Over time, most of the barriers to equality have been torn down in this country.

The Founders would see that tolerance remains a strong American value. The nation they helped create was one of the most diverse. The United States is even more diverse today. Most Americans have realized that diversity has become one of the country's greatest sources of strength. Diversity (duh VER suh tee) means having a variety of ethnic groups and cultures.

The Founders would see that Americans today value reason as much as the Founders did. This nation was built on the belief that people have the ability to reason and will use this ability as voters and citizens. ✓

Enduring Institutions

Our lives today are also shaped by enduring religious and political institutions. The oldest enduring institutions are the major world religions. Judaism, Hinduism, and Buddhism are ancient faiths. Christianity and Islam are newer religions, but they still stretch back many hundreds of years.

For most of human history, societies depended on strong rulers to keep order. Very few societies trusted the people to govern themselves. Athens and Rome experimented with governments that were run by the people. But in both places, democracy eventually failed. Today, the United States is the world's oldest nation based on the will of the people. ✓

Check Your Progress

1. How was the idea of natural rights expanded?

_____

_____

2. What is one way that the United States government differs from most past governments?

_____

_____

✓ **Checkpoint**

Name three groups who had few rights at the time of the Declaration of Independence.

_____

_____

_____

Vocabulary Builder

The word *endure* comes from a word meaning "to harden" or "to last." What does this tell you about the religious and political institutions that this section of text discusses?

_____

_____

✓ **Checkpoint**

List three ancient religions.

_____

_____

_____

Question to Think About As you read Section 5 in your textbook and take notes, keep this section focus question in mind: **How have ideas from the past shaped the present?**

▶ Use these charts to record key information from the section. Some information has been filled in to get you started.

Ideas of the Enlightenment and the Scientific Revolution	
Idea	**How Idea Affects Life Today**
Natural rights	• now called human rights. • originally _life_ , _liberty_ , and pursuit of _____ • expanded to include other rights, such as privacy and a decent standard of living • applies to more groups like _____, _____, and _____
Freedom	People can: • choose their own form of government • follow their own _____ • express _____ freely
Equality	• most _____ to equality torn down in the United States
Tolerance	• allows Americans to live in a _____ society
Reason	• Our government is based on the belief that people have _____ and use it to make decisions as _____ and _____.

Enduring Institutions	
Institution	**How Institution Is important Today**
Religion	• tries to answer questions about the mysteries of life and death • offers guides to _____ • helps human beings _____
Government	• Societies have governments to _____. • Many societies trust people to _____.

Refer to this page to answer the Chapter 20 Focus Question on page 266.

Directions: Circle the letter of the correct answer.

1. Who helped blend ancient science with Christian teachings?
   A Aristotle   **B** Francis Bacon   **C** Thomas Aquinas

2. Who first challenged the idea of an earth-centered universe?
   A Copernicus   **B** Kepler   **C** Galileo

3. Who introduced the idea of natural rights?
   A Voltaire   **B** Adam Smith   **C** John Locke

4. Colonial leaders' ideas about political rights and good government were based on the ideas of the
   A Renaissance.
   B Enlightenment.
   C Scientific Revolution.

Directions: Follow the steps to answer this question.

How might life be different today if certain Enlightenment ideas were never introduced?

Step 1: Recall information: List two key ideas from the Enlightenment.

Key Enlightenment Ideas
1.
2.

Step 2: Analyze effects: What impact has each idea had on life today? List an example of each in today's society. Then note how that example might be different if the idea had not been introduced.

	An Example of Each Idea Today	Difference in Life Without Idea
Idea 1:		
Idea 2:		

Step 3: Complete the topic sentence that follows. Then write two or three more sentences that support your topic sentence.

If the ideas of the Enlightenment had never been introduced _____

_____

_____

_____

_____

Now you are ready to answer the Chapter 20 Focus Question: **What was the importance of the Scientific Revolution and the Enlightenment?**

▶ Complete the following chart to help you answer this question. Use the notes that you took for each section.

Importance of the Scientific Revolution	
Scientist	**Importance of His Ideas**
Copernicus	• Challenged the view that Earth was at the center of the universe. • He concluded that _____, not _____, was the center of the universe.
Kepler	• used _____ to prove that Copernicus was right that _____ revolved around <u>the sun</u>
Galileo	• used _____ to discover the laws of nature • observed that not all _____ revolve around <u>the sun</u>
Newton	• discovered law of _____ that explained why planets orbit _____

Together, their work changed the way people viewed the universe. Most educated people came to accept that:
1. _____ was not the center of the universe.
2. The universe was governed by laws that could be described _____.

Importance of the Enlightenment		
Philosopher	**Ideas**	**Example of the Influence of His Work**
Locke	People form governments to protect their natural rights and have the right to _____ against governments that do not.	The <u>Declaration of Independence</u> used Locke's ideas to justify rebelling against Great Britain.
Montesquieu	Believed in balanced government with _____ branches to keep one branch from _____	Seen in the separation of powers in _____
Rousseau	_____ between people and government in which people give up <u>complete freedom</u> and rulers protect people's _____	Idea appears in _____ _____ to explain the purpose of government

Refer to this page to answer the Unit 6 Focus Question on page 267.

Unit 7 Pulling It Together Activity

Chapter 17 After the medieval period, Europe moved into the Renaissance. This period saw a new interest in art, literature, and learning.

Chapter 18 The Reformation, a protest against certain practices in the Catholic Church, had far-reaching effects on European society.

Chapter 19 European sailors explored much of the world. Europeans conquered the societies they found in the Americas and set up colonies there.

Chapter 20 A renewed interest in science gave rise to the Scientific Revolution. The growth of science led to a movement called the Enlightenment. Enlightenment ideas spread and sparked the American Revolution. Democracies have expanded and strengthened Enlightenment ideals.

Think Like a Historian

Read the Unit 7 Focus Question: **How can ideas change the course of events?**

▶ Use the organizers on this page and the next to collect information to answer this question.

In what ways did new Renaissance and Reformation ideas change the world? Some of them are listed in this chart. Review your section and chapter notes. Then complete the chart.

The Renaissance and Reformation	
Developments	**Effects**
Revival of Learning • Humanism • Secularism • Individualism	• shift from God-centered learning to study of humankind • •
Invention of Printing Press	• increased literacy and spread of ideas •
95 Theses	• Protestant movement • •

In what ways did new ideas during the Age of Exploration and the Enlightenment change the world? The chart below gives you part of the answer. Review your section and chapter notes. Then fill in the rest of the chart.

Exploration and Enlightenment	
Developments	**Effects**
Advances in Technology	• European exploration of Africa, Asia, and the Americas •
Mercantilism	• European global empires • •
Capitalism	• change from traditional to market economy • •
Rationalism, Humanism, Inventions	Scientific Revolution • •
Enlightenment	• changes in political, social, and economic thought • • •

The Beginnings of Humankind

Chapter 1: Early People

Section 1: Studying the Distant Past
- Archaeologists study prehistoric times by examining things that early peoples left behind.
- The study of fossils has helped archaeologists learn about the lives of the earliest humans.
- Archaeological studies suggest that the earliest humans lived in Africa millions of years ago.

Section 2: Hunter-Gatherer Societies
- Hunter-gatherer societies moved from place to place, hunting small animals and gathering plants for food.
- The development of tools and the use of fire helped the people in hunter-gatherer societies improve their lives.
- Modern humans developed the ability to use language, which helped them to survive.

Section 3: Populating the Earth
- By about 12,500 years ago, modern humans had spread to many regions of the world, including Africa, Asia, Europe, Australia, North America, and South America.
- Modern humans adapted to Ice Age conditions by building shelters and making warm clothing.
- By forming larger groups, modern humans adapted in order to better hunt and defend themselves.

Section 1: Early Agriculture

- Over a long time, hunter-gatherers domesticated plants and animals, and most groups became farmers.
- Although the Middle East was the first center of agriculture, farming appeared in several other parts of the world.
- Permanent farming settlements developed, and surplus food allowed some people to become craftsworkers.

Section 2: Cities and Civilizations

- Some farming villages grew into cities with large populations and large land areas.
- Wealth from farming and trade created powerful cities that gave rise to civilizations.
- The shared features of most civilizations are cities, a well-organized government, an established religion, job specialization, social classes, a developed culture, and a system of writing.

Section 3: The Maya Civilization

- Unlike river valley civilizations, the Maya civilization arose in the rain forests of Mesoamerica.
- The Maya lived in separate, independent cities, but their civilization shared many of the features of other civilizations.
- Maya achievements include a system of writing, knowledge of astronomy and mathematics, and highly developed arts and architecture.

The Ancient Middle East

Chapter 3: Ancient Mesopotamia

Section 1: The Fertile Crescent
- As people began to farm the fertile soil near the Tigris and Euphrates rivers, new methods of farming began to develop.
- Eventually, cities emerged and became powerful centers of trade and government.

Section 2: The Civilization of Sumer
- With the growth of cities, government became more important, and different social classes emerged.
- Writing may have begun at religious structures, such as temples and ziggurats, to keep records of goods that were received.
- Learning in math and science also became important.

Section 3: The Development of Writing
- Writing began in Sumeria as a way to keep track of goods in the temple.
- Writing began with pictographs. Then some symbols began to be used to represent syllables. Eventually some symbols began to represent individual sounds.
- Our modern alphabet descended from an alphabet that began in the Middle East.

Section 4: The First Empires
- As civilization advanced, strong rulers united city-states into empires.
- Sargon the Great created Mesopotamia's first empire.
- Hammurabi united the Babylonian empire. He also created a written law for his people.

Section 1: The Nile River Valley

- Egypt and Nubia rose in the valley of the Nile River, which flows from central Africa to the Mediterranean Sea.
- Early farmers grew crops in the fertile "Black Land" of the Nile Valley, but no crops could grow in the deadly "Red Land" of the Sahara.
- Around 3100 B.C., Upper Egypt and Lower Egypt were united into one kingdom.

Section 2: Egypt Under the Pharaohs

- Pharaohs based their authority on Egyptian religious beliefs. The pharaoh was believed to be a god.
- A strong government carried out the pharaoh's orders and provided for the needs of the people.

Section 3: Egypt and Nubia

- Egypt traded with lands around the Mediterranean Sea and in Africa.
- At first, Egypt gained control over Nubia. Later, Nubia, called Kush by the Egyptians, conquered Egypt.

Section 4: Life and Death in Ancient Egypt

- The ancient Egyptians believed in many gods and goddesses.
- The Egyptians believed in an afterlife and carefully preserved the bodies of their dead.

Section 5: Art, Architecture, and Learning in Egypt

- Egyptian architects built huge pyramid tombs and temples for the worship of gods.
- Paintings and statues in tombs were meant to provide for the dead in the afterlife.

Section 1: The Origins of Judaism

- According to the Torah, ancient Hebrews left Mesopotamia for Canaan under the leadership of the patriarchs.
- Centuries after the Israelites entered Egypt, Moses led them out of slavery.
- The Israelites received many commandments in the wilderness.
- Then the Israelites began the conquest of Canaan.

Section 2: The Beliefs of Judaism

- The commandments that were received at the time of Moses make up the first part of the Hebrew Bible.
- Other religious writings and traditions continue to guide Jews today.

Section 3: The Spread of Judaism

- After reaching Canaan, the Israelites were led first by judges, and then by kings.
- After the kingdom weakened, many people were taken captive into other lands. This was the beginning of the Diaspora.
- Many Jews were able to return to Jerusalem from Babylon and Persia. However, many centuries later, Roman officials again drove many Jews away from Jerusalem.
- Today, Jews live all over the world. Judaism has affected many religions and cultures.

Section 1: The Geography of South Asia

- Natural barriers strongly influenced the development of civilization in South Asia.
- The Indus River valley supported the growth of early civilization on the Indian subcontinent.
- Early agriculture in South Asia depended on the rains of the summer monsoon.

Section 2: The Indus Valley Civilization

- Studies of archaeological sites have provided information about the Indus Valley civilization.
- This civilization demonstrated central planning, as well as an extensive trade network.
- The reason for its decline is one of several mysteries surrounding the Indus Valley civilization.

Section 3: India's Vedic Age

- The emergence of the Indo-Aryans marked the beginning of India's Vedic age.
- The Indo-Aryans were a nomadic people who composed an oral literature called the Vedas.
- The caste system was a social structure that had a strong impact on Aryan society.

Section 1: The Origins of Hinduism

- Hinduism evolved from Brahmanism into the major religion of India.
- The religion continues to change over time.

Section 2: The Beliefs of Hinduism

- The four main goals that Hindus want to achieve during their lifetimes are pleasure, success, an ethical and moral life, and release from life.
- Hindus believe that there are three different paths to becoming one with God: the way of knowledge, the way of works, and the way of devotion.

Section 3: The Spread of Hinduism

- Today, Hinduism is the third-largest religion in the world.
- Hinduism has spread to many places outside India, including the United States.

Section 1: The Origins of Buddhism
- When Siddhartha Gautama saw people's suffering and sadness, he began to search for truth.
- Siddhartha studied with Hindu gurus and later joined a group of ascetics in his search for enlightenment.
- After achieving enlightenment, the Buddha spent his life teaching others what he had learned.

Section 2: The Beliefs of Buddhism
- The teachings of the Buddha formed the basis of Buddhism. He advised people to follow a Middle Way between pleasure and self-denial.
- The Buddha described the Four Noble Truths and the Eightfold Path that leads to nirvana.
- Some Buddhists join religious communities and become monks or nuns, but anyone may study Buddhist texts.

Section 3: The Spread of Buddhism
- After the Buddha's death, missionaries spread his teachings from India to many parts of Asia.
- Two major schools of Buddhism developed, Theravada and Mahayana. But as Buddhism reached other countries, it declined in India.
- Today, many people besides Buddhists respect the Buddha's moral teachings. Buddhism has also influenced art and literature throughout the world.

Section 1: The Maurya Empire

- Chandragupta conquered many kingdoms to create India's first empire.
- Chandragupta established a bureaucracy to govern the regions and provinces of his empire.
- A spy network kept the emperor informed of dangers.

Section 2: Asoka's Rule of Tolerance

- Chandragupta's grandson Asoka came to power during a time of conflict.
- After he had conquered Kalinga, Asoka converted to Buddhism.
- During the rest of his reign, Asoka practiced tolerance and worked for the welfare of his people.

Section 3: India's Classical Age

- The Gupta Empire was founded by Chandra Gupta. It arose during a time of increased learning and culture.
- The classical age saw growth in arts, entertainment, and science.

Section 1: The Middle Kingdom
- Geographic features such as mountains, deserts, and forests made the transport of goods and ideas difficult in ancient China.
- China's earliest civilization arose in the Huang He valley.
- China's location and natural barriers isolated the area from other early civilizations.

Section 2: China's First Dynasties
- The ruler Yu became the founder of China's first dynasty, the Xia.
- China's first historical dynasty, the Shang, lasted about 600 years.
- During the Shang Dynasty, China expanded its territory and developed a system of writing.

Section 3: China Under the Zhou Dynasty
- A group known as the Zhou gained control of China from the Shang about 1050 B.C.
- The Zhou kingdom grew very large and became difficult for one ruler to control. Zhou kings asked family members to rule different parts of the kingdom.
- Conflicts between the rulers of individual states marked the end of the Zhou Dynasty.

Section 1: Family and Religion

- Loyalty to one's family was one of the most important values in ancient China.
- A person's age and sex often determined his or her status in a family in ancient China.
- Religious views in ancient China focused on a belief in spirits. The worship of the spirits of ancestors was important in Chinese religion.

Section 2: The Teachings of Confucius

- Chinese thinkers such as Hanfeizi and Mo-zi proposed solutions to the state of anarchy in China during the Era of the Warring States.
- A Chinese thinker named Confucius suggested that China could restore order by returning to traditional values.
- Important Confucian ideas, such as the five key relationships, had a strong impact on Chinese society.

Section 3: Daoism and Buddhism in China

- The philosophy of Daoism encouraged people of ancient China to lead simple lives that worked in harmony with the way of nature.
- After Buddhism spread from India to China in the first century A.D., the Chinese shaped these ideas into their own sects.
- Important ideas of Confucianism, Daoism, and Buddhism were mixed and borrowed in China.

Section 1: Shi Huangdi Unites China
- Qin armies united China and founded a new dynasty.
- The powerful Qin ruler Shi Huangdi succeeded in expanding and unifying China into one people under one government.

Section 2: Expansion Under the Han Dynasty
- The Han Dynasty built upon Shi Huangdi's foundations to create one of the most successful dynasties in Chinese history.
- An imperial bureaucratic state and expansion of the empire were important contributions of the Han Dynasty.

Section 3: Han Society and Achievements
- Confucian teachings helped create a strong economy in Han society.
- Many achievements in technology, arts, and science resulted from a prosperous Han society.

Ancient Greece

Chapter 13: The Ancient Greeks

Section 1: The Aegean World
- The Peloponnesian peninsula and surrounding islands became home to early Greek-speaking people.
- The earliest people of Greece developed independent settlements that were often known for trade and sea travel.

Section 2: The Rise of City-States
- Because Greece's steep hillsides made travel by land difficult, ancient Greece was politically divided into city-states.
- The Greek city-states shared much culture but had differences in the way they were governed.

Section 3: Daily Life in Ancient Greece
- City-states of ancient Greece were often governed by wealthy landowners called aristocrats.
- Although they had little direct say in government, Greek women contributed to the culture and economy of their family and community in many ways.
- Culture, the arts, and learning flourished.

Section 4: Trade and Expansion
- The population of many Greek city-states eventually grew so great that the land could not support them.
- Some city-states began wars of conquest, while others became more dependent on trade or founded colonies in other regions.

Section 1: Political Changes in Greece

- Early Greek city-states were often controlled by governments called oligarchies, in which small groups of aristocrats held power.
- Tyrannies, or governments run by one strong ruler, replaced some Greek oligarchies.
- In Athens, citizens began to take a more active role in government, as the city-state moved toward democracy.

Section 2: Democracy in Athens

- Leaders such as Cleisthenes and Pericles carried out reforms that aided the development of Athenian democracy.
- Athens' democratic government included a large assembly, a 500-member council, and a court system with citizen juries.
- Athens used a system of government called direct democracy, in which citizens take part directly in government decision making.

Section 3: Oligarchy in Sparta

- The city-state Sparta featured an oligarchical government led by two kings.
- To overcome their population problems, Spartans carried out conquests of areas such as Messenia.
- The society of Sparta was based on military discipline and did not value growth and change.

Section 1: Greek Mythology and Religion

- The people of ancient Greece worshiped many gods, who they believed influenced the world around them.
- Greek religious practices were based upon Greek mythology and the epics of Homer.
- People in ancient Greece practiced their religion in many ways, such as building temples and participating in festivals.

Section 2: Greek Art and Literature

- Greek artists became known for the beauty of their work. Ancient Greek architecture continues to influence architects today.
- Lyric poetry and drama were important parts of the literature of ancient Greece.
- The Greeks enjoyed collections of fables, such as those of Aesop.

Section 3: Greek Learning

- Greek philosophers, such as Socrates and Plato, used reason to help them determine what is real and true.
- Historians in ancient Greece began to examine why historical events took place in addition to recording the events themselves.
- Greek scholars made important advances in the natural sciences, mathematics, and medicine.

Section 1: The Persian Empire

- The rulers of the Persian Empire set up an efficient political organization.
- The Persian Empire balanced local self-government with central government in order to govern their vast territory.

Section 2: The Persian Wars

- The Persian king Darius intended to conquer all of Greece.
- The Athenians and Spartans worked together to defend themselves against the Persians.

Section 3: The Peloponnesian Wars

- Athens and its allies formed the Delian League. Sparta formed the Peloponnesian League with its allies.
- Although together they defeated the Persians, Athens and Sparta fought against each other in the 27-year-long Peloponnesian War.

Section 4: The Empire of Alexander the Great

- The Greek city-states were finally united under one rule by Alexander the Great.
- Alexander the Great's conquests spread Greek culture east toward India and south into Egypt.

Ancient Rome

Chapter 17: The Roman Republic

Section 1: On the Banks of the Tiber
- Rome was settled along the Tiber River in the Italian Peninsula during the 500s B.C.
- Romans developed myths to explain the city's founding.
- The location of Rome allowed the settlement to grow. It provided natural defenses, nearby farmland, and access to key trade routes.

Section 2: Rise of the Roman Republic
- The earliest rulers of Rome were kings. Etruscan rule introduced new trade goods, ideas, and customs to Rome.
- After becoming tired of Etruscan rule, the Romans overthrew the third Etruscan king. They then established the Roman Republic.
- Roman society included two social classes. Struggles between these classes led Rome to move toward a more democratic form of government.

Section 3: The Government of the Republic
- The government of the Roman Republic had three branches. These branches represented monarchy, oligarchy, and democracy.
- The Roman constitution was a series of laws and practices that formed the basis of government in Rome.
- A system of checks and balances and the rule of law were among the important principles of the Roman constitution.

Section 4: Roman Society
- Roman society placed much importance on traditions, such as family relationships.
- The relationships between patrons and clients also helped form the social structure of Rome.
- Roman society valued traits such as gravitas and civic virtue. Religion in ancient Rome involved the worship of many gods, both in public and at home.

Section 1: The Conquest of an Empire

- Rome's military strength, as well as diplomacy, helped the empire succeed.
- Rome fought against Carthage in three wars know as the Punic Wars.
- Social problems led to the downfall of Rome.

Section 2: The Pax Romana

- Julius Caesar ruled Rome as "Dictator for Life" until his assassination in 44 B.C.
- Caesar's adopted son Octavian ruled the Roman Empire during a long period of peace and prosperity.

Section 3: Commerce and Culture

- Economic growth and colonization helped the Roman Empire expand during the Pax Romana.
- Greco-Roman culture spread throughout the Roman Empire as the empire expanded.

Section 1: The Origins of Christianity

- During the Roman occupation of Jerusalem a Jewish teacher named Jesus became popular.
- Jesus was crucified but his followers believed that he was resurrected.

Section 2: The Beliefs of Christianity

- Christians follow the teachings of the early church, as they were recorded in the New Testament.
- Christians believe that Jesus is God and that he died so people could be forgiven for their sins.

Section 3: The Spread of Christianity

- Apostles such as Peter and Paul helped spread the new faith across the Roman empire.
- In spite of persecution, the faith continued to grow.
- Today there are many branches of Christianity.

Section 1: Roman Arts and Engineering

- Roman art and architecture were modeled on Greek works.
- New types of roads, water systems, and advances in science, medicine, and technology improved the Romans' daily life.

Section 2: Literature, Language, and Law

- Rome's legacy of literature was based on both Greek and Latin models.
- Roman government and law influenced modern political and legal systems.

Section 3: The Decline of the Roman Empire

- Many internal problems contributed to the fall of the Roman Empire.
- Attacks by invaders further weakened the empire.